AGRARIAN SYSTEM IN PRE-COLONIAL ANDHRA DESA, 1600-1800 A.D.

AGRARIAN SYSTEM IN PRE-COLONIAL ANDHRA DESA, 1600-1800 A.D.

R. SOMA REDDY

RESEARCH INDIA PRESS
New Delhi (INDIA)

ISBN : 978-93-5171-032-5

Price : ₹ 995/-

First Edition: 2015

Cataloging in Publication Data—DK
Courtesy: D.K. Agencies (P) Ltd. <docinfo@dkagencies.com>

Soma Reddy, R. (Ravula), 1943- **author.**
Agrarian system in pre-colonial Andhra Desa, 1600-1800 A.D. / R. Soma Reddy. — First edition.
Pages cm
Includes bibliographical references (pages) and index.
ISBN 9789351710325

1. Land tenure—India—Andhra Pradesh—History—17th century. 2. Land tenure—India—Andhra Pradesh—History— 18th century. 3. Land value taxation—India—Andhra Pradesh—History—17th century. 4. Land value taxation—India—Andhra Pradesh—History—18th century. 5. Agriculture—Economic aspects—India—Andhra Pradesh—History—17th century. 6. Agriculture—Economic aspects—India—Andhra Pradesh—History—18th century. I. Title.

DDC 333.1095484 23

Published by :
RESEARCH INDIA PRESS
E-6/34, Sangam Vihar
New Delhi-110062
Phone: 011-26047013, (M) 9818085794
E-mail: researchindiapress@gmail.com

Typesetting by
G. R. Sharma

In Found Memory of

My wife

Sumathi

CONTENTS

ACKNOWLEDGEMENT

I am grateful to several institutions and individuals for their encouragement and support in the completion of this research work.

First of all, I express my deep sense of indebtedness to UGC, New Delhi, for providing the financial assistance under Major Research Project for three years to undertake this research work. I am also obliged to UGC Unit, Osmania University and Department of History, Osmania University, for extending support to me in this regard.

I express my indebtedness to all the scholars whose published works and opinions on the subject have benefited me in formulating my views.

I take this opportunity to express my gratitude to my teachers Prof. T. Surender and late Prof. M. Radhakrishna Sarma, who is a great source of strength and encouragement to me in all my academic endeavours. My daughter Vasudha and Son Dheeraj made possible the effort that created this book. I dedicate this book to the fond memory of my wife late Sumathi.

Dr. K. Veeresha, Technical Assistant, Department of History, Osmania University, helped me in computer type setting.

Finally, it is with great pleasure that I thank Shri Research India Press, New Delhi, for bringing out this book in a short time and Mr. Suman Pathak who helped me in this regard.

Hyderabad (RAVULA SOMA REDDY)

ABBREVIATIONS

Appendix to Fifth Report – Appendix to the Fifth Report from the Select Committee.

Barbosa – An Account of the Countries Bordering the Indian Ocean and their Inhabitants.

Cudd. Ins. – Cuddapah Inscriptions, N. Venkataramanayya.

DRS – Departmental Research Support, Department of History, Osmania University.

Forgotten Empire –The Forgotten Empire, Robert Sewell.

Fifth Report – Fifth Report of the Select Committee on the Affairs of the East India Company.

IAP – Inscriptions of Andhra Pradesh.

IJ. Collection – Mughal Documents of Inayaat Jung Collection.

JAHR – Journal of Andhra Historical Research Society.

J.F. Richards – Mughal Administration in Golkonda - J.F. Richards.

Landmarks – Landmarks of the Deccan, A.A. Bilgrami.

Mack. MSS – Mackenzie Manuscripts (Potti Sreeramulu Telugu University copy).

Nellore Manual – Nellore District Manual, John A.C. Bosswell.

NDI – Nellore District Inscriptions.

Qutbshahi Dynasty – History of the Qutbshahi Dynasty, H. K. Sherwani.

Relations of Golkonda – Relations of Golkonda in the Early Seventeenth Century, ed.

Moreland, 1608-22, London, 1931.

SII – South Indian Inscription.

T.T.D.E. – Tirumala Tirupati Devasthanam Epigraphical Series.

Tavernier – Jean Baptiste Tavernier's Travels in India 1640-69, 2 vols.

Thevenot - The Indian Travels of the Venot and Careri, ed. S.N. Sen.

CHAPTER – I

INTRODUCTION

Agriculture refers to the production of goods through the growing of plants, animals and other life forms. India was and also is predominantly an agricultural country and agriculture gives occupation, directly and indirectly to an immense majority of its population. In the year 1600 A.D. which marks the beginning of the period under the present study, it is estimated that 85 percent of the Indian population lived in the villages;[1] and 65 percent of the total Indian population was directly engaged in agriculture. The remaining village communities also depended, for their employment on cultivation and contributed to the agricultural production indirectly. Some of them combined agriculture as a subsidiary pursuit with some other occupation.[2] Agriculture was and is also a source of raw material for industries like textiles, sugar etc. This description can be applied to the Telugu speaking region of India of seventeenth and eighteenth centuries.

It is an accepted fact that the economic backwardness of independent India was a consequence of colonial rule of the British for nearly two centuries. Especially, it is it's agricultural economy that was most acutely affected by the colonial rule. Andhra Pradesh of Independent India is no exception to this phenomena. The agrarian exploitation and the consequent crisis of the colonial period is however more truly the vestige of the agrarian system prevalent in this region during the pre-colonial period. The roots to the malady of the colonial period are, thus, to be traced to the pre-colonial agrarian system. The British and their subordinate Asafjahi rulers mostly borrowed it from the earlier rulers and made it more oppressive because of their colonial demands. Therefore, a thorough probe into the agrarian system of Andhra Desa during the period of two centuries preceeding the colonial rule is essential for a proper understanding of the nature of the colonial exploitation in its proper perspective. This study, infact, of agrarian conditions at the regional level will contribute to the reconstruction of the economic history of pre-colonial India in particular and the economic history of India in general.

Scholars have been working, in recent years, on the history of Indian agrarian system. The agrarian relations of the pre-colonial India have drawn the attention of scholars who have indicated in their studies the complex nature of land tenures and revenue assessment, oppression of the agrarian communities and the continued dominance of certain castes as intermediaries and their control over agricultural resources. Therefore, it is necessary to undertake the systematic studies of the agrarian system at the micro-regional level. A thorough and comprehensive study of the agrarian system of Andhra Desa of this period is yet to be undertaken. The proposed study, it is hoped, will contribute to a better understanding of the pre-colonial Andhra Agrarian System. In fact, there are very few writings on these aspects and they have not thoroughly probed into the complex nature of the land tenures, revenue system and the changes in the agrarian social structure in Andhra Desa of this period.

The extant historiography on the agrarian system of the pre-colonial Andhra is thus atleast confusing and even contradictory. Several questions regarding the land tenures, basis of land revenue assessment, mode of its collection and changes in its agrarian social structure and crop pattern have never been thoroughly investigated. How many villages/lands can be classified under each of the tenures, government, service and charitable, period-wise? Why was Nayankara tenure, widely prevalent under Vijayanagara rule, continued under the Qutbshahis? How was it replaced by the system of Jagirdars, Mansabdars, Zamindars, Polegars under the Mughal and Asafjahi rule and it's impact on the agrarian system? What was their exact number and the extent of territory held by them and amount of tribute paid by them? What was the structural framework within which they operated and method of internal management of their territory? What was their caste/religious/race composition? What was the reason for the continued dominance of certain castes/communities as intermediaries. Why did the revenue farming system become indispensable throughout the period in spite of its oppressive nature? Why was the age-old village management system called 'Ayagar' system in spite of it's hereditary nature, retained during this period? The present study aims to provide answers to all these questions and remedy these deficiencies in research and provide the foundation for a correct and new interpretation of Andhra History. This will be based upon agrarian society and culture as the central concern.

METHODOLOGY

A critique of the established historiography will provide the need for exploring an alternative historiography to arrive at a real picture of the agrarian system of the pre-colonial

Andhra. This will also provide the methodological framework of the study.

The study of agrarian relations in India by the British administrator-scholars and also by nationalist Indian historians have been inevitably concerned with land revenue organization. The aspects of land revenue, government expenditure etc constituted only one chapter of their political and administrative histories. The study of agrarian system and the peasant society became, no doubt, central theme of the works of historians like W.H. Moreland and Irfan Habib. But the concept of agrarian system framed for their works reflect the concentration upon political analysis. While Moreland's pioneering work *Agrarian System of Moslem India* mainly discusses the importance of revenue assignees, Irfan Habib's famous work *Agrarian System of Mughal India,* besides being a critical study of land revenue administration, analyses the agrarian economy and social structure. Burton Stein in his penetrating and fascinating work *Peasant State and Society in Medieval South India* focuses upon peasant society and culture in relationship to land. But the study is devoted mostly to Tamil area of South India under the Cholas and the Vijayanagara Empire. Similarly, Noboru Karashima's works *Towards A New Formation, South Indian Society under Vijayanagara* and *South Indian History and Society, Studies from Inscriptions, A.D. 850-1800* are also confined to study of agrarian aspects in the Tamil districts. J.F. Richard's *Mughal Administration in Golkonda* deals with the agrarian aspects of Andhra of only the Mughal period. Finally, M.P.R. Reddy's *Peasant and State in Modern Andhra History,* and A. Satyanarayana's *Andhra Peasants under British Rule 1900-1940* deal with the agrarian conditions of only Andhra region under Madras Presidency, during the period of English East India Company.

Thus, there is no thorough and comprehensive work on the agrarian system of pre-colonial Andhra of two centuries i.e. 17th and 18th, covering all its aspects such as Land tenures, Land revenue, basis, rates of its assessment and nature of collection, revenue farming, peasant oppression, Land survey and settlement, agricultural process, crop-pattern and commercialization of crops, agricultural development, land reclamation and irrigation, village settlements, peasant mobility, agricultural communities including labour, wages etc.

While the traditional historiography has neglected this specific aspect through a grand narrative of Indian history and culture, the Marxist historians have done a similar exercise through a grand narrative of modes of production and class formation. Therefore, it is necessary to reinquire into all the aspects of the agrarian system and critique the above mentioned partial perspective. The present study is to be seen as an important attempt in this direction.

SCOPE

This study, will be confined to the investigation of the agrarian system prevailing in Andhra Desa under several dynasties, Vijayanagara, Qutbshahi, Mughal, Asafjahi and finally the English East India Company during the period of Seventeen and Eighteen centuries A.D. All the aspects of agrarian system prevailing in Andhra Desa have to be thoroughly analysed and a comprehensive picture is to be given. Andhra Desa, the area of study denotes the entire Telugu speaking area included in the present day Andhra Pradesh state of independent India. It includes all the three sub-regions i.e. Telangana, Rayalaseema and Coastal Andhra.

OBJECTIVE OF THE STUDY

The main purpose of the study is to examine the agrarian aspects such as Land-tenures of various categories like those of government, service, charity etc, and revenue, basis of assessment, rates, mode and nature of collection and specially the revenue farming system.

The study also seeks to examine, in particular, the exact number of personages holding the land under different tenures, the extent of land/territory held by them during the period, the structural framework within which they operated, amount of tribute/tax paid by them, other obligations and their caste/race composition. The study also intends to examine the transformation/replacement into or by each other of these systems-Nayankara, Polegar, Maniawar, Jagirdar, Mansabdar, Zamindar and the difference between them, their caste/race composition and also the continued dominance of socially advanced communities like Reddi, Velama, Kamma, Balija and Brahmin on land and also as intermediaries.

The pattern of migration of agricultural communities, village settlements, land reclamation, irrigation and agricultural development entrepreneurship, rural credit, land sale and transfer, process of agriculture, crop pattern, commercialization of crops, and the impact of political changes and the European trade on agriculture are also to be studied. One vital agrarian institution prevalent throughout the period was that of hereditary Ayagarlu or the village functionaries, which even the British administrators could not dispense with.

Thus the main objective of this study is to give a clear and comprehensive picture of the agrarian system of Andhra Desa of 17th and 18th Centuries.

The two centuries i.e. Seventeenth and Eighteenth, constitute an important epoch in the agrarian history of Andhra Desa. This period witnessed an enormously varied and complex agrarian situation which look different in many respects from that of the preceeding and succeeding periods.

This situation was mainly due to the political instability and confusion that characterized this period which witnessed the rule of a miscellany of political powers like that of Vijayanagara, Qutbshahi, Mughal, Asafjahi, the Muslim kingdom of Mysore, the French and the English East India Company. These developments had a powerful bearing on the economic life of this region in general and its agrarian life in particular. Andhra Desa during this period witnessed many basic changes in its agrarian economy. The land tenures system, land revenue assessment, revenue rates and the nature of its collection became quite complex. The system of revenue collection because of the practice of revenue farming and its off-shoot Visabadi system and addition of a few more intermediaries like Mokasadars, Jagirdars, Deshmukhs, Deshpandias and holders of new Charitable tenures etc. to the already existing ones like Nayakas, Palegars and the village level revenue officials, and also the Muslim religious institutions holding lands was characterized by widespread oppression. Life of the agricultural communities became miserable due to oppression, which also gave a setback to agricultural development of the region. There was no major development as far as the system of irrigation and methods of extension of cultivation and the process of agriculture were concerned.

One significant development of this period was that, Andhra Desa known for certain traditional crops like those of Paddy, and other cereals, pulses, oil-seeds like gingili and cash crops like cotton, indigo sugarcane etc, also saw the introduction of new commercial crops like tobacco, chillies etc from the new world. Another phenomena of the period was that, while the cultivation of some of the new crops spread rapidly, the production of indigenous crops like that of cotton, indigo, gingili, etc. got a tremendous impetus because of the establishment of direct trade with Europe and the consequent growth of agro-based industries like textiles etc. There were also sub-regional variations in the crop pattern.

The beginning of this period saw the decline of Hindu rule over Andhra Desa. The Vijayanagara Empire which at its height comprised a major part of the Telugu speaking area i.e. Coastal Andhra South of Krishna River, Rayalasima region and northern Telangana region began to loose its hold on this area after the battle of Rakshasa Tangadi in 1565 A.D. After the death of its last great emperor Venkata II of Aravidu Dynasty in 1614 A.D., the dismemberment of the empire was very rapid.

The Vijayanagara rule left a major imprint on the agrarian life of Andhra Desa in many of its aspects such as the land tenures, agricultural development, taxation etc though many of the developments in the agrarian field had their origin during the Kakatiya period, they attained their climax during the Vijayanagara period. The military service tenure called Nayankara held by Amaranayakas and which consumed 75% of the agricultural resources of the Vijayanagara empire was at its height. The descendants of these Nayakas and their successors the poligars came to dominate the agrarian life of a major part of this region during the period. Similarly the village Ayagar system, an important Civil service tenure, also reached its maximum growth during this period. Hindu temples and the learned Brahmins became the major charitable tenure holdes of the religious endowments lands. Vijayanagara rule also contributed to extensive agricultural development especially in the region south of river Krishna which came to be bestowed with innumerable irrigation works through a system called Dasabandam. This is another important contribution of the period. Innumerable tanks both big and small were built in the Rayalaseema region during this period. Thamos Munro writing in 1801 about Cuddapah district says that he had never come across a district in which there were so many tanks.[3] The Vijayanagara period also is associated with the Revenue farming system and the consequent tax oppression which was necessitated to bear the burden of a military state. Similarly the Visabadi System of Revenue settlement and cultivation of village lands, an off-shoot of Revenue farming system, also originated during the Vijayanagara period. It was widely prevalent in all the three regions of Andhra Desa. Many of these systems were continued in one form or the other by the succeeding governments that ruled over Andhra Desa.

The longest political rule over Telugu region, compared to other ruling powers of the period under study was that of the Qutbshahis of Golkonda. Though the Qutbshahi rule was confined to only Telangana region in the 16th century, it came to embrace the whole of Telugu speaking area after the decline of the Vijayanagara empire at the beginning of the 17th century. Though the Golkonda rulers accepted the Mughal suzerainty in 1636 A.D., during the reign of Abdullah Qutbshah the kingdom enjoyed administrative autonomy till its absorption by the Mughal Empire in 1687.

The Qutbshahi rule saw, in its wake, the introduction of many new agrarian developments in this region. Though they introduced the Mokasa system of military tenure, and endowed lands and villages to Muslim religious institutions, some of the old tenures like that of Nayankara system, Dasabandha tenures and charitable endowments made to Hindu religious institutions like, Devadana and Agrahara and the service Manyams of village officials and servants could not be dispensed with by this government. The agricultural development continued mostly in Telangana region, though in a limited way. The private entrepreneur system of irrigation development under Dasabandha was not completely discarded. The major agricultural development of the Qutbshahi period was the introduction of commercial crops in the area. The expansion of external trade due to the establishment of direct contacts with Europe and West Asia and South East Asia and the emergence of European trading companies like those of the English, the Dutch and the French in the 17th century gave a major impetus to commercial agriculture. This period saw the introduction of many new crops in the region brought by European from the New world.

Golkonda kingdom also became notoriously famous for its oppressive taxation on agricultural produce especially under the Revenue farming system called Ijara and also its off-shoot the Visabadi system. This is indicated by the contemporary European accounts.[4] Deterioration of the condition of Peasants continued unabated during this period.

After the Mughal conquest in 1687 Andhra Desa lost its political identity as this region which was under an independent regional kingdom was integrated into the Mughal Empire as an imperial province. The Karnatic territories south of Krishna and Gundla Kamma rivers which were once a part of Golkonda kingdom were placed under a Mughal Fauzdar. The wealth of this region began to be systematically drained now. Unlike the local aristocracy both Muslim and Hindu, the new elite class, the Mansabadars were drawn mostly from Northern India. The Mughal emperor though continued the agrarian structure of the Qutbshahs introduced several significant changes in the agrarian system. The old Qutbshahi intermediaries, Deshmukhs, Deshpandes, Kavalgar/Mannewar and the village level officials were all retained. Revenue farming or Ijara system, though officially prohibited in the Mughal empire, continued unabated but concealed in the distant coastal districts. 1689-90 Revenue settlement which selectively raised the revenue demand for the entire province added to tax burden. Introduction of Jiziya – first time in the area, placed another 4 per cent tax burden on the Hindus. A new superstructure of Mughal Revenue officials functioned at the capital and other administrative centers in the provinces. The Mughal conquest and the consequent Mughal rule 1687-1724 did not augur well for the Agrarian life of the region. Long period of troubles accompanying the annexation; Maratha and Bedar raids after 1700 their attacks on villages and distant towns, the revolts by local Zamindars, Desmukhs, renegade Mughal officers etc, severe drought, famine and pestilence, added to the general misery. The reduction in population, dwindled cultivated area and production led to Agrarian distress.

In 1724 the Nizam became the subadar of Deccan, and finally founded the new dynasty i.e. the Asafjahi Dynasty. He appointed his own men as governors of the provinces – Rustum Khan known to local tradition as Haji-Hussain was appointed over Rajahmundry. In northern Circars Temporary Amins were for a time appointed in place of the refractory Zamindars to collect the revenue. But soon he reverted back to old system and restored most of the Zamindars.

After the war of succession that followed the death of first Nizam in 1748, the Northern Circars (North Coastal Andhra) were ceded to the French by Salabat Jung who became the Subedar with the help of the French. While the French Company became the masters of the Northern Circars for a period of seven years (1751-1757) the remaining Telugu speaking area i.e. Telangana and Rayalasima was retained by the Nizam along with his Maratha and Canarese dominions.

Rayalaseema districts came under the rule of Hyder Ali of Mysore from 1780 to 1800 and Nellore Chittor districts remained a part of Carnatic under the Nawab. The French rule of the north Coastal Andhra districts was not peaceful. They had to face stiff resistance from Jafar Ali, the Nizam's governor of Chicacole and some of the local Rajas like that of Bobbili, which were overcome by the use of force by Bussy, the French general. The local records also allude to the religious fanaticism exhibited by the French towards the Hindu religion and its institutions in the region. The also attempted to introduce some land survey and a detailed accountan of gross collection of land revenue but without much success.[5] The Zamindars, though dismissed from their employment, were permitted under French Sanads to enjoy their hereditary privileges including Rusoom and Savarums (8 to 12 %). The revenue superintendents called the Deshmukhs and Deshpandes and Revenue farmer Ijaradars and Tahud-dars continued to be there appropriating much of the State revenue and oppressing the peasants. There was, on the whole, an increase in the State demand or annual settlement during this period.

For more than two decades the Rayalsema districts were under the rule of Mysore Sultans Hyder Ali from 1775 to 1782 and then under his son Tipu Sultan (1782-99). These rulers of Mysore by curbing the turbulent Polegars established an effective rule over these districts. Regarding this Munro points out... "Hider Ali was the only Indian sovereign we know of who ever subdued all his petty feudatories and was really master of his country".[6] The vigorous measures of the Mysore Sultans included resumption of Rusums and un-authorised Inams and the partial reduction of the Poligars. By the treaties of Mysore and Srirangapatnam in 1799, these were ceded to Nizam by Tipu Sultan.

The English East India Company became the ruler of the north Coastal Andhra then known as Northern Circars consisting of the present districts of Srikakulam, Vijayanagaram, West Godavari, East Godavari, and Krishna, in the year, 1765. In that year this area was granted by a Sanad of the Mughal Emperor at the request of Lord Clive. English agreed to pay an annual tribute or subsidy of nine lakhs of Rupees or to furnish military assistance when required to the Nizam, the subadar of Deccan who confirmed the Mughal grant of the Northern Circars in November, 1766. The English had to face, in the initial period of their occupation, a number of rebellions by the Zamindars and the tribal Chieftains who maintained large bodies of troops and holding large tracts of this region. The Zamindars were originally either the hereditary government revenue officials or renters of the Muslim period and the native chieftains were of pre-Muslim period origin.

Native-Administration

As the Company's servants did not know anything about the local land tenures, revenue settlement and its collection, they let the native administration take its course and did not concern themselves about the manner of revenue collection. For first three years, the Sarkars were leased out to the native renters who agreed for the payment of certain amount of annual revenue.[7]

Chief of Council

In 1769, the native administration was abolished and the management of the Circars was placed in the hands of the Company's servants – the provincial Chiefs and Councils. During this period, the Company's servants unable and reluctant to take up the detailed management of the revenue administration allowed the Zamindars and renters to appropriate the revenues on condition of their paying a stipulated amount to the Company government. The provincial chiefs, because of their inexperience in revenue management and ignorant of the local language had to depend upon the native Dubashis (interpreters) to manage the affairs of the Company. The revenue renting and sub-renting led to much oppression of the cultivators.

Circuit Committee

The State of affairs in the Northern Circars drew the attention of the Court of Directors. They, eager to see a better system of administration in their Madras territories appointed in 1776 a Committee of Circuit to enquire into the general conditions of the Northern Circars. But this Committee, whose efforts were thwarted by the provincial courts as well the Zamindars, was a failure Though Circuit Committee was revived in 1773 and continued its work until 1788, no fixed system could be introduced. During this period, annual leases for revenue collection was granted first and then the settlements for three or five yeas were made. The Haveli lands were let out, in most cases, on the system of village settlements and then given on a ten years lease to Condregula Jaggappa, son of a Dubashe.

In 1786 a Board of Revenue (after the Bengal fashion) was established at Madras. The Board was in continual collision with the provincial councils which were ultimately abolished in 1794 and collectors were appointed in their place. These European Collectors who were also not much acquainted with the local language had to depend on the Dubashis and other native underlings who exploited the ignorance of their masters for their own benefit. The evils arising from these fluctuations and temporary arrangements led to the introduction in 1802 of the permanent Zamindari Settlement in Coastal Andhra districts.

Guntur district area was ceded to the Company in 1788. Rayalasema districts were ceded by Nizam in 1800 in perpetual sovereignty to the East India Company, under the stipulation that the British Government should guarantee all the remaining territories of the Nizam from every attack. Nellore district and Ongole areas were Ceded by the Nawab of Karnatic in 1801. In 1838, the territory of the Nawab of Kurnool came under the English. With this, the whole of Coastal Andhra which were rich in agricultural resources and relatively poor Rayalasima region came under the English East India Company's rule and the backward Telangana region remained under the Asafjahi rulers who ultimately became the feudatories of the English. While the Ceded districts were brought under the Ryotwari system of revenue settlement in 1801 and Coastal Andhra under Permanent zamindari System in 1802, the Telangana remained under the same old system under the Asafjahis.

The establishment of British rule in Andhra Desa was an event of great significance in its agrarian history. British rule introduced certain basic changes in the agrarian life of this region. It had sought to reorganize the agriculture in its territories to suit its imperial requirements. In the initial stages, the principal concern of the English company was to realize, by quick and expeditious methods, as large revenue as possible. But the economic objectives of British rule changed gradually in view of the industrial revolution in England. British territories in India were used as a sources of raw materials for its industries and as a market for its manufactured goods which ultimately drained its agricultural and other resources.

SOURCES

The material for the study has been derived from the contemporary epigraphic and literary sources which are more abundant and varied compared to those of the preceeding period.

The inscriptions of the period, compared to those of the pre-sixteenth century period are a very few. Their region-wise and period-wise distribution also is uneven. Some of them hailing from region South of River Krishna belonged to Vijayanagara rulers and their feudatories like the Malti Chiefs of Cuddapah and Kalahasti-Venkatagiri chiefs. The remaining epigraphs belong to the Qutbshahis. All the inscriptions are in Telugu. Only some of the Qutbshahi inscriptions are bi-lingual – Telugu and Persian. Most of the inscriptions of the period throw light on the agrarian life of the period. They record the grant of villages and lands under various tenures – military and civil service and charitable. A number of epigraphs record grant of Manyam/Inam for agricultural extension, for providing irrigation and subsequent maintenance of irrigation works, under Dasavanda tenure and also record revenue rates and remissions etc. under the Vijayanagara and Qutbshahi rulers.

The major portion of the contemporary sources were literary which again consist of government documents like Farmans/orders, English East India Company's records such as Districts Collectorate Records, Fifth Report of the Select Committee on the Affairs of East India Company, Circuit Committee Report, District Manuals and Gazetteers etc. Accounts of European Travellers Hyderabad Affairs volumes and finally, the indigenous literature such as the village Kaifiyats or Mackenzie Manuscripts and literary works like Hamsavimsati by Ayyala raju Narayanamatya, Sukasaptati by Kadaripati etc.

Portuguese Chronicles and European Accounts

The two Portuguese Chronicles – one of Domingo Paes and another of Fernao Nuniz, both of the first part of the Sixteenth Century, though belonging to preceeding period, shed very useful light on Nayankara system under

Vijayanagara. It is through these two chronicles that we get much information about this important military tenure which was prevalent in some form through out the period under study.[8] The accounts of European travelers who visited Telugu speaking area during the period under study contain useful information for the subject. Dutch Schorer, English Methwold and the anonymous author visited this region between A.D. 1608 to 1622. Their relations or accounts published under the title *"Relations of Golkonda in the Early Seventeenth Century A.D. 1608-1622* edited by W.H. Moreland, London 1931 furnish the information having direct bearing on the subject. It is these relations that throw more light on the Revenue farming system prevalent in the Golkonda kingdom and oppression associated with it. They describe the variety of agricultural produce of the kingdom and their prices. Similarly, the accounts of three French travelers – Thevenot, Tavernier and Bernier and also that of Thomas Bowry who visited this region during the second half of eighteenth century A.D. also shed some light on the subject. They describe the seasons, floods, crop pattern, prices of food grains, weights and measures, coinage etc. which is very useful for the subject.

Farmans

The Farmans are another source of information for the subject. A Farman is a mandate or an order issued by a Muslim monarch.

The *Qutbshahi Farmans* numbering 22 published along with Bahmani and Adilshahi Farmans, under the title 'Farmans and Sanads of the Deccan Sultans (1408-1687 A.D.) edited originally by Dr. Yusuf Hussain Khan in 1963, published by A.P. State Archives in 1980 throw a very useful light on the agrarian life of the period. They record the grant of villages/lands under various tenures. The grant of Inam lands to Muslim saints, mosques and temples are mentioned. Similarly the revenue officials, such as Deshmukhs, Chaudaris, Sthalakarnams, Despandias, Kotwal etc and their perquisites also are mentioned in these Farmans. These Farmans are mostly from A.P. Stae Archives.

The *Qutbshahi Farmans* numbering about 70 from A.P. State Archives and Mughal Document of Inayat Jung Collection, pertaining to Andhra, obtained from National Archives, New Delhi and translated by Syed Tashirulla Hussaini under the Departmental Research Support (DRS/SAP) Sponsored by UGC, Department of History, Osmania University, also have been utilized for the study.

The *Manuals* and *Gazetteers* of Coastal Andhra and Rayalasima districts, published in the second half of the Nineteenth Century A.D. are a very valuable source for the study. They throw a flood of light on land revenue system, land tenures, political conditions prevailing in the region during the pre-colonial period. Though these works were not contemporary, they are treated as primary sources as they were compiled on the basis of original records such as the District Collectorate Records etc.

Athavanavyavaharatantram was a local Record collected by Kavali Venkata Borraiah (1776-1803) assistant of Col. Mackenzie. This Ttreatise on Vijayanagara revenue administration is known to have been translated by him into English and presented to Col. Mackenzie in April, 1802. This document throws considerable light on the system of revenue administration, local government not only in the Vijayanagara Empire but also the agrarian conditions and the Pargana hereditary revenue officials like Deshmukh and Deshpandia, village community, their perquisites, Visabadi System, Revenue Farming tax rates, etc. in the 17th and 18th centuries under the Muslim rule.

Another important source utilized for the study are the Mackenzie Manuscripts or village Kaifiyats. These are the digests of the village registers or Dandakaviles and inscriptions collected by Col. Colin Mackenzie (completed by the year 1814 A.D.), an engineer of East India Company battalion. Besides giving a narrative of the political history of the period, they throw a flood of light on the agrarian life of the period in Coastal and Rayalaseema districts. They contain useful and authentic information regarding the land tenures such as the Nayankaras, Palegars, Mokasa, Jagirs, Deshmukh, Deshpandia, Majumdar, Mannevar, Kavali, floods, famines, migrations, land and grain measures, famines, etc. For example, the Rusooms, Savarams, and Inam villages enjoyed by the Deshmukhs, Majumdars and Mannekavali held by several families in Guntur district during the period under study are mentioned by Guntupalli Kaifiyat.[9] Similarly, the land and grain measures of the period are mentioned in Guntur Kaifiyat.[10]

The District Collectorate Records are an indispensable source of information for the study. These records are dated from 1766 to 1870. These are also known as pre-Mutiny Records. They are in handwritten form. The records pertaining to Coastal Andhra and Ceded Districts were transferred in 1968 from Tamilnadu Archives to A.P. State Archives. The main reference media for the District Records are Guides in respect of Circar Districts and Handbooks to the Revenue Records of the Ceded districts. The District Collectorate Records consist primarily of their correspondence with government, the Board of Revenue, the Court of Wards, the Zamindars. A variety of subjects like the Zamindaris, Akbari, Land Settlement, Land Revenue useful for the study are dealt with in these volumes, numbering totally about 600. Among the Diaries (1) The Diary of the Collector's Proceedings in the Kondapalli and

Mustafanagar Circars 1797-1797, and Guntur Diary 1788-89; and among the Reports(2) The Circuir Committee Report on Nuzividu and Charmahal (1785-86), Circuit Committee Report on the Haveli Lands with Mr. Oram's Report and the Circuit Committee's Report on the accounts of Zamindaris are very useful for the present research. The District Collectorate Records have got, on the whole, an inexhaustible and abundant source material.

Similarly, Appendix to Fifth Report from the Select Committee on the Affairs of the East India Company issued in 1812 (Vol.III) also contain abundant information on the subject.

Chapterization

The book has five chapters. The introductory chapters explains the significance of the subject, reviews the existing work, gives the justification for the study, indicates the scope and methodology of the study and evaluates its sources.

The Second chapter entitled "Land Tenures" explains the various tenures under which the land in Andhra Desa of the period was held and its income enjoyed. All these tenures and the fluctuations in their number and size are discussed in this chapter.

In the third Chapter "Land Revenue System", land survey and measurement Modes of Revenue Assessment, Visabadi System, Revenue rate, Modes of revenue collection, Revenue Farming government revenue organization, Tax oppression etc. under various governments are discussed.

The Chapter "Agricultural Development and Agricultural Communities" deals with extension of cultivation, irrigation maintenance and Repairs of irrigation works, agricultural process, crop-pattern, famines, peasants and Agricultural labourers, live stock etc.

Finally the Summary of the report and the conclusions are given in the last chapter.

Notes & References

1. Tapan Raya Chaudhuri and Irfan Habib, *The Cambridge Economic History of India-I (1200-1700)*, p. 169.
2. *The Imperial Gazetteer of India,* The Indian Empire Vol. III, Economic, New Edition, New Delhi, p. 1 & 2.
3. *Cuddapah Manual*, p. 113.
4. Moreland, *Relations of Golkonda*, pp. 11, 57, 81 & 82.
5. *Godavari Manual*, p. 119
6. C.F. Brakenberry, *District Gazetteer*, Cuddapah, p. 40.
7. Mustafanagar, Ellore and Rajamundry Circars were let out for 3 years to the Nizam's Fouzdar, Hussain Ali Khan.
8. *Forgotten Empire*, Appendix, pp. 237-393.
9. *Grama Kaifiyattulu*, Guntur Taluka III – A.P. State Archives and Research Institute, Hyderabad, 1988, pp. 179-180.
10. *Ibid.*, II, pp. 28 & 65.

CHAPTER – II

LAND TENURES

One of the important aspects connected with the evolution of the agrarian system is the land tenure system. Government being considered during this period as the owner of the land, the Ryot had only the occupancy rights. And as long as he paid the government share of the produce he could not be evicted. If Government gave villages and lands to others under various tenures, they were given along with the Ryots, whatever be the governments, whether Hindu, Muslim or Christian, the land tenures existing in Andhra Desa during the period were of two main categories.

I. Government or Crown villages

II. And villages and lands alienated to others for some purpose.

I. GOVERNMENT VILLAGES OR CROWN LANDS

To the first category belonged all the villages which did not belong to second category. The revenue of these villages belonged to the government and was not alienated to others. They were held and managed by the government. This income from these villages went to defray the costs of building and maintaining strategic fortresses under the royal control. The number of villages belonging to this category was very small compared to that of second category. These villages are referred to as *'Bhandaravada Gramas'* and also *'Simhasananiki Chelle Gramalu'* in the Telugu districts of the Vijayanagara Empire as their revenue was paid to the royal/ central treasury called *'Bhandaram'*.

Haveli or Old Demesne or Household Property of the Sovereign

The crown lands under the Qutbshahis are referred to as Haveli. It appears, all the important forts Medak, Ghanpura, Kailkonda, Malangur, Kaulas, Elegendal, Warangal, Narsapur, Bhongir, Pangal, Haveli Hyderabad and Haveli Muhammadnagar (Golkonda), Kohir and Khammam in Telangana region; Kondapally (Mustafanagar) Kondavidu (Murtuzanagar) Udayagiri etc. in Coastal Andhra had Haveli parganas/villages attached to them and were meant for the maintenance of the garrisions stationed in them.

The area immediately surrounding the head-quarters of a district which was usually a fort was called the Haweli Pargana. It was a crown property. They were the source of revenue reserved for the support of the district governor/ fort commander and his garrison. Regarding the Haveli Parganas acquired by the company, the Circuit committee records thus ... "Havelis composed of lands in the vicinity of Moorish capitals were attached thereto as a ready source of expenses and supplies independently of the Zamindars, and to prevent any unnecessary intercourse between their licentious army and the quiet laborious Hindus of the Original Zamindaris".[1]

Khalisa

The crown tenure villages were known as 'Khalisa' under the Mughals. There were altogether 87 Khalisa Parganas in Telangana and Coastal Andhra regions put together. In the year 1690, out of these, Telangana had 53 Parganas and coastal Andhra 34. Against those, there were 124 Paibaqi Parganas which were ready to be assigned as Jagirs.[2] This indicates, to some extent, the extent of the Khalisa territories at the beginning of the Mughal period. This was more likely the arrangement under the Qutbshahis.

This is further confirmed by the revenue collection of these two types of territories. While the revenue of 87 Khalisa Parganas yielded Rupees 64,41,217 (Hasil), that of Paibaqi Parganas was Rs. 8,8,12, 447.[3] The concentration of Khalisa Parganas was more in the Telangana districts compared to that of coastal Andhra. This was probably in view of the proximity of the region to the capital Hyderabad. While only selected Parganas which were more productive from 9 out 13 Telangana districts appear to have been kept under Kalisa. The whole districts of Machilipatam, Rajamundry, Nizampatam and Srikakulam have been maintained under this category. It is to be remembered that due to short duration of Mughal rule, the Mughal term for crown lands i.e. the 'Khalisa' did not become as popular as the term 'Haveli' of Qutbshahi period, which was in use relatively for more number of years. That is the reason why this term 'Haveli' was still in use in the Company's records when the northern Sarkars came under it.

Under the Asafjahis, the crown lands were disignated as 'Kalisa' or 'Diwani' territory. They were under the administration of the Diwan or Prime Minister of the Nizam's government, and hence called 'Diwani'. The Khalisa Parganas included, with in them, small portions of Inam lands not paying revenue or fully exempted from revenue payment as well as some isolated Jagir Villages. The total area under Khalisa tenure in Asafjahi Hyderabad State was 70,168 square miles. The area of land paying government revenue, uncultivable, cultivable and cultivated including follow for one year, under this head was 2,13,20,425 acres or 12,631 villages[4].

The Haveli villages continued to be maintained as a separate tenure in the coastal Andhra districts even after they came under the English Company's rule in 1766. When the Permanent Zamindari Settlement was made, the Haveli estates were parcelled out as Mutahs auctioned and sold as Zamindaris.

II. VILLAGES AND LANDS ALIENATED TO OTHERS

The second of the above two main categories i.e. the villages and lands alienated to others, admits again two-fold classification based on the purpose of the alienation (a) one was service tenure (b) and the other was beneficiary or charitable tenure. The service tenures in land were granted in consideration of service rendered or expected of the one in whose favour the land or villages were granted. These service tenures may be classified further under two heads viz. One, the military and the other civil.

(a) Service Tenures

1. Military Service Tenures: The most important of the military service tenures was known as 'Nayankara' or 'Amaranayankara' under Vijayanagara Empire. Nayankara and Muqasa or Mokasa under the Qutbshahis, chieftains/ Zamindars of coastal Andhra and Telangana, Polegars of Royalasima, Jagirs under the Mughals and the Asafjahis also belonged to this category.

Nayankara or Amara Nayankara System

It was the most important military land tenure of the Vijayanagara period. It originated during the Kakatiya period. It resembled the Iqta system of Delhi Sultanate and prevailed in most of the post-Kakatiya period kingdoms It reached the climax of its evoluation during the Vijyanagara period. For this system of tenure prevalent in the Vijayanagara Empire, we have much evidence from the Portuguese travellers besides the indegenous sources of the sixteenth century. This system was also known as 'Amara Nayaka' tenure. Under this system, Vijayangara Emperors apportioned the country among their Nayakas who in turn had to provide the former with army and money. An account of the period of Achyutadeva Raya by the Portuguese traveller Fernao Nuniz confirms this. Nuniz says "All the land belongs to the king and from his hand the captains hold it.... The kingdom of Bisnaga is divided between more than two hundred captains who are heathen".[5] This is further confirmed by another Portuguese traveller, Domingo Paes of Krishnadeva Raya's period. He states "these captains whom he has over those troops are the nobles of the kingdom; they are lords and they hold the city, and the towns and the villages of the kingdom".[6]

The List of the Vijayanagara Nayakas from the Telugu region belonging to the first part of the 17th century are given below

Sl. No.	*Name of the Nayaka*	*Nayankara Sima*	*District*	*Date & ruling king*	*Source*
1.	Muddayadeva	Prabhakarapatnam	Anantapur	1602-03 Venkata-II	-
2.	Ramarajayya deva	Guttik Sima	Anantapur	1602 Venkata II	SII, XVI, 308
3.	Gangappa Nayaka	Dupati Sima	Kurnool	1614 Venkata II	SII, XVI, 313
4.	Malla Ravella	Kohcharla Kota Sima	Kurnool	1622 Ramadeva	SII, XVI, 316

5.	China Tirumalayya	Prabhakarapatnam Sima	Anantapur	1625-26 Ramadeva	Butterworth & Setty CP & SI of South India Nellore 34-A, p. 802.
6.	Immadi Papinayudu	Penakacherla Sima	Anantapur	1626 Ramadeva	SII-SVI, 313
7.	Velugoti Venkatapati Nayudu	Rapuru, Nelluru, Poruru, Kalahasti Kondampadu, Venkatagiri Korturu Simas	Nellore & Chittoor	1628 Ramadeva	Butterworth & Setty CP & SI of South India Atmakur 53.
8.	Timmaraju Deva	Jagtapigutti Sima	Anantapur	1640 Venkata II	SII-XVI, 327
9.	Hande Sidda Ramappan-ayaka	Kovilakuntla	Kurnool	1643 Sriranga III	SII, XVI, 330
10.	Ravela Muddu Krishnappa Nayaka	Sariyapalli Sima	Nellore	1645 Sriranga III	SII-XVI, 331.

The Nayankara tenure which was hereditary and became so deep rooted in the Telugu region that the Qutbshahis, the next ruling power, could not dispense with it completely in their dominions newly conquered. Jagdev Rao of Elgandal (Karimnagar district) Asva Rao of Palvancha (Khammam district) were some of the Nayakas under Qutbshahis. An epigraph of 1613-14 A.D. from chundi town (Nellore district) refers to a certain Nayudu holding Chundi town granted a Amaram to him by Mohammad Quli Qutbshah.[7] An epigraph of 1642 A.D. from Chundi (Nellore district) refers to 'Amaram' tenure held under the Qutbshahi rule by a Hindu Nayaka.[8] Similarly, in 1688-89 A.D. one Ravella Muddu Krishnappa Nayudu was holding as Amaramu the villege Narikellapuri in Sariyapalli Sima (Nellore district) which was part of Qutbshahi kingdom. This is refered to in an epigraph of that year from the above villege.[9] Gandikota Durgam Kaifiyat states that one Sanjeeva Nayaka had two villages – Mudiyamu and Paluru as Amaram for the maintenane of himself and his 100 soldiers serving in the Gandikota fort under Mirjumla during Abdulla Qutbshah period.[10] The Nayakas mentioned as 'Nayaka warrian-1,-Azam' maintained large contigents of troops for Qutbshahi compaigns.[11] It appears, the Nayakas of Qutbshahi kingdom were apparently the Hindus and many of them belonged to the Velama caste. As the Qutbshahi State replaced the Velama kingdom that ruled over Telangana region before it, some of the Velama nobles of Rachakonda and Devarakonda might have continued as Nayakas under the Qutbshahis. As far as Vijayanagara empire is concerned, the Nayakas belonged to many castes such as Kshatriya, Balija, Kamma, Velama, Brahmin and Boya. There were also Muslims in the Vijayanagara Empire holding these military tenures.

Here it is to be observed that, we do not find any prominent Reddi Nayaka either in the service of Vijayanagara or of Qutbshahis. Inspite of the fact that, they were ruling over coastal Andhra in the pre-Vijayanagara period as independent rulers simaltaneously with the Velamas in Telangana, none of their descendents could rise to the level of the Velamas, Kammas and Balijas who played a prominent role as Nayakas during the Vijayanagara period covered under study. The Balija Nayakas could establish the independent Nayaka kingdoms of Madurai, Tanjore, Ginjee and Vellore in Tamil region in the post-Vijayanagara period.

With the help of the information available, it is difficult to estimate the total number of Nayakas under either the Vijayangara empire or Qutbshahi kingdom and also the total territory alotted to them. Nuniz tells that there were total 200 Nayakas (captains) in the Vijayanagara Empire. But it is difficult to indicate their number in the Telugu districts of the empire. N.Venkataramanayya concludes on the basis of the number of forts held by them as mentioned in *Rayavachakamu* that nearly three-fourths of the Vijayanagara Empire was under the Amara-nayakas.[12] Krishnaswami says that nearly three-fourths of the land in Tamil country was held during this period by the Nayakas under this tenure.[13] Probably this proportion holds good for the Telugu speaking area of that empire.

The size of each Nayankara or the number of villages held by each Nayaka, depended, probably, on the importance of the Nayaka and the additional position held by him. It appears, most of them held only one Sima which was equalent of a modern Taluka. Only very few Nayakas held more than one Sima. In 1628-29, one Velugoti Venkatapati Nayadu was holding seven Simas (in modern Nellore and Chittoor districts) in his Nayankara.[14] Nuniz mentions some of the important Nayakas who were occupying key positions such as ministers, treasures etc., holding larger areas.[15]

Some idea can be formed about the number of troops maintained by Nayakas and the tribute paid by them on the basis of Portuguese Sources. Nuniz states that the total revenue of the villages held by the Nayakas (during the period of Achyuta Raya 1529-42) was 120 lakhs Pardoas (a spanish coin) out of which 60 lakhs was paid by them as tribute to the emperor every year and with the remaining 60 lakhs they maintained 6 lakhs of infantry and 24 thousand horses.[16] From this account we are given to understand that they paid as tribute only half of the revenue they collected from the territories assigned to them and the bulk of the army was maintained and supplied by them in times of war.

At another place, Nuniz mentions the names of some of 11 of the important Nayakas of the 200 mentioned above and the territories of the empire held by each of them, the positions held by them at the court, the total revenue yield from the territory of each of them, the amount of rent paid by each in gold Pardoas and finally the number of foot soldiers, horses and elephants maintained by each them. These Nayakas, as indicated in this account, also held important positions like minister, treasurer, marshal, chief master of the house, chief counseller of the king and also commanders of army.[17]

The revenue yield from the territory of each Nayaka ranged from 11,00,000 to 20,000 pardos and the tribute from 3,00,000 to 7,0000. These 11 Nayakas paid a total of 11,62,000 tribute out of 45,35,000 which was the total revenue, from their lands. Thus, these 11 Nayakas, contrary to the statement of Nuniz above, paid as tribute only one-fourth or 26 percent of the total revenue on an average, on the areas assigned to them. This difference might be due to the fact that the 11 Nayakas were holding some additional positions besides fulfilling the stipulated conditions of Nayakas.

The Nayakas of Vijayanagara empire paid the tribute annually. Paes states that they paid it in the first part of the month of October on the occasion of a festival at the capital.[18] Nuniz states that the tribute was paid in the month of September on the occasion of a great festival.[19] Probably both of them are referring to the Mahanavami or Dasara Festival.

Nayankara system continued to function, along with the Mokasa system in the Qutbshahi kingdom. During the early Qutbsahi period, some of the Nayakas like Jagdev Rao, the Velama Nayaka of Elgandal (Karimnagar District) were in the Qutbshahi service. A Farman of 1688 A.D. refers to Nayakawaris along with revenue officials of Tarkunda Pargana (Telangana region).[20] We find the remnants of Amara Nayaka system even during the Asafjahi period. An epigraph dated 1777 A.D. mentions one Nandyala Narayana Raju making a land grant to a Brahmin from his Amara village Anantasamudram.[21]

Palegars of Ceded Districts

The Palegars system of Rayalaseema and Chittoor district also was of military tenure. The land held by the Palegar was Palemu (in Telugu) The Palegars were military chieftains of different degrees of power and consequence. Their position and origin is almost similar to those of the Zamindars of Northern Sarcars. The system had its origin in Tamil region. Visvanathanayaka of Madurai (1529-64) is said have started this system. In many respects it resembles the Nayankara system. This system had travelled to ceded districts during the later Vijayanagara period (post Tallikota period). The Palegars were bound by the ties of military to the king and held lands on 'Amaram' or military tenure, in return for a fixed annual tribute called 'Peshkash' and the maintenance of stipulated military contingent. Their office and land grant had become hereditary like that of Nayaka though in theory and practice they could be expelled and their grants resumed by the suzerain power.

During the period of Seventeenth and Eighteenth centuries, when this area came under the rule of Qutbshahi, of Golkonda and Adilshahis of Bijapur first, and then the Mughals, Marathas, Mysore (Hyder Ali and Tipu Sultan) and Asafjahis in succession, the Palegars were at war with each other for the extension of their respective powers or against the soveriegn power. They paid the tribute not according to any fixed principles, but according to the power of the government in force. The Management and administration of the their Palaiyams or Palems and the control of their subjects were left entirely to the Palegars.

The Palegars of Rayalasima, like the Zamindars of coastal Andhra were of different origins. Of the 80 palegars existing in Ceded districts at the time of their cession to the East India Company in 1800, majroty of them were of Vijayanagara period origin and the remaining were of subsequent period.

Half of them were Palegars from the beginning and the remaining started their career, some as Kavalgars/Talaris, some as intermediary Zamindars or revenue collectors, some as Dalavayis, some as Patels etc.[22] The Palegars belonged mostly to the Boya, Golla, Baliza and Reddi Communities.[23] Three of them were of Muslim Community.[24]Of the total 80 Palegars 49 Palegars belonged to the Cuddapah district and the remaining 31 belonged to the Kurnool and Ballary including Anantapur districts (only four belong to Bellary district).

An Abstract statement of the Palegars in the Ceded Districts taken from the *Appendix to Fifth Report from the Select Committee* is given in the following pages. They indicate the total number Palegars, the number of villages of their respective Palems, their full valuation or rent, the amount of tribute they were to pay and the number of cavalry and foot soldiers they were to furnish by the condition of their tenures. These tables also indicate the changes which took place in the extent of their territories, amount of tribute and the nature of their tenures from the period of Vijayanagara rule till the year 1800 when Rayalasima was Ceded to Company.

An Abstract Statements of the Palegars in Ceded Districts

(Xerox copies of chartrs to be included in the text)

Simiarly there were a few Palegars in Nellore district. They include those of Turavaru Palegars of Rapur, the Tadiboyana Palegar, Chittadu Palegar, Udathawarpalegar, Gangulavari Charuvapalli Palegar and Buchireddipalem palegar.

Zamindars of Coastal Andhra

There were a large number of military chiefs/Zamindars in Coastal Andhra region and also considerable number of them in the Telangana region who held villages under military service tenure during the period under study. There were 70 Zamindars in the districts of chicacole, Godavari, Mustafanagar and Murtuzanagar Sarkars represented by modern A.P. districts of Srikakulam, Vijayanagaram, Visakapatnam, East and West Godavari, Krishna, Guntur and Prakasam districts. Similarly there were four Zamindaris of Venkatagiri,Kalahasti, Bomray and Sayidapur (formed into the district of Western Pollems in 1800) in Nellore and Chittoor districts, and also Chundi Mutyalapadu and Guduru (both Nellore). Towards the end of the period, all of them were holding territories on military tenure paying tribute and maintaining armed forces to be supplied to the sovereign power. Seventy per cent of the Parganas/villages in coastal Andhra region were under this tenure.

The Zamindars of coastal Andhra were of different origins and evolution. The origin of some of them can be traced to pre-Muslim period. The tribal military chieftains mostly in the hilly tracts north of Godavari river were of this category. These hill Zamindars were the descendants of the kingdoms of Orissa and who were entrusted with the protection of the area from robbers and wild beasts. Due to the difficulty of keeping them in strict subjection, the Muslim rulers allowed them to perform their traditional duties and enjoy the government share of the produce from their territories on condition of paying a tribute.[25] Majority of the coastal Andhra Zamindars were of Qutbshahi period origin. The major Zamindaris like that of Vijayanagaram, Peddapuram, Peetapuram, Narsaraopet, Bobbili, Repalle, Devarakota (Tsallapalli) Mailavaram and Polavaram belong to this category. The founders of these hereditory estates were originally renters or Revenue Farmers (Izaradars) under the Qutbshahis and were promoted as Deshmukhs, Mokasadars, Mannewar subsequently. Some of them like those of Sattenapally, Chilkaluripadu, Vissannapet, Medurghat were originally of Qutbshahi period Deshpandes or Majumdars. A few of them like those of Anakapalle and Vallur were of East India Company's period origin. Finally, all of them became Zamindars by the time of Company, paying tribute and maintaining armed forces.

The military force of the Zamindars, like that of the Palegars of the Ceded districts, consisted of three categories. First, the common peons, who were paid in money and whose constant attendance was expected. They were like the standing army; Secondly; the Mokasa peons, who were paid by assignment of revenue of the villages or lands, subject to quit rent only. Third, the Manovarthy peons who consisted of military tenants of a higher order (mostly relations of Zamindars) and who were bound to bring their adherents with them to the field and who also enjoyed lands under Mokasa.[26] The Majority of the Zamindars of Coastal Andhra belonged to the communities like Velama, Raju, Kamma, Brahmin and Reddi. There were a few Zamindars belonging to Vaisya, Goldsmith, Perika, Golkonda Vyapari communities. The Chieftains of Andhra, Sarvapally, Salur, Panchipenta, Chemudu, Samgamvalasa, Belgam, Merangi and Kurupam situated in Srikakulam district were tribals called Kondarajus of Oriya origin. Charts indicating the number of these Zamindaris in 1802 Sarkar/Distric-wise, caste/community of the Zamindars, number of Parganas and villages, under the categories such as assessable, Agraharas, Mokasas etc. under each Zamindari, and finally the tribute paid by each of them are given below. Another chart showing the sibbandi/armed forces, their categories, maintenance cost under each Zamindari also is given.

CHART-1
Chicacole Sarkar
Number of Villages tenure-wise held by the Zamindars in 1802

S. No.	*Estate*	*Caste*	*Assessable or Tirayati villages*	*Agra-hara*	*Mokasa*	*Peshkush Rs.*
1.	Vijayanagaram Pusapati	Kshatriya	834	250	73	7,16,705
2.	Jeypore – Deo	Kshatriya	140	51	1	90,000
3.	Magole	Kshatriya	77	26	-	-
4.	Andhra Garaya Dora	Kondadora	9	2	22	1,500
5.	Sarvapally Bhimavaram	Jogiraju	-	-	-	400
6.	Salur 3 Parganas	Kondaraju	122	27	-	40,000
7.	Bobbili	Velama	140	51	-	90,000
8.	Panchipenta 2 Hill Mutas	Kondaraju	15	(total 19+132 hamlets)		3,000
9.	Chemudu	Kondaraju	13	2	-	5,000
10.	Sangamvalasa	Kondaraju (Oriya)	19	1	-	6,700
11.	Belgam (1796= 14 villages)	Kondaraju	-	-	-	10,500
12.	Merangi	Kondaraju	42	19	-	18,500
13.	Kurupam Sanyan Dora	Kondaraju	48	10	-	14,500
				439	105	

Lapsed Estate in Chicacole Sarkar after 1802

S. No.	*Estate*	*Lapsed in*	*Caste*	*Assessable of Jirayati villages*	*Agrahara*	*Mokasa*	*Peshkush*
1.	Palkonda	1833	Khond Jatapu	108	49	68	57,000
2.	Golkonda	1837	Doras	24	13	24 5	10,000
3.	Vemalapudi	1831		14	-	-	7,000
4.	Kottakola	-		12	-	-	13,500
5.	Sarvasiddi (purchased by Vijayanagaram)	-		13	-	-	25,600
6.	Rajala	1831		-	-	-	-
7.	Kottur	-		8	-	-	9,067
8.	Velchur Kodur-(Company)	1844		-	-	-	7,267
9.	Konda Kirla			13	1	-	-
10.	Raghavaram			12	1	-	-
11.	Dimili			10			

Krishna and Guntur Zamindars

S. No.	*Estate*	*Family*	*Caste*	*Jirayati*	*Agrahara Parganas*	*Mokasa Total*	*Peshkush*
1.	Masulipatnam	Nawabs	Muslim	-	-	-	-
2.	Nuzividu	-	Velama	18	231	-	
3.	Nandigama	Vasireddi	Kamma	-	551		
4.	Narasaraopet	Malraju	Velama				
5.	Repalle	Manikrao	Velama				
6.	Sattenapalle and Chilakuripadu	Manuri	Brahmin				2,53,400
7.	Medurghat and Jamalvayi Kanakagiri	Vellanki	Velama				
8.	Devarakota-Tsallapalli	Yarlagadda	Kamma				1,02,690
9.	Charmahal	Kamadana	Velama	4	260	-	
10.	Mailvaram	Surineni	Velama				
11.	Bezwada	-	Velama?				
12.	Munagala	Garlapati/ Keesara	Reddi				
13.	Lingagiri	Mantri-pegada	Brahmin				
14.	Vissannapet	Varigonda	Brahmin				
15.	Vallur	Bomma-devara	Kamma				

Godavari District Zamindari

S. No.	Estate	Family	Caste	Pargana/Villages Peshkush
1.	Peddapuram	-	Raju	372
2.	Pitthapuram	-	Velama	128
3.	Polavaram	-	Reddi	128
4.	Kotaramchandrapuram	-	-	66
5.	Rampa	-	-	338
6.	Totapalli	-	-	103
7.	jaddangi	-	-	88

There were total 18 Zamindaris and 80 Muttahs in 1802.

CHART-2
General Abstract of Zamindaris – Rajahmundry Circar

Name of the Zamindari		No. of Parganas	No. of Villages
Raja Jagpati Raju	1. Peddapur	14	388
	2. Petlapur	7	127
	3. Paroor	1	32
	4. Ramchandrapuram	1	38
	5. Kottah	1	28
Reddi	6. (Polavaram)	2	65
Reddi	7. (Gootala)	2	66
Reddi	8. Cottapally	1	32
	9. Corukonda	1	55
	10. Pullekonda	1	-
	11. Thottapalli	1	45
	12. Velampollam	-	-
	13. Rajamundry	7	-
		31	913

Ellore Circar

S.No.	Zamindari	Pargana	Villages
1.	Mogalatore	7	246
2.	Chintalapudy	1	62
3.	Selakcharla	-	5

Mustafanagar Circar

S. No.	Zamindari	Pargana	Villages
1.	Nandigama	3	123
2.	Challapalli	1	66
3.	Bezawada	3	48
4.	Mailavaram	1	53
5.	Madoorghatt	1	33
6.	Samoolvoy	1	38
7.	Munagala	1	19
8.	Lingagiri	1	6
		12	386

Source: (Masulipatam Circuit Committee Report, Vo.3009, Mr. Oram's Report on the Accounts of Zamindar s 1776-87.)

Number of Villages Pargana-wise in each Zamindari

Peddapuram Zamindari

Pargana	No. of villages
Kimmoor	53
Bickavole	42
Mandapetha	23
Chagalnadu	44
Cottam	34
Eseapally Muttah	13
Mollarao	15
Injaram	6
Murumullam	10
Eutacolah	60
Tanlly Panka	42
Cotteravooconda	18
Moonudevarum	8
Paravaram	20

Gootala Zamindari

Pargana	No. of villages
Couamdalah	49
Goosoogbilly	13

Polavaram Zamindari

Pargana	*No. of villages*
Polavaram Goosoogpally	65

CHART-3
Sibbandi of Zamindars

1.	**Peddapur Zamindari** - (Godavari District)		
1812	Mokasamdars and their allowances		Rupees Annas Paisa
	The amount of their villages		12,869-12-73
420	Mannovurthydars – The Rajas Relations and Dependentants		13,947
1282	Peons paid in ready money		17,230-30-30
3515	Total	Total	44,046-42-79
2.	**Pithapuram Zamindari – Godavari district)**		
100	Mannovurthydars –the Rajas relation and dependents		7,611-9
445	Peons paid in readymoney		5,547-19-39
545			13,158-28-39
3.	**Domahal or Ramchandrapuram Zamindari (Godavari District)**		
12	Mannovarthydars ..		208
383	Peons …..		4,103-24-60
395			4,313-24-60
4.	**Korconda Zamindari – (Godavari District)**		
300	Mokasamdars the amount of their village		2,298-2-12
400	Seerast Peons, the amount of their grounds		2,270-15-5-
331	Peons paid in ready money		2,483-19-40
10	Mannovurthydars – Rajas Relations and Dependents		317-30
1041			7,369-19-22
5.	**Polavaram Zamindary (Godavari district)**		
500	Mokasamdars, amount of their villages		2,013-26-20
720	Peons…..		6,302-15-54
1220			8,315-41-74
6.	**Gootala Zamindari**		
400	Mokasamdars		500
480	Peons		4,240-
880			4,740

7. Kottapalli Zamindary

521	Mokasamdars	739-18-25
172	Peons	1,613-46-40
693		2,353-16-75

8. Mogultore Zamindary

385	Mokhasam Peons – the amount of their villages	593-13-15
400	Mannovarthydars – the Rajahs Relations and dependents	14,132-
1886	Peons paid in ready money	16,276-43-0
2671		31,002-8-50

Note: The whole of Zamindari Artilary? Including the followers Of his dependents may amount to 4000 Men.

9. Chintapudi Zamindary

We have no accounts of this

10. Salekcharla Zamindari

None

Nuzividu and Charamahl No Reports …..

11. Devarakota Zamindari

151	Mokasam Peons	1,891-30-40
8	Mannovarthydars	1,380-
652	Peons paid in money	7,299-2-35
811		10,570-32-75

12. Nandigama Zamindari

This Zamindar maintained a large body of men in his Guntur possession we therefore Cannot determine. The numbers may occasionally be employed in the Nandigama.

13. Mailavaram Zamindari

776	Mokasam Peons…..	2,863-25-7-
259	Peons paid	479-1-40-
1035		3,342-26-47

14. Bazoara Zamindari

60	Mannovarthydars	1,200-
392	Peons paid in money	3,844
452		5,044

15. Madoor Ghatti Zamindari

No accounts – they have possessions in Khammad Circar.

16. Munagala Zamindari

3	Mannovarthydars	18-36-
497	Peons paid in money	688-3-
500		707-24-

The Zamindaris of Nellore district included those of Venkatagiri, Saidapur, Chunci and Mutyalapadu and Gudlur. Each Zamindari was held by a single individual, the eldest in the family usually holding the post. But, towards the end our period they have been divided among several sons of the Zamindar after his death. This was not allowed earlier either under Hindu or Muslim Governments.

The Samsthanams of Telangana region

Amarachintala, Gadwal, jatprolu, Vanaparthi (Mahboobnagar district) Paloncha (Khammam district) also were the Hindu Chieftains holding territories on military tenure. Some of them were of pre-Qutbshahis period, some of Qutbshahi period and some of Asafjahi period. During the Asafjahi period, all of them were maintaining armed retainers and paying tribute to the overlord., the Nizam. While the Rajas of Jataprolu and Paloncha were of Velama community, the remaining were Reddis. The following chart indicate the extent of their territories, tribute etc. during the Asafjahi period.

Samasthanam	*Number of villages*	*Total Revenue*	*Tribute - Army*
1. Amarachintala	60	Rs.1.4 lakhs	Rs. 6,363
2. Gadwal	214	Rs.3 lakhs	Rs. 86,840
3. Jataprol	89	Rs.1.9 lakhs	Rs.73,537
4. Paloncha	6 sub-talukas 800 sq.miles	Rs.70,000 lakhs	Rs.45,875 2000 cavatry 3000foot soldiers
5. Wanaparthi	124	Rs. 1.5 lakhs	76,883

There were Samsthanas of Papannapeta, Dubbaka, Donti in Medak district. All these chiefs both from Telangana and

Coastal Andhra regions, wether they were originally tribal chieftains and tributary chiefs of pre Muslim period or Deshmukh's, Deshpandes, Mannewar etc. of Qutbshahi period came to be designated as Zamindars during the Mughal period. All of them were holding villages, paying tribute and maintaining armed forces. Therefore their tenures can be described as military tenures. All these territorial proprietors, in general, (whether tributary Rajas, Deshmukhs, Deshpandia's etc.) in their different capacities were all ultimately confounded with each other and classed under the same common well known appelation of Zamindar or landholder during the Mughal period. Therefore the using of common term for all those chiefs was the creation of Mughal period.[27]

Zamindars/Deshmukhs/Deshpandes of Telangana under Mughals

1. Gopal Rao, 1687, Deshmukh and Muniyawar of Haveli Pargana surrounding Pangal and Kothakota Pargana (Mahboobnagar district) Assessed Annual taxes 26,777 gold Hun for Pangal and Jatprolu 50,000 gold Huns for Kothakota)
2. Nirmal Rao, Narasing Rao (three sons of above Gopal Rao) Joint Deshmukhs of Jatprolu Pagana, 1688
3. Timma Rao, Deshpande for Haveli pargana of Pangal, Kothakota and Jatprolu Parganas[28]
   - Same Gopal Rao in 1688 was made by Mughal Deshmukh and Munniwar of those 2 parganas, Pangal and Kothakota in Mahboobnagar and 8 more Parganas located in 4 other districts – total 400 village to pay a Peshkash of 100,000 Rupees.[29]
   - Kishan Rao, Deshmukh of Gandikota.

- Nursing Rao (same as above) Deshpande of Gandikota
- Gopal Rao (same as above?) Deshmukh of Rajamundry district in 1690.
- Venkatapathi, Deshmukh of Muhammadnagar Pargana at the capital.
- Venkat Rao in 1691,Deshmukh of Pargana Elegandal district[30]
- Anand Aswa Rao, Zamindar 1692 – paying tribute of Rs.50,000 Peshkash
- Bhim Reddi 1697 – Deshmukh of Kandur and Ghanpur Parganas (Mahboobnagar district) and Rs. 20,000 Peshkash.
- Nirmal Rao – Deshmukh of Nurkol Pargana (Koilkonda district)

The process of signing up Deshmukhs and Deshpandes extended over seven or eight years. In the interior (Andhra) the Mughals dealt directly with the Deshmukhs and Despandes of over a hundred individual parganas.

The Armed forces of Zamindars and Palegars

All these chiefs holding military service tenures, Palegars/ Zamindars were maintaining in their service, armed retainers. The 80 Palegars of Rayalasima were having in their service a total thirty thousand armed men in the year 1800. Similarly, the Committee of Circuit found in 1777 that the total of seventy Zamindars of Northern Sarkars were maintaining about Forty one thousands of armed retainers in their service. The total cost of their maintenance was calculated as Rs.19,68,000 at the rate of Rs.4 on each armed peon per month.[31]

These armed followers were meant for the performance of police duties in addition to military function. The armed men of the Palegars of Ceded districts consisted of three categories.

1. The first category were paid entirely in cash and had no other means of living. They were full-time employees and were like the standing army. But they were the least numerous.
2. The second category were assigned service lands (Manyam/Inam). These composed of Ryots who also rented out other lands besides having the service Inams. These were part-time soldiers.
3. The third category also were part-time soldiers having Inam-lands. Unlike those of the second category, these men confined themselves to the cultivation of there Inam lands only.[32]

It appears that the quantity of the land alloted to the armed followers in the Ceded districts was a field valued at six Pagodas annual rent according to the survey conducted by Thomas Munro.[33]

However, each one of them was entitled for Batta when he served outside his village. They also paid quit-rent on these Inam lands. The Palegars were able to mobilise, whenever necessary, a much larger force than their fixed establishment since every regular armed retainer had relations able to bear arms and was required to bring them into the field in times of emergency. The armed followers of Palegars were also known as 'Kattubadis' or Jangi Kattubadis and the lands granted to them were known as Kattubadi Inams.[34]

Tankas

In Western Pollams or Palems (consisting of Venkatagiri, Kalahasti,Bommaraj, Sayidapur, Chundi, Mutyalapadu and Gudlur in Nellore and Chittoor district), three modes of defraying the remuneration of their respective establishments including their personal, revenue and military were followed. The first mode was in money, second in grain and third in assignment of land. The money payment by the Polegars to their servants are extremely rare but the mode most generally resorted to, and considered equalent to money payment was to issue *'Tankas'*. It is to give eight or ten peons in an order to the amount of their pay on a renter or Ryot who was in arrears of several years revenue. Because of their inability to collect their amount, the receivers of Tankas were compelled to sell their Tankas at a discount of fifty or sixty percent which were some times circulated in this manner through the country from one purchaser to another. Some time, unable to dispose of the Tankas, their receivers waited on the Ryot or renter in a body and during that stay period they exacted Batta at the rate of one Seer of rice and one Piece daily per man. All this resulted in oppression of the Ryots and renters and also corruption. Tankas were also issued.for grain payment. The distress ensued in this case also.[35] Another peculiar usage resorted to in some of the Palems like that of Bommaraj was to deduct two or three month's pay from all the servants to make up the deficiency in the crops from drought or other causes.[36]

Interesting details regarding the Amaram and Kattubadi tenures are given in the Nellore Manual. The assignment of land under Amaram and Kattubadi tenures were made mostly for the military establishment in the Western Palems.

Amaram Tenure

Under **Amaram tenure**, the whole villages were assigned to the peons or armed retainers in the proportion of eight or ten to each village. They are considered as the Mirasidars of that village and were jointly bound to pay the stipulated quit-rent.[37] The term 'Amaram' means army and this military tenure in this region must have been a continuation of that tenure of Vijayanagara period. As mentioned already, the Amaram tenures were continued in the post-Vijayanagara period. Gandikota Durgam Kaifyat refers to one Sanjeeva Nayaka of Boya caste as one who was serving with his one hundred armed followers in the Gandikota fort under Mir Jumla, the Qutb Shahi governer and enjoying four villages as Amaram for the maintenance of himself and his followers. According to this source, he was paying a quit rent of 25 Varahas and collecting fifty percent of the agricultural produce of those villages.[38] Here it is the duty of the holders of Amaram tenure to encourage agriculture by giving the just share to the cultivators. Otherwise, the latter would desert their villages and go to the places where they got favourable treatment.

However, the Polegars usually assigned villages which were in ruin and decay for several years instead of productive villages to their soldiers who by their own means had to improve the agriculture. Those first two or three years, the Amaram peons could enjoy the income of their assignments free of any imposition beyond the original stipulated amount. But once the agriculture was improved he was compelled to pay additional impositions like the Katnam or Nazzars to the Polegar under the threats of being ejected from their villages.[39]

The Amaram villages were divided into equal allotment agreeably to the number of peons each. These allotments were made in some villages annually by mixing good, bad and indifferent land in each lot, so that the income from all may be nearly equal. In some villages, the allotments were made less frequently, in others, the first alotments made on the original grant were never changed. If any disputes regarding these cases arose, they were settled, some times, by the interference of the Palegar. And many a time they were settled by the Curnam and head of the neighbouring villages who were called in to adjust them by arbitration.[40]

Duties of Amaram Peons

Regarding the principal obligations of the Amaram tenure holders their names were registered at the Palegars Office (Huzur Cutchery) and also the rent they have to pay for their respective villages. Whenever the Palegar summoned them, they had to attend to the summons failing which they were punished with dispossesion from their lands. Amaram soldiers, being of higher class, were allowed to serve with such arms as they prefered. In case, a soldier, because of sickness, minority or other causes could not attend, he had to provide an efficient man to serve in his place. While on duty they were entitled to a Seer of rice and one Piece Batta daily per man. They also were incharge of the policing within their villages and were bound to make good the amount of all stolen property.

As the Amaram tenure was hereditary, the law of premogeniture was followed as far as the succession to the post and also the Manyam lands accompanying it. When there was no male heir, the land reverted to the Palegar. If the Amaram was in the family for several generations, a portion of the land was sometimes given to nearest surviving female relative in Inam, which also, on her death, reverted to the Polegar.[41] Jawanlapalli, the villege in present Mahboobabad Taluka, Warangal District must have been allotted to Jawans or solders under Muslim governments under the same Amaram tenure, so the villege came to be known after them.

Kattubadi Tenure

The other mode of payment by the Palegars to their armed retainers was by assignment of land called Kattubadi Inams which implied gifts to binds. The Kattubadi soldiers or peons were all Ryots to whom pieces of jungle and waste lands were assigned to cultivate in lieu of a stipulated money payment. The land was given in different proportions in different Zamindaris/Palems and also caste-wise. In Venkatagiri Zamindary, for the Kyjitam Vandlu or Pike peons of the Velama, Kamma and Kshatriya castes, eight Gorrus of jungle land or its equalent --three Gorrus of Punji (wet land) and 15 Kuntas of Nunji (dry land) of waste arable land which might have been neglected were assigned. The Velugulu or Match lock peons of the Golla, Pulli, Boya and Mala communities which were considered as inferior to those above mentioned were assigned only four Gorrus of jungle land or instead of jungle, two Gorrus of Punji and ten Kuntas of Nunji of waste arable land.

In the Kalahasty Zamindari, the first class peons got waste arable land of one Gorru of Punji and 30 Kuntas of Nunji; the second class half a Gorru of Punji and 20 Kuntas of Nunji.

In the Bommaraj Zamindari, the first description of Peons got 100 Kuntas of Punji and 30 Kuntas of Munji; and the second description, about half that quantity of both Punji and Nunji.[42]

The Kattubadi Inam holders were initially given advance of Taqavi (loan) for first two or three years for the development of land. During that period, they were obliged to engage outside cultivators who were given half of the produce. But when the lands became fully productive under their own cultivation, these Inam holders were, compelled to pay to the Polegar the Katnams or annual presents called 'Mamul Katnam' in installments and also additional Katnams called 'Ghair Katnams' or extraordinary presents levied on occasions such as marriage of Palegar or his relation etc. The succession to the office and the Inam land of Kattabadis and their obligations and perquisities were same as that of Amaram holders. The only distinction with the Kattubadis was that they were bound to serve either with the pikes or match-locks at their expense as stipulated.[43]

It appears, from the above description that, the Amaram and Kattubadi armed soldiers employed by the Palegars were part-time soldiers and were Ryots cultivating the Inam lands assigned to them in lieu of their salaries. Only in times of war they were summoned. In the case of Amaram holders, the whole villages were assigned to a group of them on equal shares and they were allowed to serve with weapons of their preference. There is no information about their caste background. But in the case of Kattubadis, individual pieces of land were assigned. Here again the quantity of land assigned varied caste wise and Zamindari wise. In both the cases, Amaram and Kattubadi, only neglected, jungle and waste lands were assigned requiring the allotees to develop it with their own means. The Palegars in this way contributed to the reclamation of land and agricultural development in their territories. These tenures with all their aspects must have been a continuation of that of Vijayanagara system as already mentioned. It is estimated that the net amount derived by the peons of Kattubadi and Amaram, on the largest allotment amounted to 8 star Pagodas and 6 4/6th Annas annually, and on the smallest to 3 star Pagodas and 4 4/6th Annas after deducting all the charges of cultivation etc.[44]

Muqasa or Mokasa Tenure

The Muqasa of Qutbshahi period were of military tenure. The holders of territories under this tenure were Muqasadars who enjoyed revenue, executive and military powers. Muqasa was almost like Iqta of Delhi Sultanate and the local Nayankaram and unlike the latter the Muqasadars did not pay any annual tribute. The revenue from the Muqasa enabled the Muqasadar to defray his salary and that of his soldiers and entourage. The Muqasadars, for the collection of revenue in his area, adopted the system of Ijara or revenue farming through an elaborate series of lessees and sub-lessees which was the usual practice during the Qutbshahi period. All the highest ranking administrators both civil and military in the kingdom belonged to this cadre. Yulchi Bek, the governer of Kaulas district and the commander of the Kaulas fort was a Muqasa holder during the period of Abdulla Qutbshah. With his annual income of 40,000 gold Hun from his Muqasa lands, he maintained himself and one hundred Persian and Turqi Cavalrymen.[45] Even Hindus were also assigned Muqasa tenure by the Qutbshahis. One Antoji, agent (Karyakarta) of Ramoji Mambaji Naroji Raghoji Pantulu is mentioned in an epigraph of 1650-51 from Kondamudusu Palem village (Kandukur tq. And Nellore district) which states that the Muqasa of Kandukur was granted to Antoji, who was a Hawaldar, by Abdulla Padusha.[46] Probably Antoji was Muqasadar of the entire Kandukur Pargana of Nellore district. Both these persons Ramoj Raghoji Pantulu and his agent Antoji appear to be Maratha Brahmins as their names suggest. Raghoji Pantulu as Fauzdar (commander-in-chief) and Antoji Pantulu as Hawaldar and the agent of the former are mentioned in an another epigraph of the same year and month with fifteen days gap but belonging to the neighbouring village Machavaram. This epigraph further states that the four villages – Kandukur, Kondamudusupalem, Mopadu and Machavaram situated in the Kandukur Pargana which was in the jurisdiction of Hawaldar Antoji Pantulu were granted as Muqasa to Chella Timmireddi, Mummadi Timmireddi etc. by Abdulla Padsha.[47] These Reddis were granted Muqasa for their military service. During the Qutbshahi period, the revenue farmers or contractor were also known as 'Hawaldar'.[48] It is interesting to note here that Antoji the Maratha Hawaldar having Kandukur in the area of his jurisdiction as mentioned in the above two epigraphs was also a Mokasadar of Kandukur Pargana.

Mokasas in Zamindaris

On the model of the Qutbshahi State, its various Hindu feudatories, Rajas and Zamindars also assigned a large number of villages under this military tenure called 'Mokasa' or 'Muqasa' for the maintenance of their armed forces. There were 197 Mokasa villages earmarked for this purpose in the various Zamindaris of Chicacole Sarkar itself.[49] There were a few villages under this tenure in Nellore district granted to Kavalgars.[50] For other Zamindars, we do not have this type of information but the amount spent in Rupees on Mokasam armed forces in various Zamindaris of Godavari, Krishna and Guntur districts is given. That was the amount which was equalent of the income/revenue derived from the Mokasa villages.[51] The Mokasa assignements to armed retainers of this region was similar to Amaram and Kattubadi tenures of Nellore and Chittoor Palems.

Police Service Tenures – Kavalgar/Mannewar

This tenure is similar to military service tenure, since it is also refered to as 'Mokasa'.[52]

The Kavalgar system originated during the Vijayanagara period. Each Kavalgar was appointed by the king over a certain territory, a few parganas or even a full district. These Kavalgars belonged generally to the criminal tribes and they were required to prevent theft by their castemen and restore the stolen property within their locality for which they were assigned lands and also for their maintenance.[53] The Kavalgar system appears to have been prevalent in Ceded district and other districts south of river Krishna, which formed a part of that empire while similar functions were performed by Mannevar in North coastal Andha. Sometimes, these police duties were performed by the Polegar or Zamindar or Deshmukh and they held the additional position of either Kavalgar or Mannewar and enjoyed the Manyams and other perquisites of both the offices i.e. Mannewar and Zamindar. Venkatanarasimha Rao, Zamindar of Malraju family was appointed by a 'Parvana' from Basalat Jang as the Deshmukh and Mannewar of Vinukonda Pargana (Guntur district).[54] Similarly, Manik Rao Rama Rao was made both the Mannewar and Deshmukh of the whole of Murtuzanagar Sarcar (Guntur district) by a Farman dated 1690 A.D. of Aurangzeb's period.[55] The members of both these families holding Mannewar tenure were of Velama community. The Zamindar of Chintapalli who held the additional post of Mannevar of Murtuzanagar Circar in 1789 enjoyed, according to a Sanad of Mughal Emperor Shah Alam, a Rusum of 3% up on the Ryot's share and Savaram of 12 Cochals of ground in every large villages and half a Chaver in a small village. He also held 2 jagir villages and Rusoom of 180 Pagodas. They were continued under the company rule.[56]

The Duty of Desakaval or district watch system prevalent in Nellore district was performed by Kavalgars. Kavalgar (and also Mannewar) a hereditary officer was made responsible to maintain law and order in part of a district, for the apprehension of offenders and recovery of stolen property; failing which he was bound to make good the loss to the sufferers. This part of his duty was called in Telugu "Achu Kavali".[57] The Palegars of Venkatagiri, Saidapuram and Kalahasty (all Nellore district and Chittoor district) also performed the duties of Kavalgars.

Kavalgar's emoluments included villages held as Mokasa or Vadapattu which were rentfree; of Mera or Kalavasam on the crop (a part of it) at varying rates (never higher than 6 7/8 percent, nor lower than 2 ½ ; of Manyams in the villages under their watch and in some cases a 'Rusum' on certain of the government collections.[58]

The Kavalgars maintained Kavali peons on fixed wages who were employed in guarding their territories. There were about ten Kavalgars responsible for maintaining peace in different parts of the Nellore district. The statement given below indicates the names of Kavalgars, number of villages covered in the area of their jurisdiction, their Inam, Vadapattu villages, tribute, in Nellore district.[59] Kavali fees were partially levied in addition to the customs to defray the expense of maintaining Kavalgars on the roads for the protection of merchants. This collection was made at Custom Choukies near passes and places particularly calculated for depradators to harbour in.[60]

S. No.	*Kavalgar*	*No. of Villages*	*Vadapattu/ Inam*	*Peshkash in Pagodas*	*Present Taluqs*
1.	Urtavari Kavalgar (Reddi)	160	4	p. 1021	Nellore, Gudur, part of Atmakur and Rapur
2.	Chittetivari Kavalgar (Reddi)	64	3	p. 775	Parts of Gudur and Rapur
3.	Tarravari Kavalgar	88		p. 50	Parts of Gudur and
4.	Tadeboyinavar	Rapur-ghat	3	p. 40	
5.	Mukkasadar of Gangulavari Kavalgar and certain	Dornal pass highways	8		
6.	Zamindar of Chundi Kavalgar				
7.	Zamindar of Gundlur Kavalgar				Gudlur & Kavali

8.	Kavalgar of Aduru	3	Gudur
9.	Kavalgar of Pakur	1	Saidapur
10.	jaghirdars of Udayagiri	their respective 3439 territories	
11.	Zamindars of Mutyalapadu		

The Kavalgar tenure system served the purpose for which Vijayanagara rulers created it. Many of the Vijayanagara epigraphs which refer to the land grants refer to Mannegars (Kavalgar) along with the Parupatyagars (the revenue official of a district).[61]. But this system became a source of great abuse and oppression in the later years. This is explained in the Manual of Nellore District thus.... "The resources of the Kavalgars, originally given to secure the restoration of stolen property or its value, and probably sufficient for the purpose, were swallowed up by alienations to Brahmins and Pagodas, by the overgrown establishmet of the peons which they kept up, and the feudal pomp which they deemed befitting their station. The exactions of the renters and Fouzdars were an additional source of embarrasment, and what was left to them was scarcely sufficient for their maintenance to say nothing of making good just claims against them. They became overwhelmed with debt and completely inefficient for police purposes. In fact they became depredators instead of protectors. They became heads of organised gangs of decoits, and their peons went on raids into the surrounding country, the plunder being shared with their masters.[62] This description applies to the Kavalgars of Rayalasima also. Some of them became Palegars.

All the Zamindars (including pre-Qutbshahi period chiefs and the Deshmukhs and Deshpandies of Qutbshahi period) who were paying tribute or Peshkash, have been mentioned in the Mughal and Asafjahi sources as "Peshkashi Zamindars". These Zamindars who were holding a number of villages. Parganas and paying peshkash were also known as "Ismi Zamindars". A Peshkashi Zamindar was not subject to the detailed assessment of land revenue actually under cultivation. They were to pay the Peshkash on an adhoc basis as fixed through the negotiations between the government and the Zamindar. The Peshkash collected from the old Nayakas of Venkatagiri, Kalahasti, Nayakas of Karnatic,[63] the Palegars of Rayalaseema and the chieftains of (Deshmukhs & Deshpandians) coastal Andhra was in the nature of tribute which was a token of the recognition of Mughal overlordship. All these chiefs of Mughal period may be classified as Peshkashi Zamindars. During the Asafjahi period also the status of Chiefs continued to be the same. And the Deshmukhs and Deshpandias of Coastal Andhra also joined these ranks. It was because of this reason that these tributary chiefs of Coastal Andhra districts were called Zamindars even under the East India Company's rule and the permanent revenue settlement was made in 1802 with all these Zamindars.

Jagir System

Jagirs of Mughal and Asafjahi periods also belong to the military tenure and the Jagir system was insaperately connected with the Mansabdari system. The Mughal bureaucracy was basically military in its origin and nature. Every civil and military official of the Mughal government had to be enrolled in the list of Mansabdars. The Mansabdari system had two district features. First, all the mansabdars owned direct subordination to the Empercr, who was the sole authority for appointing or dismissing a Mansabdar and to sanction the increase or decrease in the rank of the Mansabdar. Second., the Mughal Mansab was duel rank represented by two numbers known as Zat (personal) and Sawar (cavalry). The Zat rank indicated ones position and determined the personal pay while the Sawar rank was additional rank indicating the military obligation of the Mansabdar and the maintenance of the required number of contingent out of the emolument paid to him separately for the purpose.

All the members of the administrative machinary transferred to Hyderabad after the fall of the Qubshahi kingdom in 1688 and also those members of the Qutbshahi state service who were absorbed into the Mughal system were now Mansabdars. There were several hundred Mansabdars in Mughal Golkonda province. The staff of lower ranks were paid monthly cash salaries,[64] and the Mansabdars of higher rank were assigned the land revenue of a specified area in lieu of their salaries. The territories whose land revenues were assigned to Mughal Mansabdars were called Jagirs or Jagir-I-Tankhwah. The holders of these Jagirs were Jagirdars. They made their own arrangements for the realisation of their revenue. The assignment of a Jagir conferred on the Jagirdar only the right to collect the government share of the agricultural produce without any additional administrative responsibilities or right of occupation and land holding. In fact the Mughal Jagirdars were frequently transferred to forestall the development of their Jagirs into local landed estates and finally fiefs.

The Subadar of Hyderabad Subah, the Kotwal and Fauzdar of Hyderabad city and its suburbs, the Bakshi (military inspector and intelligence officer of the province) the Buyutat (superintendent of imperial stores, palaces and workshops) Fauzdar of the Sarkars, Qaladars of forts and several military officers were all Mansabdars holding Jagirs. All the Mansabdars except one or two were Muslims whether North Indians or of Golkonda. One Bidr-ud-din

Khan was holding in 1720 the Jaghir of Udayagiri (Nellore District) consisting of 63 villages. He was confirmed as Jaghirdar and Mansabdar of 700 by Mughal Emperor in 1731.[65] The Jaghirs of Rapur and Kaitapalli in Nellore District also were of this type. Bangaru Yachama Nayudu, the Zamindar of Venkatagiri (Nellore District) of the Mughal period was a Mansabdar of 5000 (Panchhazari Mansabdar).[66] He must have been the same Yachama Nayaka who became a Mansabdar in Aurangzeb's service and was eventually executed for treason.[67] This Nayaka as his name suggests was probably a Velama Nayaka of Venkatagiri principality in Nellore District. Similarly, the Zamindar of Nizividu (Krishna district) one Narasimha Appa Rao was made a Mughal Mansabdar of 3000 (Tin Hazar Mansabdar) during the post-Aurangzeb's period.[68]

The Mansabdari system and the assignment of Jagirs to Mansabdars under the Asafjahis had undergone certain changes in it to suit the local exisgencies and the need of the time. However, the broad basic structure and the principles of Mansabdari system of the Mughals remained the same.

During the Asafjahi period, there were five types of Jagirs. They include.

1. Al-Tumgha Jagir or Inam-al-Tamgha which were permanent, perpetual and hereditary grants.
2. Zat Jagirs or grants made of large portions of lands for the maintenance of the grantees and mostly personal.
3. Jagir Nigehdasht Jamait or Paigah. These were the assignment of the groups of villages/Parganas to some of the nobility in lieu of maintaining a certain numbr of troops whose expenses were to be defrayed from the income of the Jagir.

4. Tankhahi Mahalat which were the assignments of villages/parganas in lieu of certain state debts or advances made to government for the pay of offices or establishmets or troops. These Jagirs were of later origin.
5. Sarfkhas Jagirs which were assigned to Nizam in lieu of Cash payments from public treasury for his personal maintenance. They also include some personal Jagirs.

These Jagirdars did not pay any tribute to the government. All of them held military service tenures. There were total 6,848 Jagir villages of all descriptions in Asafjahi state and about 2,391 villages in Telangana districts.[69]

The Paigah Jagirs were assigned for the maintenance of Nizam's cavalry called household troops. They were first assigned by Nizam Ali Khan Nizam-ul-mulk Asaf Jah to Abul Khair Khan, the first Shams-l-Umra. This Jagir comprised an area of about 2,373 square miles or 1007 villages with a revenue of 54 lakhs of rupees a year.[70] Of the total villages mentioned above under this tenure, 107 villages were situated in Telangana districts (Medak and Indur or modern Nizamabad).

Sarfkhas Jagirs as mentioned already were assigned to the Asafjahi king, in lieu of cash payments from the public treasury. They also include some personal Jagirs. These Jagirs were assigned originally probably, to the first Nizam as Subedar of Deccan and also a Mansabdar of 7000 rank. The area under this tenure spread over several districts of Hyderabad State and covered 7,113 square miles area and contained total 1,443 villages. They included 2 Talukas in Aurangabad 1 in Bir, 2 in Bidar, 2 in Nanded, 4 in Naldurg districts and several villages in Parbani and Gulburga outside Telangana. In Telangana region 5 parganas of Atraf Balda (area surrounding Hyderabad City) and 3 villages in

Medak, 24 in Elgandal, 8 in Khammam, 3 in Nalgonda and 13 in Nagarkurnool belonged to Sarfkhas Jagirs.[71]

2. ***Civil Service Tenures:*** The other category of service tenures were that of civil service. All the hereditary Revenue officials from the district level to that of the village during this period were assigned tax free villages/lands on hereditary basis within their jurisdiction, and other perquisites. The officials, included – Sardeshmukh, Sardeshpandia at Sarkar/District level, Chaudari or Deshmukh, Sthalakanam or Deshpandia and sometimes also Majumdar at Pargana level, Patwari/Kulkarni and Reddi/ Muqaddam patel at village level, who were hereditary officials.

Sardeshmukh and Sardeshpandia

Sardeshmukh and Sardeshpandia were appointed over a Subha or some times over a Sarkar or several Mahals/ Parganas and sometimes several of them over a sarkar. For example in 1687, (last year of Qutbshahi rule) one Venkata Manohar Das (must be a marwadi) was holding the Sardeshmukhi of twelve Mahals including Devarakonda, Ibrahimpatnam, Kandur etc. with his Rusum.[72] During the Mughal period, Warangal Sarkar with 16 Mahals/Parganas had three Sardeshmukhs – Karmaji, Ramanna and Narsanna and five Sardeshpandias – Tirumak, Sikkoraj, Chinnaya, Malpa and Sapna; Rajamundry Sarkar with 24 Mahals, had only one Sardeshmukh Gopal Rao and one Sardeshpandia Barmahji. Machilipatnam sarkar with 8 Mahals had only one Deshmukh Venkayya and one Deshpandia Bhagwan and two Majumdars – Laxminarayana and Chandrappa.[73] A mughal period land grant record dated 1701 A.D. from Gandikota (Cuddapah district) mentions Deshahi, Sardeshahi, Asari Majumdar along with Kanungo, Palegars and Kavaligars.[74] These Deshahi, Sardeshahi and Majumdar must be the local variants of the Deshmukh and Sardesai and Despandia mentioned above. The Sardeshmukh and Sardeshpandia, it appears, were of Mughal period origin. While Deshmukh and Deshpandia were of Qutbhshi period origin. Sardeshmukh and Sardeshpandia had their emoluments, Inam lands and other perquisites, though we do not get information in this regard. Deshpandia and Majumdars are mentioned in one of the above mentioned Mughal records indicating that they were two different offices.

Deshmukh and Deshpandia

Over each pargana or Mahal, a Deshmukh and a Deshpandia were appointed, during the period under consideration. The importance of these two offices can be gauged from the fact that all the Qutbshahi and Mughal Farmans or Parwanas or Parwanchas concerning grants of land revenue were addressed to these officials for the implementation of those grants. There were 400 to 500 parganas in Andhra Desa during the Mughal period and during the early Asafjahi period, there were about 205 parganas or Mahals each of which was under a Deshmukh or Desai and a Deshpandia. They were appointed both in Haveli as well as Zamindari territories.

Deshmukh

He was the executive and the Revenue Collector and agent of the government. He was a buffer between the local inhabitants and the Muslim Government. We find Desais (same as Deshmukh) functioning in Qutbshahi kingdom as early as 1585 A.D. A Qutbshahi Farman of 1585 A.D. which was issued to confirm the assignment of the village, Madhol to the Chisti Sufi saint Hussain Shaha Wali, was addressed to Desaiyan and Karkunan (villege Accountants or Karnams) of Arki Pargana.[75] During the period of Muhammad Quli Qutbshah, the fifth ruler of the dynasty, a Farman dated 1593 was addressed to Desais and Karkuns of the village of Patlur regarding the grant of revenue to a Muslim religious saint.[76] Similarly the Farman of Muhammad Quli Qutbshah dated 1594 A.D. refers to Desaias and Karkuns of Arki Pargana.[77] Another Qutbshahi Farman dated 1614 A.D. refers to the Desais of the Jalpalli Pargana.[78] An interesting Farman of Abulla Qutbshah dated 1617 A.D. refers to the grant of 'Deshpandiagiri' together with the grant of land in Inam, Rusum etc. in perpetuity to one Appakonda, son of Timmanna from the district of Kondamel, Muhamadnagar Sarkar and Hyderabad suba.[79] These evidences clearly establish the fact that Desais or Deshpandias were appointed even before the Qutbshahis accepted the Mughal suzerainty in 1636 A.D. These positions Desai and Desh Kulkarni appears to have been also created in the neibhbouring and contemporary Adilshahi kingdom of Bijapur. Adilshahi Farmans dated 1664, 1671 and 1678 A.D. confirm this.[80]

We do not have any evidence to show that any counter part of Deshmukh existed in Andhra Desa during the pre-Qutbshahi period. In the Tamil districts of Vijayanagara Empire, there existed an officer called 'Sthala-gauda'.[81] He was the revenue collector of a Sthala (a territorial subdivision smaller than modern Taluka) His position was similar to that of Deshmukh of post-Vijayanagara period. It appears, similar position did not exist in Andhra Desa during the Vijayanagara period. The Qutbshahis appear to have borrowed this system of Deshmukh and Despandia from Western Deccan where similar institutions existed during the period of Bahmanis.

An inscription of later Qutbshahi period from Kandukur (Nellore district) dated 1683-84 mentions the Deshais, the Sthalakarnams along with the village Karnams, Kapus and

Desasthas.[82] As mentioned already the Desai must be the same as Deshmukh and Sthalakarnam was a continuation of Vijayanagara period institution and almost an equalent of Despandia.[83] *Athavanavyavaharatantram* of 18th century A.D. a source book on revenue administration of Vijayanagara Empire mentions Deshmukhs and Deshpandias besides Majumdar of the period of Akkanna and Madanna.[84] These evidences prove the prevelance of the Deshmukh and Deshpandia and Majumdar system during the period of Abul Hasan Tanesa, the last Qutbshahi ruler.

According to the Fifth Report from the Select Committee on the affairs of the East India Company the origin of the office of the Deshmukh was to be traced to the time of the Hindu Rajas of Pre-Mughal period in Northern India. It originally went by the name of 'Chowdrie' or 'Chaudary' which was changed by the time of Mughals to that of 'Crorie'. This was instituted in 1582 by Akbar. Crorie was an intermediate agent of government to superintend a certain portion of the country, redress the petty grievances of the inhabitants, furnish the peasants with necessary advances for agriculture and help collecting the revenue to the government. As a compensation for the discharge of his duties the Deshmukhs of our region enjoyed certain rent-free lands termed "Savarums', which were conveniently dispersed through out his area of jurisdiction so as to make his presence necessary every where in order to give the greater effect to his superintendence. He was also entitled to receive certain 'Russooms' or fee on the crops and other perquisites drawn from the Sayer or customs and from the quit rents of the houses. These personal or rather official lands and perquisites amounted altogether to about ten percent on the collections he made in his area.[85] The Deshmukhs were mostly the local influential non-Brahmin

Zamindars or landholders and belonged to advanced Sudra communities such as Reddi, Velama, Raju, Kamma etc.

This office became hereditary civil service tenure Qutbshahi period Royal orders provide information about the appointment of Deshmukhs and Deshpandias and granting of their emoluments. A Farman of 1686 of Abul Hasan Tanasha mentions the appointment of Ramachandar Rao, Prasad Rao, Ragh Nayak Rao, and Siyanat Rao in the combined position of Deshmukh, Majumdar (Auditor) and Nargud (Nadgoud?) for the Ninety six villages situated, probably in Charikunda pargana, Hyderaad, because the Farman was addressed to the officials of that Pargana. It further states that from the total number of villages, the revenues from twelve villages were set aside for the emoluments of Deshmukh and the revenues of nine villages for Majumdar. Those four individuals were also to receive 10 percent of the land tax collections of the Pargana and the proceeds of a number of specialised markets, transit and liquor taxes for their services.[86] Krishna Bhupal Bala Rao and Jupalli Appa Rao the joint Deshmukhs of Udayagiri and Cumbum (Nellore and Prakasam districts) were to collect a Jama of Rs.2,54,607. Their Rusum was Rs.25548-8-0 and the rent from their five Inam villages was Rs.10,531-8-0 and their total income being Rs.36080. The Rusum was calculated at 2 percent on full Jama (revenue) during the period of Carnatic Nawabs.[87] This gives an idea of the emoluments of the Deshmukhs.

Deshpandia

Deshpandia was the next revenue officer of rank of civil service tenure over a Pargana as that of Deshmukh. This hereditary tenure was held mostly by Brahmins. In one exceptional case, there was a Muslim Despandia in Ramgir Circar (Karimnagar district) whose Brahmin ancestor was converted to Islam by Mughal Emperor Aurangazeb. (Hyderabad Affairs-I, p.582) Deshpandia (Despand, Persian and Deshpandi Marathi) maintained complete records of all types of taxes paid and lands cultivated on yearly basis for each village in the Pargana. He was to assist the government tax officials or Revenue farmers in the proper assessment of the land and other taxes of the Pargana. His office must have maintained the land revenue records of all the villages of his pargana. His remuneration was similar to but usually less than that of a Deshmukh. It consisted of a small percentage of the taxes collected, (Russoom of two and a half percent) tax-free lands or villages etc.[88] The appointment of one Appakonda son of Timanna, as Deshpandia from the district of Kondamal, Sarkar Muhammadnagar,Suba Hyderaad, and grant of Inam land and Rusum etc. to him in perpetuity is refered to in a Farman of Abdulla Qutbshah, in the year 1617 A.D.[89] as mentioned before.

After the Mughal conquest, some of the Zamindars revolted and caused disturbances, but they were subdued by the local governer. The remaining Zamindars including the Pargana Mannewar, Deshmukhs and Deshpandia's were willing to accept the authority of Mughal government which confirmed them by Sanads in their respective posts but by collecting appointment fees and taking a written bond from them. The Deshmukhs had to pay 2 ½ per cent as Deshmukhs fees for getting their offices reconfirmed by the new Mughal government. Nirmal Rao, Deshmukh of one half of Nurkol Pargana in Koilkonda district, Gopal Kishan of Ibrahimpatnam Pargana and sahib Rai of Devarakonda Pargana purchased the Deshpandia/Deshmukh rights.[90] This additional payment of purchase money and the strict assessment of revenue under the Mughals must have resulted in the collection of more revenue from the cultivators. For example, in the case of Kandur pargana

(Mahboobnagar district) which had about 50 villages, its revenue demand (Hasil) from the Deshmukh Jakka Reddy was raised 23 per cent from that of pre-Mughal period.[91] In 1690, a member of Manik Rao family (Velama) was made both the Deshmukh and Mannewar (police) over the 44 haveli villages and 14 Samutus of Murtuzanagar Circar and a member of (Brahmin) Manuri family was made Deshpandia (Registrar) and Majumdar (auditor) and Sheristadar (Secretary and office manager) over Murtuzanagar Circar. In 1725, the office of Deshmukh and Mannevar of 225 villages of Murtuzanagar Circar were conferred on a member of Vasi Reddy family (Kamma)[92] Zamindari parganas also had Deshpandias to look after the revenue accounts and land records and they also settled the account of Zamindaris with the company government. Nizampatam Circar Collector sends a circular of 1795 A.D. suspecting fraud in the accounts settled by Zamindars through their Despandias for last 3 years.[93]

Mazumdar and Sheristadars

During Mughal period and subsequent period, Mazumdar (Auditor) and Sheristadar (Secretary) also were appointed over each circar. As mentioned above, in 1690 a member (Brahmin) of Manuri family was made Deshpandia and also Mazumdar and Sheristadar of Murtuzanagar (Kondavidu) Circar. One Kandregula Jogipantulu was both Mazumdar and Sur Sheristadar of Rajamundry Circar under both Nizam and English East India Company in 1765. Kandregula Venkatarao (former's brother) succeeded to those offices in 1773 and continued till 1778, when those offices were abolished.[94] When Kandregula Jagannath (Jogi Pantulu) was appointed as both Mazumdar and also as Sur Sheristadar (or Head Sheristadar) of Rajahmundry Sarkar in 1766 A.D. by Nizam's government, he was remunerated with some 37

Candies (Puttis) of land spread over several Parganas (one catty of land in each village) with tax concession and one percent on all revenue collections including that of customs and land revenue granted to him. The government order was addressed to all local revenue officials like Deshmukhs, Majumdars; village accountants etc. His signature was necessary on all accounts including Jamabandi, daily receipts etc. to be valid according to the Farmans.[95]

All the superior revenue officials like Deshpandia, Deshmukh, Majumdar, Sheristadar appear to have been assisted by Gumastas in the Collection of revenue and the maintenance of accounts.

The Despandia and Majumdar were entitled for pension for themselves and family pension after their death. Potaraju Hanumaiah, the Deshpandia of Divi Pargana who was in receipt of pension, died and his son claimed pension in 1818.[1] Pension was drawn by their descendants. In 1819, the Board of Revenue sanctioned the payment of one half of the amount of pension to one Narsingha Rao after the death of his father who was Majumdar of Ellore.[97]

Sthala Karnams

The Sthala Karnams of Vijayanagara period and also of Karnatic Nawabs held civil service tenures on hereditary basis. Sthalakarnam during the Vijayanagara period was the accountant at the level of Sthala, a territorial sub-division which consisted of 20-60 villages, while Sima, the next higher subdivision was equalent of a Pargana or Taluka of later period. The counterpart of Sthalakarnam in the Tamil districts of the Vijayanagara Empire was the Senabova of Nadu or Nad-Senabova or Nad Karnam who was accountant or Karnam at the level of Nadu a territorial sub-division.[98] Sthalakarnam maintained the records of revenue and the state of cultivation in each village in his Sthalam, which were transmitted to him by the village Karnams. His office was hereditary. The post of Sthalakarnam was either replaced or renamed as Deshpandia and appointed over a Pargana during the Qutbshahi period which succeeded that of Vijayanagara in this region. But the post of Sthalakarnams was continued in Nellore district and also parts of Guntur and Prakasam district even under the Muslim rule – the Qutbshahi, Mughal and Carnatic Nawabs. One Ram Raj Jangam is mentioned as Thalkarni (same as Sthalakarni) of Macherla Pargana (Guntur district) who was ordered to submitt the accounts of that pargana, in the Takids (royal orders) dated 1674 and 1675 A.D.[99] These positions survived in Nellore and Ongole til 1800 A.D. The district of Nellore proper was divided between two Sthalakarnams, the northern portion under Akkaraju and the southern portion under Muttaraju families during the period of Karnatic Nawabs. Both of them were apparently Brahmins as their family names indicate. Similarly the Ongole district area was under four sthalakarnams belonging to four different families during that period.[100] It appears that Sthala Karnam's, post was continued in some areas of Telangana even during the Qutbshahi period. A Qutbshahi Farman of 1688 A.D.mentions Tahelkarnis, (same as Sthalakarni) along with Deshais, Nayakwaris of Tarkunda Pargana and Muqaddams, (village head) Karkun (village accountants) and populace of the Yaedrah village[101].

The Sthalakarnams, like the Deshpandias of later period got emoluments for the maintenance of their office. They consisted of Rusums or money fees, Meras on the crop, Maniyam and Shrotriam lands during the period of Karnatic Nawabs and also when that area was transferred to the East India Company. The two Sthalakarnams of Nellore in 1801 possessed Rusum at half percent on the jama (total Revenue collection) and Shrotriyams and Maniyams in Circar (government) lands; Shrotriyams .. and Maniyams in Kalahasty, Chundi; and Rusum at half percent in Kalahasty, Chundi and Bala Rao's country; and a Katnam of Madras Pagodas 240 from the Jagirdar of Udayagiri. Their total emoluments were 7,204 ¾ Pagodas and disbursements were 1606 ½ Pagodas. Similarly, three of the four Sthalakarnams of Ongole had Meras on the crop at four Muntas per putti (1/30th), besides Rusum derived from Salt pans at varying rates, usually on the bullock load; all four Sthalakarnams had Maniyams of different values and their total emoluments were Madras Pagodas 2,350 ¼ and disbursements were 262 ½ Pagodas. In some cases, the Sthalakarnams had Rusum as high as one percent on the price at all the salt stations north of the Pennar river. The total demand on account of Sthala Karnams and village Karnams Rusum for the year 1801 A.D. was 9,592-18-55 Pagodas.[102] This account gives an idea of the emoluments and expenditure of the Sthalakarnams. The disbursement amount mentioned above must have been spent either on their establishments or towards quit rent on their Inam villages and lands. These Shalakarnams were obliged to maintain a certain establishment consisting of writers or Gumasthas. Their emoluments and establishments and also functions must have been a continuation of that of Vijayanagara period when they originated.

The office of Sthalakarnams, like those of Deshmukhs and also village Karnams, we are told, were undermined and corrupted by the renting system or revenue farming system resorted to by the Carnatic Nawabs in their dominions. The Sthalakarnams frequently became renters… "the falsification of the accounts and registers became a direct advantage to these very officers whose duty it was to keep them. Further, the intimate knowledge which these men had of the condition and resources of the villages gave them a lever for exactions, such as no other renters possessed".[103]

The Village Ayagars

The village Ayagars who were assigned Manyam lands and other perquisites for undertaking public service were also Civil Service tenure holders.

Ayagar system played a major role in the management of the village affairs not only in Telugu speaking area but also in other parts of Deccan. It is one of the most important village institutions in Medieval Andhra Desa. It became so indispensable that even the British administrators could not dispense with it. This hereditary system continued to function in this area till the Andhra Pradesh Government abolished the hereditary aspect of the headman and the accountant during the tenure of N.T. Rama rao, as Chief Minister.

The history of Ayagar system in Andhra Desa can be traced only from Kakatiya period onwards. The term 'Ayam' means 'demsn' extent, or measure as of a field. The Ayagars, therefore denote people who hold Ayam or fields of a certain extent granted to them free of tax by the villagers or by the state as payment for undertaking public service.[104]

These Ayagars are referred to as "Panniddaryayagandlu" indicating there number as twelve. The later Vijayanagara period records and also those of Qutb Shahi period mention them as 'barabalvantulu'. This term was most probably derived from 'Barabalutedar', the term used for them in Maharastra area. They are also referred to in the Kaifiyat of Kamalapurm, as 'Simasthas'.[105] This system is same as the Jajmani system of North India.

The Ayagars were appointed on hereditary basis. This system appears to have existed in all the villages. But in Agrahara villages which were granted to the learned

Brahmins, the post of village headman was probably not there as the management of the Agrahara was conducted either by the sabha and its Mahajanas if it was a Ganabhoga and a single done if it was Ekabhoga Agrahara. Except the village headman all other Ayagars were probably there in the Agraharas. For example, an epigraph of A.D.1546 from Balyampalli, Cuddapha District, refers to the Karnam of Bhogapura Agrahara village along with the Mahajanas.[106] Similarly, a Copper Plate grant of A.D.1652-53, records the grant of Manyam Land and Mera grain to Karnam and other 'Ayagandlu' in the Agrahara Ayyavairpalli newly created by one Peda Venkatadri Nayanigaru. Both these epigraphs do not mention the headman.[107]

The composition of the body of Ayagaras and also the designation of its individual members varied according to the locality. An examination of the following two lists of Ayagars furnished, one from *Athavanavyavaharatantram* and another from *Kamalapuram Kaifiyat* (Cuddapah District) indicate the caste composition of Ayagars.

I. The list of Ayagars given by *Athavanavyavaharatantram*[108]

1.	Shanabogu	(Accountant)
2.	Gavudu	(Headman)
3.	Kammari	(Black smith)
4.	Badige	(Washerman)
5.	Agasa	(Goldsmith)
6.	Panchanga	(Priest)
7.	Vayidya	(Barber)
8.	Madiga	(Cobbler)
9.	Agasarlu	(Carpenter)
10.	Talari	(Watchman)
11.	Neruganti	(Water distributor)
12.	Kumbara	(Potter)

The list of Ayagars given in the Kaifiyat of Kamalapuram[109]

1.	Purohit	(Priest)
2.	Lekhaka	(Accountant)
3.	Devalakadvayam	(The Archakas of the Siva and Vishnu temple)
AND		
4.		
5.	Ayahkarah	(Black Smith)
6.	Vardhaki	(Carpenter)
7.	Khsuri	(Barber)
8.	Rajaka	(Washerman)
9.	Padajah	(The protector of the village boundary i.e. Reddi)
10.	Padavijneyah	(The knower of the foot prints i.e. the Talari)
AND		
11, 12,	Antyajati-dvayam	(The two of the last cast, i.e. Vetti and Dohi)

The first list provides the usual composition of Ayagars. But the second list doesnot contain in it the village headman, potter and the gold-smith but it contains in their place two Archakas or priests of the local temples, one of siva and another of Vishnu. On the whole, five of them i.e. potter; carpenter, blacksmith, goldsmith and the shoemaker were the village artisans. The first four of these belonged to the sub-castes of the fourth caste of the traditional Varna system i.e. Sudra and the fifth one i.e. shoemaker belonged to the fifth caste as he is referred to as of Antyajati in the above second list and Madiga in the first list. Washerman and barber belonged to the fourth caste. The priest and the village accountant known as Karnam or Sanboga or Lekhaka were invariably of Brahmin caste. The village Watchman known as Talari usually was of Boya or Mudiraj community; whose members were also known as Bantus as thy also served as soldiers in the army. It was also a hunting community. Water distributor or Neerati also referred to as of Antyajati in the above second list belonged to the fifth caste and probably a Mala. In some villages this water distributor belonged to the caste of Vaddera or Vodde Boya or stone-cuttor.[110] The position of village headman known variously as Kapu, Peddakapu, Reddi, Gavudu, Muqaddam, Patel[111] etc., was held, it appears, mostly by the people of farmers communities like those of Reddy, Velama, Kamma, Balija etc. His designation 'Peddakapu' and 'Kapu' also indicate that he was of farmer's community. Therefore he was of fourth caste. But in some villages of Ceded districts people of non-Kapu communities; such as Kuruba also held the village headman's post.

The duties of the Ayagars were clearly prescribed. Their duties were mostly agriculture or ryots oriented. The relations between these Ayagars constituted the basic structure of the division of labour in the local agrarian society of the period. It was a division of labour based on the exchange of commodities. The village headman was almost the uncrowned monarch of the village. This is indicated by the popular story 'Anaganaga oka uru A urikoka raju.....'. His basic duty was the protection of the village as is indicated by designation 'Padajah' given in the Kamalapuram Kaifiyat. He had to collect all kinds of taxes in the village and pay them to the government and settle the accounts every year.[112] An epigraph from Dharmavaram village, Prakasam district of 1600 A.D. belonging to the period of Muhammad Qutb Shah which records the revenue settlement of the village Eklaskhanapuram clearly states that the Pedakampu and the Karnam of the village had to collect the revenue of the village and deposit it in the government treasury.[113] He was also obliged to have the village lands cultivated. Under the village lease system or Visabadi system which was one of the modes of revenue settlement and collection, the village headman distributed the lands to the ryots every year according to their means, the number of the tilling cattle etc possessed by them. The Visabadi villages, which Sir Thomas Munro observed in the ceded districts, divided the village's land into 16 shares which were apportioned among ryots.[114] If the headman was the monarch of the village, the village accountant was like its minister. He maintained the records, called Kavile of the village lands, accounts of the taxes, remissions made etc as one of his designation 'Lekhaka' suggest. He was also known as Kulkarni, Karnam and Patwari.[115]

These two, Headman and the Accountant, on the whole, held a dominant hegemony in the village life. Their revenue collection powers, their control over the land, their official connection with the superior government revenue officials and revenue contractors contributed to their dominant position. This many a time also led to exploitation and oppression of the village community by them.

The work of the village headman and the accountant was supervised by their superior officials, at Pargana level, Deshmukh and Deshpandia respectively.[116] Their role at the village level was similar to that of Deshmukh and Deshpandia at the Pargana level.

The village Headman and the accountant played a major role in the extension of agriculture in the village. Their involvement and supervision in the work of agricultural extension was necessary. An epigraph of A.D.1647 from Chakibanda village, Cuddapah District, which records the gift of some grain for the repairs of the local tank bund by one Appakonda nayudu states that those repairs had to be carried on with the consent of the 12 Ayagars.[117] An epigraph of A.D. 1780 from Peddachepalle, Cuddapah District, records the grant of 'Pallekattumanyam' i.e. Manyam lands for the establishment of a village by the Reddi and Karanam to one Srinivasarayudu.[118] Similarly a Dasavanda grant made by the Karnam and Reddi for the construction of a irrigation tank is recorded in a copper plate grant of A.D.1731 from Cuddapah District.[119]

The Headman and the Karnam were made responsible, in some cases, for the maintenance of the irrigation tank. An inscription of A.D.1635-36 from Nellore clearly states that Velugoti Venktapati Nayudu made it binding on the village headman and Accountant (Kapu and Karnam) that they should collect the Mera grain and give it to the Upparas and maintain the tank properly.[120]

Particularly, the village Headman and the Accountant appear to have played an important role in the rehabilitation of the villages. An interesting record of 1533 A.D. from Kanaganipalle, Ananthapur District, records the agreement made by Reddis and Karnamas of 32 villages exempting the Panchanamwaru (artisans) of those 32 villages from payment of all the taxes in those villages in order to rehabilitate them in their former places from which they had migrated to the other Simas due to tax oppression.[121]

If the government made any remission of taxes, it conveyed the orders to the Head and Accountant of the village who were made responsible to implement them. An Epigraph of 1542 A.D. from Bukkapatnam, Ananthapur district which records the remission of taxes on marriages and the earnings of the Brahmanas, states that the Government conveyed the orders to the Reddi and Karanam of the village Krottacheruvu.[122] In some cases the Headman and the Accountant also were warned not to violate the remissions of taxes made by government either to individuals or institutions.[123] It appears in some cases these village officials misappropriated them.

The village Purohit performed the marriages and other religious ceremonies in the village. As his other designation 'Panchanga' suggests he had to maintain the calender and explain to the ryots the suitable time for sowing, harvesting etc and auspicious days for commencing journeys, performing marriages etc.

Talari, as his designation 'Pada Vijneyah' meaning the knower of the foot prints, suggests, protected the village from danger of thieves and robbers and assisted the headman and accountant in the work of administration and revenue collection. If any thefts were committed with in the village, the Talari was held responsible. He also kept a watch on the aliens in the village, Talari was usually of Boya community.

The artisans – carpenter and blacksmith, manufactured ploughs and other agricultural implements for the ryots. The goldsmith who was usually 'shroff' besides testing the soundness of the coins collected as revenue in the village also measured the government's share of the produce from the ryots as the 'Kyldar'. The Potter supplied the pots necessary for the use of the ryots . The barber shaved the ryots and also provided music at the time of marriage and other auspicious occasion in the village as his other designation (besides 'Kshura') 'Vayidya' suggests. Washerman washed the clothers of the Ryots. The cobbler furnished the Ryots with ropes, buckets, sandals etc. Finallly the Waterman protected the village tank-bund and regulated the water supply to the fields.

As far as the remuneration of Ayagars is concerned they were given Manyam lands or Bhatavritti Manyams.[124] Besides this, they were also given remuneration in the form of 'Buyam' or 'Nijayam' and 'Ardhayam', 2 Muntas on both accounts (Probably 2 Kunchas are equivalent to 20 kg) on the produce from the ryots known as 'Mera' either on each kapile (Mota or lift) or field or Khanduga[125] depending on the Pargana. It is not known if headman and accountant got some percentage of the revenue collected. They also got other small perquisites from the Ryots and others. The headman and the accountant appear to have appropriated to themselves the income from the lands cultivated by the Ryots but not mentioned in the government records. Similarly, the Talari or Watchman got from the villagers every day thick porridge of Ragi flour, curry and ears of corn and also blankets from the Kurubas. This was probably justified because he had to watch the village day and night. Villagers gave them probably out of fear that he might single them out at first to carry the luggage of the government officials. Similarly, the washerman and the barber used to get food from the households on the day when they washed their cloths and shaved them respectively. The other artisans also used to get additional income if they attended to the work other than prescribed to them as Ayagars. The carpenter and blacksmith were paid wages if they constructed houses or bullock-carts etc. If the potter was engaged in making tiles for house roofs, sold jars for the storage of the grain and sold pots he must have definitely got additional wages. It is the same with goldsmith when he was engaged in making ornaments.

The Ayagars, excepting the priest, had to pay Jodi or quit rent on their Manyam lands.[126] Some of the village accountants were also exempted from this tax and their Manyam lands were made Sarvamanya or tax-free.[127]

Except the headman, Accountant and police man, the remaining Ayagars were given 'Hore hollu" and 'Morabatta'.[128] The meaning of these Kannada language terms is probably wages fees.

Some of the Ayagars also paid professional taxes on their trade. The potters had to pay 'Cakrakanika' on his potter's wheel to the government. Similarly, the Washerman paid the tax 'Revu-gutta' probably for using the Revu of tank or river for washing clothes and 'ayila-gutta' on firewood for boiling cloths.[129] The Barbers, throughout the medieval period paid the tax 'Mangalapannu' which the Vijayanagara monarch Ramaraya abolished. The Cobbler, who belonged to the Madiga Community who were treated along with Malas and their dependent communities as untouchables also paid a tax on their community called 'Jatimannelu'. *Athavanatantram* (p.12) states that, he had plenty of income (Ayam) Besides Horehollu, Mora batta, Nijayam, he used to get 'Kolatamigulu' (left out grain after division between the government and Ryot), 'Motakuli' (wages for carrying the luggage of the government officials).

We get more specific account of the emoluments of Ayagars for the Company period. A Report dated 29-9-1789 addressed to the Board of Revenue gives them as follows. Out of every 10 candies of grain produced in the village the Karnam received 3 Maunds and 30 Seers; Carpenters and blocksmith 1 Maund and 10 seers; barbers and washermen 25 seers; potter and Vetti Pariah got 20 seers.[130]

The Madigas, the leather worker, along with the Malas who constituted the agricultural labour and also water distributor in some villages played an important role in the agrarian economy of the village in Andhra Desa of the period. Their services such as skinning of dead cattle and its tanning and making of leather goods were indispensable for the agricultural communities whose economy was interlinked with cattle breading and dairy, as in other parts of India. They made leather ropes, and buckets for lifting water from wells and footwear. Inspite of the fact that, they were treated as untouchables and lived outside the village, they were important members of the village Ayagars. And inspite of the discrimination shown to them, they also performed an important duty in the rituals such as bufallow sacrifice conducted to pacify the village deities to prevent the epidemics such as cholera etc. On those occasions, they attained a state of high spirtuality.

The village headman and accountant appear to have managed to get, apart from the legal Manyam/Inam land assigned to them, a considerable extent of illegally acquired land as well. According to the survey of 1807 A.D., all the Inam land-both authorised and authorised with the Patels and Karnams in the Ceded districts amounted to 64,701, 138 acres of which the estimated rent was star Pagodas 3,02,587-21-33.[131] But it appears, the figure 64,701,138 acres given in the Appendix to Fifth Report is a mistake. Most probably it was 4,701,138 acres instead. Regarding the unauthorised land in the possession of the Patels and Karnams in the Ceded districts it is reported in the Appendix to the Fifth Report that (p.273). "These Inams are in many villages, thirty or forty per cent of the revenue, but in others, not more than two or three per cent. In general, all above five per cent may be regarded as unauthorised. The frequent changes of government, and the loss or rather concealment of accounts, have during a long course of years, facilitated the fraudulent extension of these Inams, at the expense of the Circar lands.....".

Specific Service Tenures

Performance of specific services was also remunerated by the assignment of the income rights on land granted to persons for public service. It was called 'Umbali' under Vijayanagara Empire 'Pallaki-Umbali' for the upkeep of Palanquin, 'Garadi-Umbali' for the maintenance of acrobatism, 'Salligi-Umbali' for the deceased warriors who sacrificed their lives in the service of the state, for Physicians etc. come under this category.

Dasabandam Tenures

For agricultural development or extension of cultivation i.e. founding of new villages, revival of deserted villages, reclamation of land by clearing jungles, levelling, providing irrigational facilities such as tanks, canals and wells, lands were assigned with tax concessions under the 'Dasabandam' or Dasavanda' tenure to the private enterpreneurs. Various types of Manyams under Dasavanda tenure were granted depending on the nature of work undertaken. For example, for establishing new villages, the enterprencurs were granted 'Pallekattu Manyam' lands. For bring new land under cultivation by clearing jungles and by levelling, they were granted lands under 'Achchukattu Manyam'. For extending cultivation by providing irrigation facilities such as canal and well, they were granted 'Kaluvakattumanyam' and 'Bavikattumanyam' respectively. The extent of the land granted to the investor under the above tenures was not always uniform. It was sometimes, half of the land reclaimed, sometimes one fourth and sometimes a fixed measure. For example, an epigraph of the first quarter of the Seventeenth century from Nandalur village (Cuddapah district) refers to 'Pallekattumanyam', 'Bavikattumanyam' and 'Kaluva Dasavandam' granted by one Matli Venkata Raju, a local Vijayanagara feudatory chief to one Appala Raju who undertook, the work, of establishing a village called Anantarajupeta, digging an irrigation well and a canal. For establishing this village, he was granted 7 kuntas of land, both dry and wet as "Pallekattumanyam' and half of the land brought under cultivation under the new well and canal as Desavanda grant. Further, for the cultivation of the remaining half of the reclaimed land (in which trees were cut and levelled) he was given tax concessions for several years.[132] Another 'Kavulu' grant of the same period and place which also records the grant of 'Pallekattu Manyam' under Dasavanda tenure to a private investor, states that the latter was given half of the land brought under cultivation by levelling and providing irrigation with canal water as 'Dasavanda'.[133] A large number of Manyam lands were assigned under Dasavanda system in Rayala Sima region under Vijayanagara during the first quarter of the Seventeenth Century.

Even the Qutbshshi rulers followed this method of assigning lands under Dasavanda tenure for agricultural development. For example an inscriptions dated 1554 from the village Panugallu, Nalgonda district states that during the reign of Ibrahim Qutbshah, one Muslim official Rahmatulla got repaired the dam across the river Musi near the village Namali near Ramannapet of the same district and also an old canal repaired to feed the tank of Panugallu. For the maintenance of the dam, canal and the tank, he granted a Dasavandam Manyam out of the irrigated land under that tank.[134] Similarly, Abdulla Qutbshah granted in 1653 A.D.50 Kuntas of land as 'Dasabanda Manyam' for the maintenance and repairs of the tank of Peddavoorampadu in Ceded districts, according to Venubaka Kaifyat.[135]

The Dasavandam Manyam, came to be known as Inams under Muslim governments were continued throughout the period under study. Even the British administrators found them to be very practicable and useful. As late as in 1834, the Nellore district collector states that the grant of Inams for constructing tanks etc was well calculated to meet the object in view and that one-fourth of the land brought under cultivation as Dasabanda Inam was a sufficient inducement. He further recommends that in cases where the construction etc. was attended with very great expense as by clearing jungles etc. the collector might be at liberty to recommend ½ of the land as Dasavandam Inam.[136]

Thus a large number of Manyam or Inam lands were held under Dasabandam tenure in all parts of Andhra Desa during the period under study. They were continued till the end of the period under study. We find a Dasavandam grant as late as 1788 A.D. in a village in Siddavatam Taluka of Cuddapah district for the construction a tank. It records the grant of land under this tenure – at the rate of one fourth land for bringing new land under cultivation and one-half for old land brought under cultivation under the tank built by several Reddis[137] The holders of these Dasabandam tenures also maintained the irrigation works under which the Dasavanda Manyam lands were granted. Besides, provision was also made for their maintenance by a system of yearly contributions called – 'Cheruvu Mera' usually one 'Kunchamu' of of grain on each Putti produced under that irrigation work.

(b) Charitable Tenures

Hundreds of villages and thousands of acres of land were assigned under Charitable tenure to the religious institutions and persons belonging to both Hindu and Muslim religions and also feeding houses-Hindu Satrams and Muslim Langars. These were assigned by both the Hindu and Muslim states and also their feudatories. The Hindu religious institutions that were benefitted by these tenures include temples, Mathas and the Agraharas and beneficiaries among the Muslim religious institutions were the Masjids, khankas, Dargas and Asurkhanas. The villages/lands assigned to the religious institutions and personages belonging to both the religions were of perpetual nature and were described as 'Achandrarkasthayiga' in the case of Hindu institutions. All of them were exempted from full state tax burden and enjoyed maximum tax concessions. Those grants were described 'sarmanya' in the case of Hindu institutions. The charitable assignments of Hindu Temples, Mathas and Agraharas/learned Brahmins are refered to as Devadaya, Mathapura and Brahmadeya respectively. The villages and lands assigned under charity to the Muslim institutions were collectively called Milk or Madad Mash or Suyurghal.

Charitable Tenures held by Hindu Religions Institutions

For the first quarter of the 17th century we do not get evidence to know the extent of the charitable tenures of the Hindu religious institution in Andhra Desa a major part of which was under Vijayanagara Empire. But from the evidence of the previous centuries an idea of it can be formed. According to Kakatiya Chronicle, *Pratapa Charitramu*, some four thousand villages as Agraharas were in the enjoyment of the learned Brahmins and another two thousand villages were in the possession of the temples during the reign of Kakatiya Prataparudra who ruled Andhra Desa upto 1323 A.D. This chronicle further states that the above monarch used to spend, every year, four crores of coins (probably Rukhas) out of forty four crores which was the total income of his kingdom for the maintenance of the Temples situated in his kingdom and some even outside.[138] This amount spent on temples must have been the government share of the produce from those 2000 villages assigned to the temples if not an additional amount. Fernao Nuniz, the Portugues chronicler states that emperor Mallikarjuna (1546-1565) used to spend one fifth of the state revenue only on temples of the Empire.[139] *Rayavachakamu* another chronicle (17th century) gives the annual expenditure of the Vijayanagara government on Devadaya, Mathapura and Bhrahmedeya and other Sarvamanya endowments during the period of

Tuluva Veeranarasimha as 60 lakh Varahas (gold coin)[140] and that of Krishnadevaraya's period as 84 lakh Varahas out of 10,84,000,000 Varahas which was the gross total income of the state per annum.[141] These amounts were not cash payments, but the government share of the revenue from the villages and lands which was assigned for the support of those institutions/persons.

The Mallikarjuna Temple of Srisailam (Kurnool district) had 52 villages under its control during first quarter of the Fourteenth century A.D. when that area was under Kakatiya Prataparudra II.[142] The temple of Srivenkateswara of Tirumala Tirupati had in its possession 150 villages in the middle of the sixteenth century.[143] Similarly the temples of Narasimha of Simhachalam (Visakhapatnam district) and Ahobilam had ten villages each during the Sixteenth century.[144] The number of villages and lands whose revenue was assigned to the temples depended on their size and popularity. Same is the case with other Hindu Institutions.

In view of the above evidence and also the existence of large number of Hindu religious institutions in this region the statement of *Pratapa Charitramu* does not appear to be an exaggeration. Many of these Kakatiya period asssignments, though confiscated to State during the brief period of 13 years of Tughluq rule are said to have been revived and new ones granted under the new kingdoms such as Musunuri, Reddi, Velama, Gajapati and Vijayanagara that emerged in this region in the post Tughlaq period. This was claimed in the contemporary records by the founders of those kingdoms[145] and also by the evidence of Nuniz and Rayavachakam, mentioned above. A large number of these revenue assignments were made under Charitable tenures by the rulers of those kingdoms and their subordinates during the subsequent period. And there is every reason to suggest that these large number of assignments continued in this region atleast till the death of Venkata II of Vijayanagara Empire in the year 1614 A.D. and subsequent occupation of this region by the Qutbshahis.

The number of assignments to Hindu religious institutions under the charitable tenure were drastically reduced after the fall of the Gajapati rule in north Coastal Andhra and that of Vijayanagara in South Coastal Andhra and Rayalaseema regions. Some of the Muslim governers appointed by the Qutbshahi government proved to be fanatics. They destroyed some of the temples of these regions and deprived them of their source of income. An epigraph of 1599 A.D. from Srikurmam (Srikakulam district) clearly states that Amin Malka, a Qutbshahi general (Amin-ul-mulk) while returning from a compaign against Mukunda Bahubalendra and Vidyadhara, destroyed the temple of Srikurmanatha of that place and built a mosque.[146] An epigraph of 1605 A.D. from Simhadri (Visakapatnam district) gives similar picture. It states that Asvaraya, a Hindu official of the Qutbshahi kingdom revived the worship in that temple which was affected earlier. He granted a village to that temple which used to have ten villages under Hindu rule.[147] Regarding the fate of these institutions in South Andhra, the Kaifiyat of Pedapudi (Guntur district) states that the Qutbshahi government (Turakanyam) which was established in this region after the fall of the Vijayanagara rule, destroyed the temples, built mosques over them and confiscated all Inam or Srotriya lands including that of Pedapudi Agrahara.[148]

The Qutbshahi kings who are generally known for their liberal religious policy might not have directly encouraged their officials to indulge in iconclastic activity. They were quite benevolent to extend patronage to some extent, to Hindu religious institutions and also to allow some of their officials to do the same.[149] As mentioned already, Asvaraya, a Hindu official under Qutbshahis granted a village in 1605 A.D. to the Simhachalam temple. Similarly, a Muslim officer Lalkhan granted an Agrahara for several Brahmins for the religious merit of Muhammad Quli Qutbshah in the year 1586-87 A.D. A Farman of Abul Hasan Tanashah, the last ruler of the dynasty, addressed to the officials of the Chandipargana and Ramraj Sankaraiah the governor of Karnatic regarding the grant of 50 Kochal (Kuchchalas-land measure) in three villages for the maintenance of the Temple Sri Bramara Malleswara and the revenue of the villages Malleswarapuram to the same was issued in 1684 A.D.[150]

The existence of a large number of Agraharas and Devadana villages in various Zamindaris of Andhra Desa at the end of the 18th century indicates the continuation of these Charitable tenure assignments during the Qutbshahi, Mughal and Asafjahi periods. Many villages Kaifyats of Coastal districts mention the Agraharas and the fixing of their Srotrayam/quit rent.[151] Chart-II (p. 37) shows the existence of 503 Agraharas distributed over all the Zamindaris in Chicacole Sarkar. (Modern Srikakulam and Vijayanagaram) itself.[152] The Zamindars and other Hindu high officials of Coastal Andhra continued to assign villages and lands for charitable purposes, though on minor scale, till the end of the period under study. Mr. Travers, the collector of Nellore district, found 207 villages alienated on the Shrotriam tenure in the year 1801 A.D. in that district. There were 57 Shritriyam villages in the Zamindari of Saidapur of Nellore district. These villages were held at a fixed and unusually favourable rent and in most cases were granted by the Revenue renters and Fouzdars.[153] The Statement of tenures of 1874-75 A.D. given in *Godavari District Manual* (pp. 373-75) contains the list of 89 Agrahara/ Shrotriam villages, along with 36 Inam villages in Godavari

District. Similar statement of Cuddapah district contains a list of 259 Shrotriam villages in that district.[154]

Charitable Tenures held by Muslim Religious Institutions

Considerable number of villages and lands were assigned by both Hindu and Muslim governments under the Charitable tenure to the Muslim religious institutions. The Babayya Darga of Penugonda (Anantapur district) had in its enjoyment the revenue of more than six Hora village besides a number of individual plots of cultivable land and gardens granted by the Vijayanagara monarchs.[155] Similarly, the Khanqah of Syed Shah Raju I, the Chisti Sufi Saint was in receipt of a Jagir from Sultan Muhammad Quli Qutbshah.[156] Large number of Mosques, Dargas, Khanqahs etc built during the Bahmani, Qutbshahi, Mughal and and Asafjahi period at many places in Andhra Desa came to have it is not wrong to infer, large number villages and lands assigned under Charitable tenure. We have severalQutbshahi Farmans granting individual pieces of land and villages to the Sufi Saints and Dargahs.[157] In the year 1617 A.D., the Qutbshahi Fauzdar of Srikakulam granted four villages and several lands as Jagir for the maintenance of Mohammad Madina Sahab Darga at Kalingapatnam.[158] A statement of revenue and expenditure of theGolkonda kingdom for the year 1685-86 states that Rs.3,97,801 were given as Nadhar to Miran Shah Raju (Shah Raj-II) the Sufi Saint, Rs. 6,35,001 as Inam to Muslims and orphans, Rs. 64,650 for expenses of Ashur Khanas and Rs. 2,08,901, for Langar (feeding house) of two Imams.[159] These amounts, it is very clear, were the government share of the land revenue from villages and lands which were assigned to them. These Inam villages/lands were to a great extent continued under the succeeding governments.[160]

Asafjahi rulers also assigned the revenue of villages/ lands called Milk or Madad Mash for the maintenance of holy saints, Dargahs, Masjids and men of learning. Sometimes they were granted Wazifa (in cash) also. Both these grants i.e. cash and land together constituted what was generally called as 'Suyurghal'.

With the help of the available sources, it is difficult to give the total extent of the land which was under the Manyam/Inam tenures whether they were of service tenures or charitable tenures, during the study period in the entire Andhra Desa. Some idea can be formed of it with the help of the 1807 survey report in Ceded Districts. According to this survey, the total Inam land in Ceded districts was 2,599,747 acres with an estimated rent of 12,35,458 star Pagodas (gold coins). This was out of 12,066,923 acres which was the total land both under the government control (sarkar) and Inam land capable of cultivation with a rent of 39,54,417 star Pagodas.[161]

Notes & References

1. *Circuit Committee Report*, p. 48.
2. J. F. Richards has calculated these on the basis of Inayath Jung Collection 1/7/72 to 1/7/105 *Mughal Administration in Golkonda*, pp. 160-161.
3. *Ibid*.
4. Moulavi, Chirag Ali, *Hyderabad (Deccan) under Salarjung*, Vol.IV, Bombay, 1885, p. 27.
5. Robert Sewell, *Forgotten Empire*, p. 370.
6. *Forgotten Empire*, p. 280.
7. Butterworth and Setty, *A Collection of the Inscriptions on Copper Plates in the Nellore District*, pp. 484-85.
8. *Nellore District Inscriptions*, Kandukur, 80.
9. Butterworth & Shetty, *A Collection of Inscriptions on Copper Plates in the Nellore District*, p. 437.

10. N. Venkataramanayya., *Cuddapah Inscriptions*, p. 102.
11. J.F.Richards., *Mughal Administration in Golkonda*, p. 19.
12. N. Venkataramanayya, *Studies in the Third Dynasty of Vijayanagara*, p. 171.
13. Quoted from Burton Stein, *Peasant State and Society in Medieval South India*, p. 420.
14. *Nellore District Inscriptions*, pp. 198-199.
15. *Forgotten Empire*, pp. 365-70.
16. *Ibid.*, 354.
17. Barradas refes to a Dalavay who was the commander of the army paying a tribute of five hundred thousand cruzados (Forgotten Empire p.216). This commander appears to have been a Nayaka holding some territory in the first quarter of the Seventeenth Century.
18. *Forgotten Empire*, p. 270.
19. *Ibid.*, pp.357, 360 & 370.
20. *DRS* copy Doc. No. 7.
21. *Cuddapah Inscriptions*, p. 1022.
22. J. C. Dua, *Palegars of South India*, p. 60.
23. *Ibid.*, p. 48.
24. *Appendix to Fifth Report*, pp. 383-385. (111)
25. *Fifth Report from the Select Committee on the Affairs of the East India Company*, Vol.III, p. 22.
26. *Fifth Report*, p. 147.
27. *Appendix to Fifth Report from the Select Committee on the affairs of the East India Committee*, Vol.III; p.23; also see for its definition Irfan Habib, *Agrarian System of Mughal India*, 1556-1707, p. 169-186.
28. *I. J. Collection*, 1/1/15.
29. *I. J. Collection* 1/16/806.
30. *I. J. Collection* 1/1/17.
31. *Appendix to Fifth Report*, p. 54, 111.
32. J.C. Dua., Palegars of South India, p. 120.
33. *Ibid.*

34. In Palegar villages, the village servants were known as Grama Kattubadis who were required to perform service through out the year.
35. *Nellore Manual*, pp. 262-265.
36. *Ibid.*
37. *Ibid.*, p. 265.
38. *Cuddapah Inscriptions*, p. 102.
39. *Ibid.*
40. *Ibid.*, pp. 265-66.
41. *Ibid.*, p. 266.
42. The measurement of the allotment varied in each Zamindari. In Venkatagiri24 Kuntas made a Gorru and 76 square feet to a Kunta; in the Bommaraz Zamindary Gorrus were not in use; and only 64 square feet were allowed in a Kunta (-see Nellore Manual, pp. 266-267.
43. *Ibid.*, p. 268.
44. *Ibid.*, pp. 268-269.
45. Nizamuddin Ahmad, *Hadiquat-us-Salateen* (ed.), S.A. Bilgrami, Hyderabad, 1961, pp. 220-1 and J.F. Richards, p. 13.
46. *A Collection of the Inscriptions on Copper Plates and Stone in the Nellore District* Part-II, p. 533.
47. *Ibid.*, p. 577.
48. *J.F. Richards*, p. 23.
49. See Chart 1 & 2.
50. *Nellore Manual*, p. 475.
51. See Chart 3.
52. Nellore Manual, p.190.
53. T.V. Mahalingam, *Administration and Social Life Under Vijayanagara*, I, p. 138.
54. *Kistna District Manual*, p. 317.
55. *Ibid.*, p. 319.
56. *Guide to Masulipatam District Records*, p. 148.
57. *Nellore Manual*, p. 490.
58. Rusum of fixed rate per village on Pullari collections (grazing tax); Kuppakattalu or an allowance of a bundle from each

stack of grain; fees paid by Komati traders, shepherds, tax on betel, tobacco etc. ; see *Nellore Manual*, p. 490.

59. *Ibid.*, pp. 491-492 and 511.
60. *Ibid.*, p. 277.
61. *SII*, Vol.VI, No. 246.
62. *Nellore Manual*, pp. 492-493.
63. The Venkatagiri Zamindar having a territory of 9 taluqs was paying a Peishcash of 21,673 Pagodas to the Qutbshahi government and it was raised to 1,11,058 star Pagodas under the East India Company; *Nellore Manual*, pp. 71-722.
64. The lower staff like Tahwildar, Tahsildar, Mushrif, Futadar, Karkun, Muharir etc were paid monthly salary.
65. This Jagir became hereditary and was also confirmed by the English Company see *Nellore Manual*, pp. 498-9.
66. *Ibid.*, p. 719.
67. J. F. Richards, *Mughal Administration in Golkonda*, pp. 65-6.
68. *Krishna District Manual*, p. 296.
69. See Moulavi Chirag Ali, Hyderabad under Sir Salar Jung, Vol.IV, Bombay, 1885, p. 4-13.
70. *Ibid.*, pp. 5-12.
71. *Ibid.*, p. 13.
72. *DRS O.U.* copy Doc. No. 60.
73. *I.J. Collection* VIII/2/464-648; VIII/2/680; Nayeem, *Administration of Deccan under Nizam-ul-Mulk*, p. 49.
74. *Cuddapah Inscription*, p. 79.
75. *Qutbshahi Farmans in Hazarat Banda Nawaz Collection* No.15.
76. Sitapati, P.(ed.), *Farmans and Sanads of the Deccan Sultanas 1408-1687 A.D.*, 1980, p. 19.
77. *Ibid.*, p. 20.
78. *Ibid.*, p. 21.
79. *Ibid.*, p. 22.
80. *Ibid.*, p. 14, 15.
81. T.V. Mahalingam, *Administration and Social Life under Vijayanagara*, p.246.

82. A Collection of the Inscriptions on Copper Plates and Stones in the Nellore District, Part-II, p.563.
83. In Nellore and Ongole district areas the office of Sthalakarnam continued to function in the post-Vijayanagara period (see *Nellore Manual*, p. 480).
84. *Athavanavyavaharatantram* (ed.), M. P. R. Reddy, p. 21.
85. *Fifth Report*, pp. 148-149; *Appendix to Fifth Report*, pp. 22-23.
86. M. Sitapati (ed.), *Farman and Sanads of the Deccan Sultans 1408-1687)*, Hyderabad, 1980.
87. *Nellore Manual*, p. 480.
88. *Appendix to Fifth Report*, p. 24.
89. P. Sitapati (ed.), *Farmans and Sanads of the Deccan Sultans 1408-1687 A.D.*, Hyderaad, 1980.
90. *I.J. Collection*, 1/6/48, 1/6/50, 1/16/636 – taken from J.F. Richards, p. 115.
91. *I. J. Collection* – 1/7/98 (taken from J.F. Richards, p. 114.
92. *Ibid.*
93. D.C.R. 2992, p. 131).
94. R. Subba Rao, "Correspondence Between the East India Company and the Kandregula family in the Eihteenth Century", *Journal of Andhra Historical Research Society*, Vol. No. III, p. 2-4; GRMD, I, p.143; DCR, 2788, pp. 547-67.
95. R. Subba Rao, "Correspondence Between the East India Company and the Kandregula family in the Eihteenth Century", *Journal of Andhra Historical Research Society*, Vol. No. X.
96. G.RMD II, pp. 126-41).
97. *Ibid.*
98. T.V. Mahalingam, *Administration and Social Life under Vijayanagara*, 1940, Madras, p.247; *Nellore Manual*, foot note, p. 479.
99. *Farmans and Sands of the Deccan Sultans, 1408-1687 A.D.* , P. Sitapati, (ed.), p. 24.
100. *Nellore Manual*, p.480.

101. *Qutbshahi Farmans*, DRS Library, Department of History, Osmania University Doc. No. 7.
102. *Nellore Manual*, p. 481, foot note no. 1).
103. *Ibid.*, p. 481.
104. G. Yazdani., ed. *The Early History of the Deccan*,. Vol.VI-XI, p. 675.
105. *Kaifiyat of Kamalapuram*, L.R. I, PP. 94-95; also see S. Pratapa Reddy, *Andhrula Sangika Charitra*, pp. 330-31.
106. N. Venkataramamanyya, *Inscriptions of Cuddapah District* II. p. 228.
107. N. Venkataramanyya, *Inscriptions of Nellore District*. Vol. I No. 8.
108. *Athavana Vyavaharatantram*, p. 5.
109. *Kaifiyat of Kamalapuram, (Mack Mes.)* LR.I. pp. 94-95.
110. *Nellore District Inscriptions II*, p.577-83, and *Cuddapah Inscriptions*, pp. 247-248.
111. *Qutb Shahi Farmans* – Documents Nos.4, 13, 7, 45, 54. (English Translation, DRS Library, History Department, Osmania University; Appendix to Fifth Report, p. 24.
112. *S.I.I.*, Vol.X, No. 753.
113. *Ibid.*
114. Cited in Athavanavyavaharatantram, *p.18.*
115. *Appendix to Fifth Report*, p. 24.
116. *Athavanavyavaharatantram*, p. 18.
117. *Inscription of Andhra Pradesh, Cuddapah District*, Vol.III, p.165.
118. *Cuddapah Inscriptions*, 506-507.
119. *Cuddapah Inscriptions*, p.900.
120. *N.D.I.*, II, pp.820-21.
121. *South Indian Inscriptions*, Vol.XVI, No.104.
122. *Ibid.*, No.128.
123. *Ibid.*, No.302, 311 & 331.
124. *Athavanavyavaharatantram*, p.5-8.
125. *Ibid*, Buyam (Bhu+ayam) means income from land; Arthayam means income in cash.

126. *Ibid.*, p. 10.
127. Inscriptions of A.P. Cuddapah, pp. 228-258.
128. *Athavana Vyavaharatantram*, p. 8.
129. *Ibid.*, p. 114.
130. *Guide to Masulipatam District Records*, Vol. II, p. 142.
131. *Appendix to Fifth Report*, p. 273.
132. *Cuddapah Inscriptions*, pp. 1013-1014.
133. *Ibid.*, p. 865.
134. *Inscriptions of A.P. Nalgonda District II, Hyderabad*, 1994, no.84 and 82.
135. *Venubaka Kaifyat Mack.Mss*, vol.103, pp.192-93.
136. *Guide to the Records of the Nellore District 1801-1835*, p.239.
137. *Cuddapah Inscriptions*, p.247.
138. *Siddeswara Charitramu*, pp.154-155.
139. Robert Sewel, *Forgotten Empire*, pp.291-292.
140. Visvanatharayani Sthanapati, *Rayavachakam*, ASPP III, p.29.
141. *Ibid.*
142. *SII*, Vol. XVI. No.504.
143. *TDER*, p. 33.
144. Sundaram, K., *The Simhachalam Temple*, Waltair, 1969, p.141.
145. Errapragada, Harivamsamu, quoted from S. Pratapareddi, *Andhrula Sanghikacharitra*, p.90,; also see my book *Hindu and Muslim Religious Institutions, Andhra Desa, 1300 to 1600 A.D.*, p. 21.
146. *SII*, V. no. 1312.
147. *Ibid.*, VI, no. 1184.
148. *Mack. Mss*. 20 (S.A.), pp. 8-37.
149. *Mack. Mss*. No-4 (S.A.), p. 19.
150. P. Sitapati, (ed.) *Farmans and Sanads of the Deccan Sultans 1408-1687*, p. 24.
151. *Grama Kaifiyathulu, Guntur Taluka*, Vols. I, II & III.
152. R. Soma Reddy, Origin and Evolutions of the Zamindari System, *Minor Research Project of DRS Report*, 2002, p.19.

153. *Nellore Manual*, p.499.
154. J.D.B. Gribble, *A Manual of Cuddapah District*, 1875, Madras, Appendix No. II.
155. A.R., 1911, p. 87.
156. *Land Marks*, p. 74.
157. P. Sitapati (ed.), *Farmans and Sanads of Deccan Sultans*, pp.19-23.and also *Qutbshahi Farmans, DRS*, History, O.U. Copy.
158. *Srikakulam Zilla Grama Kaifiyattulu* (Telugu), A.P. State Archives, pp. 4-5.
159. Girdharilal Aqar, *Tarikh-i-Zafarah* (1771-72 A.D.), Chapter-I, quoted from *History of the Qutbsahi Dynasty*, of H.K. Sherwani, pp. 654-57.
160. In 1695, the Mughal government confiscated some land for the Khalisa, 14, 711 Bhigas in Telangana and 9,979 Bhigas in Coastal region, (*Mughal Administration in Golconda*, p. 207).
161. *Appendix to the Fifth Report*, p. 273.

CHAPTER - III

LAND REVENUE

The principal source of government revenue during this period was from the government share of all agricultural produce.[1] As the government was considered as the proprietor of the soil, it collected a share of the produce of the soil.[2] After taking the government share which was quite large and considerable and after deducting the village expenses and other inputs; what was left with the cultivator was his income. The land revenue system during the period under consideration is an extensive and important subject and it is very difficult to give a comprehensive picture of it. The land revenue system which was in vogue in this part of the country during the period can be studied under the following heads.

(A) Land Survey and Measurement.
(B) Revenue Assessment
(C) Revenue Rates (or share of the State and the Ryots)
(D) Mode of Payment.
(E) Machinery for Assessment and collection or Revenue organization.

(A) LAND SURVEY AND MEASUREMENT

The extent of arable land during the period under study was much less than what it is today and much land was under jungles and scrub. It was inspite of the fact that much land was brought under cultivation during this period and also during earlier centuries under Vijayanagara rulers and their predecessors Kakatiyas who founded a number of villages by clearing jungles and providing irrigation facilities. With the help of the available evidence, it is difficult to indicate the total extent of the land under cultivation in this region during the period of study. According to the land survey of 1802-1807 conducted in Ceded districts, the total land under cultivation was 3,203,859 acres of which the total government revenue was star Pagodas 18,52,955. (Appendix to Fifth Report p. 272).

We do not have direct evidence to show that there were any periodical and scientific land survey and measurement of land in Andhra Desa till the years 1802-1807, when the East India Company government undertook it in Ceded districts for land revenue assessment. But it can be definitely stated that all the cultivable land in this region as in other parts of India was surveyed and measured during certain periods of the earlier governments. The Mauryan Emperor Asoka employed officials like Rajuka for surveying the arable lands so as to introduce a uniform system of land measures and tax assessment. The length of the Rajju or measuring rope, according to Kautilya was equal to 10 Dandas (each Danda is equal to 96 Angulas or 1. 82 Metres).[3]

We have evidence to show that during the Qutbshahi period, arable land was surveyed and measurement was made. An epigraph of 1577 A. D. from Malkapur village, (Guntur Taluq and District) records the measurement of the land in each of the 19 villages of Ravipadu Sthalam by the standard rope (Paggamu) of 38 cubits (Pidimura). According to it, the measurement was made by the villages themselves by mutual agreement under the orders of Ibrahim Qutbshah.[4]

We are told that the Qutbshahi government of Golkonda conducted the land survey in territories including Cuddapah conquered from Vijayanagara in the first part of the seventeenth century and completed it in four years. The Qutbshahi revenue assessment was based on land survey and measurement.[5] Similarly, a rock edict of 1696 from the village Burrakayalakota, Chittoor district, records that during the period of Aurangzeb, on the representation of Reddi and Karnam of the above village that the old measurement of the land of that village was incorrect, Inayat, the Fauzdar of Gurramkonda had the lands remeasured with a two feet pole at the rate of 30 Guntas per Tumu.[6]

Classification of Arable Land

For measurement of land and for assessment of land revenue the arable land was classified during the pre-Muslim period into three categories.

(1) Dry land called 'Velipolamu' or 'Velichenu' or Cheluka.

(2) Wet land called 'Nirunela' or Magani.

(3) and garden land called 'Totabhumi'.

This classification continued to be followed for assessment during the seventeenth and eighteenth centuries and even afterwards.[7] Under the Hindu rulers, the land measures followed were different for dry land and wet land. The extent of dry land was known in Tumus (or Khandik or Khanduvu) and Puttis which were also used for the measuring of the grain.[8] The extent of wet land was known in Marturu (Telugu) or Nivarthanas (Sanscrit). The literature and epigraphs of Kakatiya, Reddi and Vijayanagara periods explain these land measures as given below. With a small difference these measures were followed throughout the above period.

One Putti of dry land consisted 20 Tumus;

One Tumu of land measured – 112 and a half Kuntas

One Kunta was a square Gada or Dandaka or Pole or Single pole lengthwise and breadthwise.

One Gada or Dandaka consisted of 32 Jenas or Vitastis or foot

One Jena was equalent of 12 Angulas

One Angula was half of the circumference of the thumb or half the length of the middle finger.

The representations of the above poles or Dandakas or measuring rod or pole were sketched on pillars in temples and their extent was described in contemporary literature. One Kesaripati Gada appears to have been the standard one during that period. [9] Similarly the Marturu or Nivartana which was the measure for indicating the wet land is explained as follows.

One Gocarma made 10 Nivartanas or Marturu

One Nivartana was equivalent to 20 Dandas

One Danda measured 10 Hastas

One Hasta was equalent of 2 Jenas or Vitastis.[10]

(Gocharma was equalent of 4 ½ puttis of land)

(B) REVENUE ASSESSMENT BY ANCHANADARS

During the Vijayanagara and Gajapati periods the revenue assessment was made and the government share was estimated before the harvesting commenced. The quantity of the crop of each cultivator was ascertained. This was done by the survey by the persons who were unconnected with the village and who were outsiders. It was done in the presence of the cultivators and the village officials such as the headman, accountant etc. The officials who surveyed the land under the crop and ascertained its quality and quantity were skilled and were experts in that job and were called Anchanadars While doing so, they were aided by the reference to the produce of the former years as recorded by the village revenue officials. If the cultivators were not satisfied with the assessment, they could get second survey by their own people and if any difference appeared in the two estimates, a third assessment was made under the orders of the village officers.[11] Anchanadars or Assessors were there through out the period under study under all the government including that of company. The term-Anchanadar was of pre-company period origin. In the year 1795, ten Anchanadars were appointed in Masulipatam Circar, to value the crops.[12]. That, they were paid Batta (daily allowances) while on duty is indicated by the fact that on 28-1-1795, the arrears of Batta of Kistnaiah and Conaiah, the Anchanadars was claimed.[13] Thus, the quantity of the government share called 'Karoo' was ascertained which it received either in kind or cash and the remaining produce was Ryot's share called 'Medipalu' (the share of the plough handle). Under the Vijayanagara government the revenue was paid in kind in the proportion of half the produce. The government half was commuted for money.[14]

The Circuit Committee Report of 1784, describing the mode of making revenue collection in Kasimkota division of the Chicacole Circar, and prevailing under the native Rajas (Gajapatis and their feudatories) describes the land revenue assessment thus... "The quantity of the crop was determined by a valuation made by indifferent persons just before the harvest and in the presence of the public servants and the inhabitants. This estimate being registered by the Karnam, the Circar servants, after the grain was trodden out, received the government moiety.... ".[15]

It appears, this basic system of assessment or ascertaining the crop before its harvest on behalf of the government and fixing the government share was almost common in all the regions of Andhra Desa under the Hindu rule. There might have been minor regional variations. It was followed in crown lands as well as in those alienated to others. And this method was also followed under the succeeding Muslim governments and also under company with minor changes in the procedure. The position of the cultivator was same in the villages belonging to all the tenures.

During the Qutbshahi period also the assessment of land revenue was made on the basis of land survey and measurement. This system of assessment known as 'Jamia-i-kamil' (perfect assessment) 'specified a normative land tax figure for each village, sub-district and district'[16] (pargana and sarkar) in the Golkonda kingdom. During this period the assessment and collection of land revenue was made in cash rather than in kind which was the system prevalent under the earlier governments. [17] For making this assessment, the Qutbshahi government appears to have depended on the assessment figures of the earlier period maintained by the local revenue accountants such as *Sthalakarnam* and the *village Karnam*. According to *Muntakhab-al-luba* (II, 367-8) by Khafikhan, the Jama of Golkonda kingdom at the time of its conquest by Aurangazeb was 28,790,000 Rupees or 8,22,714. Gold Hun (at the rate of 3. 5 Rupees per Hun) and according to Mughal documents of Inayat Jung Collection, it was 29,188, 125 Rupees or 8,339,750 Hun (Col. , 1/7/72).[18] The Qutbshahi government also respected the tax concessions enjoyed by the Hindu religious institutions like the Temples, learned Brahmins etc who held lands under Charitable tenures, and the village servants on their Manyam lands held under service tenures and also the Manyam lands granted for agricultural development. Otherwise, the assessment was based on the system of getting one half share of production. The assessment or *Jama-i-kamil* figure assigned to each territorial unit became the standard assessment figure as a ceiling beyond which payment should not be made by the tax payer. It represented a bargaining point for all parties concerned in the revenue collection – the central revenue ministry, its Amildars, Muqasadars, their agents, revenue farmers, the hereditary revenue officials at pargana and village level.

We have evidence to show that the revenue assessment (Jama-i-kamil) by the revenue officials during the Asafjahi period was made with the consent of the cultivators (Zamindars or Ryots). After the assessment was made, the amount of revenue the Ryots agreed to pay was stated on paper, their signatures obtained in the presence of Deshmukh, Deshpandia and all of them had to affix their seals. Finally the Qazi (the judicial officer of the district or pargana) had to authenticate the document with his own seal with the endorsement "ba inqrar-i-Zamindaran Muhar namuda shud" – (with the approval/consent of the Zamindars the seal has been fixed); or 'ba iqrar wo dastakhat deshmukh wo deshpandia muhar namuda" (with the approval and signature of the Deshpandia and Deshmukh the seal has been affixed); or with the consent of Majumdar and Deshpandia. [19] During the period of Asafjahis, the revenue assessment was made twice a year; at the time of Kharif (autumn) and Rabi (spring) harvests.[20]

Under the Nawabs, in the Kurnool district, the revenue settlement was made in the Saka month of Kartika or Margasira (November and December).[21] While the term 'Jama-i-kamil' was used for the standard amount figure of revenue assessment, the term Jamabandi indicated the actual amounted collected, 'Jihat' were the taxes levied to meet the expenses of the government incurred in making assessment of Mal or revenue.

Even the revenue collection during this period was made with the consent and approval of the tax payers who were the cultivators and with the consent of the Deshmukh and

Deshpandia. All the documents of revenue receipts (Jama Wasul Baqi) bear the consent of the cultivators with their seal attesting the revenue paid and the balance to be paid. And, finally it was attested with the seal of the Qazi.[22]

Corruption in Assessment

The government officials involved in the revenue assessment, some times tended to be corrupt and took bribes from the cultivators and cheated the government. This tendency on the part of the village headman and accountant during the Vijayanagara period is indicated in the work *Athavanavyavaharatantram* (p. 5 & 6). We get some stray references in the District Collectorate Records to the corruption of some of these officials like Tanadars (head of police out post) Anchanadars (assessors) Kyldars (Measurers), Deshpandia etc. of the last part of the Eighteenth century under the company's rule. The report dated 3-4-1795 refers to a complaint given by Karnam (accountant) of Kosanapally village (Krishna district) about the Tanadar and Despandia (Pargana Registrar) accepting bribes for reducing the rent. All the concerned in the case were required to go to Huzur Katchery (revenue head-quarters).[23] Another report, dated 19-3-1795 refers to the complaints given by the Tanadars of Vuyyoor that the estimates given by Anchanadars were found to be false. The Anchanadars were to be sent to the Huzur. [24] It was also reported that the actual outturn of the crops was much higher than the estimates made by the Tanadar and Anchanadars received bribes for reducing the estimates. All the concerned were ordered to attend the Huzur.[25]

It is clear, from the above, that not only the Deshmukh, Deshpandia of Pargana and village headman and accountant, but the Anchanadars, Kyldars and Tanadars involved in revenue assessment on government side indulged in corruption and cheated the government. Everybody of them got their remuneration besides enjoying their Inam lands. The report dated 22-8-1795 mentions the complaint of Kyldars against the Renters. Who were refusing to pay the usual allowances of the Kyldars. It is further stated that, the collector of Masulipatam directed the renters to pay those allowances.[26]

Modes of Assessment of Land Revenue

For the land revenue assessment several different modes were followed. They were as given below.

The revenue rates or the government share depended on the nature of the soil, crops and also the caste and condition of the Ryot and also the type of irrigation.

1. Money Assessment – (Tirva), Visabadi etc., Cist and Malwaty (in Money)
2. Division of crop (Varum, Bhagamu Gallabakshi, (in Grain)
3. Fixed Assessment – Bilmakta on garden crop (in Money)
4. Concessional Assessment Quit rent – Jodi, Shrotriyam

1. Money Assessment

In some cases the land revenue was assessed in fixed Money. It was known as 'Tirva' in Nellore district which formed a part of Karnatic and which was under the Vijayanagara and Qutbshahis, Mughals and the Nawab of Arcot in succession. The word 'Tirava' (probably a Tamil world) had its etymology from the Telugu word 'Tirpu' meaning settled or finished. It implied that all arable lands belonging to every villages had a fixed money valuation or Tirava which was sanctioned by Mamul or custom The process of this fixed money assessment was as follows:

When a Ryot came forward to cultivate a piece of waste or jungle land, it was given to him on cowle for a term of years on the principle of progressive increase of tax or graded taxation. The sum to be paid annually by the Ryot was fixed by the village Karnam and Reddi in conjunction with the government servant who took into consideration the labour and other inputs for clearing and leveling the ground. At the expiration of the Cowle period, when the land was supposed to have been brought to the highest pitch of improvement by successive cultivation by the application of manure etc, a fixed Tirva equalent of the valuation or assessed amount of that kind of arable land in the same village was then settled again by the government servants, village head, accountant and some of the principal cultivators. This fixed Tirva which was considered as 'Mamul Tirava' even after it was registered in the Register of the village Curnum.[27]

The fixed money assessment was resorted to, thus, mostly in cases of land development when new land was brought under cultivation during different periods. The money rates under this fixed assessment varied from village to villages and land to land within the same village and the rates in each village were well known to each cultivator. The government (Polegar or renter) also, it appears, did not conform to these rates strictly-sometimes less than the Manual Tirva was levied but many a time more was collected.

In the case of Fixed money assessment, the Ryots could take advantage of three factors. The first one being the quantity of the land under this assessment. Under this system, the land was not annually measured but often taken at guess by which means the Ryot managed to get more land than stipulated in his engagement. Secondly, it was the quality of the soil. As a particular rate of Tirva or assessment was fixed on each kind of land, the Ryot contrived to get the first sort for the assessment usual for the second sort and so on with the rest. Thirdly, it was from the difference in the price of grain. If the prices were high, he got some profit. Otherwise, if they were low, that proved detrimental to his interest.[28]

The village headman and the accountant played an important role in this type of assessment, in which they collided with the Ryots in the assessment and got some benefit out of it.

Nagur Cowl: Under the Asafjahis, the fixed money rent was called 'Nagur' cowl a Nagati (plough cowle in Telugu). The Sarbastidars (Zamindar having Sarbastu Cowl) assessed the revenue by taking the number of ploughs into account. Land ploughed by the instrument (Nagali) by two bullocks was assessed at from Rs. 5 to Rs. 10 and with two ploughs Rs. 10-to Rs. 25. In this type of assessment, the extent of the land cultivated was not taken into consideration.[29]

One plough, it is said, is capable of tilling two Beegas at a time that is two Bigaas in the Abe and two, in the Tabeen (first and second crop). But this is rather a rough estimate as much as it depended on the quality of bullocks and also their number – (A Beega is equalent of 6400 sqaure yards. Six consoor (measure) of paddy are looked on as one Beega's sowing capacity. This tenure was usually given from three to four years and granted for the cultivation of dry grains.[30]

Koolharee: The hatchat tenure. This existed among the Coorwars of the Pakhal in Warangal. It is as much as one man can clear with his hatchat (axe). From 4 to 8 Annas was the rent for each hatchat.[31] This system prevailed probably in forest region where the tribals adopted podu or shifting cultivation.

Visabadi System

Visabadi system was one of the important modes of revenue settlement during this period. It comes under the category of fixed money revenue assessment. It was widely prevalent in this region until the introduction of Ryotwari system by the Company. Under this system, the village revenue was assessed in a fixed lump sum per annum. The land revenue of the village and also the cultivable land of that village was divided into shares and distributed among the Ryots of the village according to their means and also on the basis of the nature of the soil. This system was called 'Visabadi' because the assessed total village revenue and all its cultivable land were divided into 16 shares called 'Visas'. Visa was the 1/16th part of a Rupee. [32] These shares of revenue and lands were distributed by lots among the Ryots. The village headman, accountant and the chief cultivators of the village played a major role in the distribution of these shares.

Visabadi was, thus, the division into fractions payable by each Ryot to make up the full assessment on the village. It was settled some times annually and some times once in four or five years. Similarly, the cultivable lands were distributed among the cultivators of the village either once in a year or once in four or five years. It was a settlement in money.

Origin and Extent of Visabadi System

It is difficult, with the available evidence, to trace the origin of Visabadi system and to indicate the exact extent of its prevalence in this region. As mentioned already, Visamu was 1/16th part of a Rupee and it was also a weighing measure. The system of land distribution among the various claimants or share holders on the basis of Visams or sixteen shares was prevalent in this region during the Qutbshahi and Mughal periods. One stone epigraph of late Qutbshahi period dated 1685 A. D. from the village Palampalle (Cuddapah district) records that the Dasavandam Manyam land which was given for the revival of a damaged tank was to be distributed among the claimants on the basis of Visas, i. e. 'Patika' or four 'visas' to one person, one Visa to the next etc, indicating the land distribution on the basis of Visa.[33] Similarly, a Kaul deed dated 1715 A. D. from a village of Cuddapah district states that the Dasavandam land given for the construction of a new tank in that village was to be divided into 16 Visas and to be distributed among the beneficiaries[34]. It appears that the Visabadi system of land revenue settlement was prevalent in the Telugu region long before the establishment of English rule.

It is reported in the *Manual of the Kurnool* district that the village lease system appeared to have been the ordinary mode of settlement during the Hindu and Muhammadan periods".[35] But we do not get any evidence to prove that the Visabadi system prevailed during the Vijayanagara period or earlier to it. As Revenue farming system was prevalent in the Vijayanagara Empire, the Visabadi system, an off-shoot of the farmer also must have been followed there.

On the other hand, it is reported that it was promoted by the Ryots themselves in order to avoid the endless demands caused by the extortionate government of the Muhammadans[36]. Probably, the Ryots preferred this fixed assessment instead of paying the additional exactions of the Muslim rulers. In the Carnatic territory of which Nellore and Chittoor were a part, this system was widely prevalent in all the villages during the period of Muslim rule. During this period, the system of revenue farming became a general rule. The revenue farmers were very often the Deshmukhs who were originally the government revenue collectors. The government also found it convenient to treat them as revenue contractors for the revenue of their respective subdivisions by allowing some percentage, or commission on the revenues collected as their remuneration. But in the course of time they became feudatories paying tribute to their sovereigns. In that situation, the practice of sub-renting naturally ensued and the farming system extended itself to single villages[37]. Thus, it appears that the origin of this system was of Muslim period and it was a off-shoot of Revenue farming system.

Regarding the extent of the prevalence of Visabadi system, it appears to have been followed in Nellore and part of Chittoor districts, which formed a part of Carnatic under the Nawabs; Palnad of Guntur district, several hundreds of villages in Godavari and Visakapatnam districts and also in Ceded districts. In Telangana districts also, it appears to have been prevalent under the Qutbshahi and Asafjahi rule as Revenue farming was widely prevalent there. It was widely prevalent through out the Karnatic including the Tamil districts like Tiruchinapally, Tinnavelly, Tanjore and Arcot.[38] Regarding the extent of its prevalence in Carnatic and Ceded districts, the Fifth Report States ... "it was found, on that territory (Carnatic) being annexed to the British possessions, that the revenues of each village were generally sub-rented to the Potails. But in the districts ceded by the Nizam and in the Mysore country, which also passed from the rule of Muhammadan princes, to that of the East India Company, sub-renting by villages, was by no means universal, though it existed to a great extent......".[39]

Working of the System

The working of the Visabadi system in Nellore district under the Karnatic Nawabs is described in the *Nellore Manual* thus..... "One system of cultivation which we find to have been very prevalent in the Nellore district was the Visabadi tenure, by which the lands of a village would be held by the community in common, and shares allotted to the different members by quarters, eighths, sixteenths, thirty-seconds and sixty-fourths. Where this system prevailed, and also under other tenures, it was often customary for the residents of a village periodically, say every five or six years, to exchange all their lands so as to secure an equal division of the soils, good and bad.[40]

Similarly the working of Visabadi system during the pre-colonial period is explained in the *Vizagapatam Manual* as follows. "A fixed sum of money was assessed on the whole village, for one or two years. A certain number of most respectable ryots became responsible for the amount, each being responsible for his own separate portion thereof, and all for each other; and the lands were divided by lot, as in the Samudayam villages of the Tamil country, the portion of land to be occupied by such being determined by the proportion of rent for which he became responsible. Thus, if ten ryots obtained their village for three years at a Visabadi rent of 100 Pagodas, the first becoming responsible for 20, the second for 40, and the other eight for 5 pagodas each, the lands of the village would be divided into ten equal shares, the first would be entitled to two of these, the second to four, and each of the others to half a share. From this division of them into shares, the settlement took its name of Visabadi, namely a village settlement by shares in ready money.... ".[41]

The distribution of the lands in the Visabadi villages among the Ryots was done with reference to their means, i. e. the number of tilling cattle, seed, manpower and other infrastructure possessed by the cultivators. The land to be distributed was classified on the basis of the nature of the soil. The classification of the lands in Kurnool district followed in the time of Nawab Ali Khan, father of the last Nawab and described in a Telugu statement taken from a Carnum in 1810 by colonel Mackenzie is thus described below.

1. Tuvva soil or soil mixed with sand, 1 to 1 1/16 Chalavani rupees, or 13 Annas 4 pies to 14 Annas and 4 pies) for a Munta (or about 2 ¼ acres).

2. Red loamy lands, 1 1/6 to 1 ¼ Chalvani rupees or 14 Annas to Rs. 1-0-8 per Munta.
3. Regada (inferior), 1 rupee to 4 rupees a Munta
4. Black Regada (alluvial soil), 10 or 12 Chalavani rupees a Munta.[42]

We are told in the above source that some of the rich lands were generally given to wealthy Ryots with Tambulam or a betel and nut, free of assessment at 5 to 6 Muntas each as a sort of encouragement.[43]

Challenging System under Annual System

The Visabadi settlement was of two kinds, annual and for a term of 5 years. Under the annual assessment, the ryots generally retained the same lands though assessment was revised every year and the revision being made by the ryots themselves. Under the Visabadi assessment for a term of years the lands were exchanged among the ryots and the assessment also was revised every few years according to custom in each village.[44]

As the assessment was revised every year by the ryots themselves under the annual Visabadi system its impartiality was ensured by the introduction a practice called "challenging". According to this system, any ryot who felt that his own holding was over-assessed and that of his neighbour or some other ryots in the village was under-assessed, the former could demand that the later's land holding should be made over to him at an increased rate. If the ryot in possession consented to pay the enhanced rate, he could retain the land and in that case a proportionate reduction was made in the assessment of the land held by the complaining party. If the Ryot in possession refused to agree to the enhanced demand, he was compelled to give up the land to the complaining party, who agreed to it on the higher terms. But this system of challenging had a very bad effect on the improvement of agriculture. The wealthy and enterprising ryots were deterred from investing in improving the inferior land as they had no certainty of possessing that improved land and were liable to loose it. Inspite of its disadvantages, this system of challenging was retained for some more years even after the abolition of the Visabadi system. As mentioned already it ensured impartiality. It was Mr. Prendegast, the Collector of Godavari district reporting in 1850 who felt that it was only method of doing justice and putting a stop to violent disputes and it was quite in unison with the feelings of the people.[45]

Merits and Demerits of the Visabadi System

The Visabadi system of revenue assessment had its merits and demerits:

Merits: Under the Visabadi system, the villages had greater bargaining power and there was also a scope for mutual adjustment in case of isolated crop failure. The government also found it beneficial and convenient to its interest, for it simplified the collection of taxes.

Under the Visabadi system, the joint responsibility of the community kept up the extent of the cultivation as much as it was possible to keep it up. That was the only way the rent fixed for the village could be totally paid. But when the Visabadi system was abolished and the joint responsibility broken up, the poor Ryots could not keep up the extent of the land allotted to them and had to relinquish much of their land as they could not get any assistance from the richer Ryots. There was a steady decrease in the total extent of cultivable land and the consequent decrease in the revenue for years from 1839 to 1843 in Kurnool when Visabadi system was abolished. We are told that some of the poorer Ryots were reduced to the state of day labourer who were hired by the richer Ryots to cultivate their own fields in Jagir area[46].

Demerits: There were certain evils associated with the system. The Ryot had the disadvantage of fluctuating and uncertain government demand due to the periodical assessment and exchange of fields frequently.

Visabadi system proved to be more advantageous to the chief Ryots of the village and disadvantageous to the poor Ryots. The head and the rich Ryots monopolized all advantages at the expense of the common cultivators. They regulated the cultivation and while distributing they managed to get the best lands for themselves. They under-assessed the lands in their own occupation and the lands of their own relations and friends and over-assessed the lands of the poor Ryots. Some times the poor Ryots were forced to cultivate the lands of the village chief Ryots free of charge. They also advanced the kists or installments of revenue for the poor Ryots and seized their produce to recover the debts and made profits by reselling that grain. They made all sorts of exactions in the name of Grama Kurch or village expenses[47] which they appropriated for themselves or used to the corruption of the governments servents[48].

Another disadvantage to the poor Ryots in the Visabadi villages was that they were forced to take highly assessed lands (lands on whom more revenue was assessed) while the rich Ryots got the low assessed fields. Though the poor cultivators were free to choose any field, he was unable to take more than what he was capable of managing due to lack of investment. More over, as the poor Ryot wasted much of his cattle dung as fuel due to scarcity of fire wood he was unable to use cattle manure for fertilizing the fields[49]. And finally, under the Visabadi system, the Ryots were not given

Pattas or registration documents of the land in their name, as the lands changed hands frequently.

Regarding the distribution of lands and the dominant role played by chief Ryots in Visabadi villages in Kurnool under the Nawabs before the Ryotwari settlement was established in 1840. Mr. Scott, the Commissioner of Kurnool writes to the chief Secretary to the government in 1843. Thus ".... It is true that each field has a Tirwah (fixed rate) tacked to it, but it is entirely nominal for No. 1 may be assessed at 1 Rupee, and No. 2 next to it and of the same description, may be rated at 3 Rupees an acre with out any one being able to assign any other reason than that it is so.... Such is the ascendancy of the Reddies and Karnams, and the subjection of the Ryots from long established custom, that nothing is easier than for the former to saddle any one with an undue proportion of highly assessed land, reserving the most lightly rated or the lands nearest to the village for themselves and those whom they may wish to favour.... "[50].

The revenue rates in the Visabadi villages appear to have been excessive. The Godavari district collector's report dated 10. 7. 1800 states that the cultivators of the Visabadi villages preferred to cultivate in the neighbouring villages. So that they might get the remission given to outside cultivators (Payakaris). It further states that in Attili and Asuntah Parganas the condition of Visabadi Ryots was worse and they were refusing to enter into fresh engagement[51]. It is reported that in the Visabadi villages the acrage under cultivation was decreasing. In Nellore district the Ryots were converting the arable lands into pasturage for cattle breeding which was found to be more remunerative to the cultivators than the cultivation. But it resulted in revenue loss to the government[52]. The assessment in Visabadi villages was fixed at 50% of the gross value of the produce[53]. The cultivator had to bear other expenses from his share.

Sist and Malvati System of Assessment

This system is said to have been prevalent in the Zamindari territories of north Coastal Andhra just before the establishment of the company's rule. By this period, all the intermediaries such as, the hereditary feudal Rajas, the hereditary revenue officials of the Pargana – the Deshmukhs and Deshpandias and also some of the revenue contractors were elevated to the same position and were called as Zamindars as stated earlier in the chapter on tenures. The Circuit Committee Report states that it was followed in the Zamindari territories of Rajamundry, Parts of Ellor and Vizagapatam districts. It states that the Zamindars eventually .... "set aside the former usage and after ascertaining by measurement the quantity of the arable land, imposed a fixed rate of Rupees 10 per Garce,[54] called Sist, the payment of which was to entitle the labourer to the unrestricted disposal of crop. This alteration, favourable as at first sight it may appear to the inhabitant, was established solely for the convenience and profit of the Zamindar, as it enabled him to take one Kist or installment of the collections in advance and served as a foundation whereon to calculate any further assessments. Soon after, when the land was supposed to be improved, the Malvati was added at the rate of 100 to 150 percent on the Sist and then forward considered as fixed payment. The nazar which is taken in plenteous years, is an exaction not fixed, but generally at the rate of 50 per cent on the Sist.... ".[55]

From this account, it appears that the system of Sist and Malvaty was introduced in the Zamindari territories only during the period of anarchy when the central government became weak during post-Aurangzeb period. It appeared a bit favourable to the cultivator. Since he already paid the Sist in advance and on which Malvati and Nazar were calculated, he needed not wait for the government officials for the division of the produce to enable him to dispose of his grain. But it was more advantageous to the Zamindar as he could get a part of the revenue quite before the Ryot harvested his crop. The sist was a nominal sum entered in the Patta; and when the crop was entirely ripe, it was valued by government servants and the enhancement called Malvati calculated on the condition of the crop was added to the Sist.

Graded Taxation

The system of graded taxation in the case of land-reclamation or bringing new or waste land under cultivation was much prevalent under Vijayanagara rulers. A number of epigraphs belonging to the later Vijayanagara period belonging to Rayalasima districts throw light on this type of taxation where tax relief was given first three or five years or it was slowly raised till it reached the normal rates. Besides giving Dasavanda Manyam lands for establishing new villages (Pallakattu Manyam) for bringing new lands under cultivation by clearing jungles and leveling it (Achchu kattu Manyam) for providing irrigation by a canal or well (Kalava kattu and Bavikattu Manyam) tax concessions for three or five years were given under graded system. Different rates of tax concessions were given depending on the nature of work involved, or duration and value of crops.[56]

When a waste or new land was allotted to a Ryot, the system of graded taxation was adopted. It was called 'Istawa' cowle in Telangana districts under the Asafjahis. It was increasing rent for first three to five years when it was fixed finally. In the case of red soils the following rates per Beegah (6400 square yards) were prevailing.

First Year	½ rupee per Beegah.
Second Year	1 rupee per Beegah.
Third Year	1 ½ rupee per Beegah.

Fourth Year	1 ¾ rupee per Beegah.
Fifth Year	2 rupee per Beegah.
In the case of black soils	
First Year	1 rupees per Beegah.
Second Year	2 rupees per Beegah.
Third Year	3 rupees per Beegah. [57]

2. Division of Crop or Sharing System

Most of the land during the period under consideration was assessed on the basis of sharing system. Under this system of assessment, the Ryot and the government shared the produce of the soil. It was grain assessment. It is referred to as 'Varun' (meaning sharing) in Nellore district Manual. It was also called 'Bhagam' under Hindu government, 'Gallabakshi' and 'Batai' under the Mughals.

During the Asafjahi period in Telangana districts, the procedure followed for revenue assessment in the case of Battai or crop sharing was as follows. The cultivator could not cut his crop until after the Sarbastidar (Assessor or valuer) estimated the probable produce. Then an undertaking called 'Kabuliyat' was signed by the Ryot agreeing to pay the assessed revenue to the government. The crop was cut in the presence of the sub-agents of the Talukdars such as probably the Naibs, peons, the village headman and accountant. Then it was kept under seal till it was threshed and measured or weighed for division between the cultivator and the government. [58]

3. Fixed Assessment - Gutta or Bilmakta Assessment:

An other mode of fixing the government share or Assessment was Gutta or Bilmakta or fixed money rent which was adopted by the government in the case of garden produce or plantations. The term used in northern India for this assessment was 'Muktai'.[59] It was a fixed annual rent for a measure of land for fixed number of years. It was known as "Gutta' (Vijayanagara) and Bilmakta (Persian term). This was not liable to fluctuation even though the garden produce might be more or less. In fixing these rates the following were taken into account.

The garden crops to be raised, required additional expenses, labour and time. There was also the hazard of carrying them to the distant market with the risk of their perishing on the way.

In Nellore district before the English Company's rule (under the Arcot Nawab) the following rates of Money rent in Rupees on garden crops per Gorru (measure) of land were followed. These rates were adopted by the district Collector Mr. Travers in the settlement of 1801 A. D.

Betel cultivation	-	from	Rs. 290 to Rs. 116
Sugarcane	-	"	Rs. 232 to Rs. 116
Tobacco	-	"	Rs. 174 to Rs. 29
Ginger and Garlic	-	"	Rs. 116 to Rs. 58
Coconut Plantations	-	"	Rs. 116 to Rs. 29
Sanu, hemp & vegetables		"	Rs. 29 to Rs. 4[60]

In Kurnool district under the rule of the Nawabs, the tax on betel gardens was levied as follows – For the first year, as in the case of dry crop (probably a fixed amount for a measure of land); in the next three years, each plot of land containing 128 Madis (beds of 9x4 cubits) each was charged 8 Mitta Pagodas or 32 Rupees and the tax was collected in three installments.[61]

These crops were many a time were watered by well irrigation and were raised in garden lands or 'Totabhumi'. Because of the extra labour involved in lift irrigation with Kapile or Mota; a fixed assessment in cash was fixed as a Gutta or Bilmakta.[62]

In assessing the garden cultivation and fixing the government share, it appears, the amount of expenses and labour involved, were also taken into account. That is the reason why we find a wide range in the revenue rates for the garden produce. On the basis of the labour and expenses involved in the irrigation of garden lands and also the yield, they were classified in 1801 in Nellore district by the collector in to three classes and the revenue was fixed as given below.[63]

1. Those irrigated by "Kannabhavulu" or Sunken wells, more than 15 feet deep from which the water was lifted by bullock power (either Mota or Kapile or Persian wheel). Two crops were obtained, each of 2 Putties and the government's share at 4/20th of the net produce was Madras Pagodas 5-12-31 per Gorru, commuted at the standard rate of 28 Rupees per Putti. (Here the Ryot's share at 16/20th of the net produce was Madras Pagodas 20-49-28-8.

2. Those irrigated by Picottahs from shallow wells, Nullahs or pools. This irrigation was called "Yetam Potalu". Two crops were usually raised and the government share at 8/20th of the net produce was worth Madras Pagodas 10-26-0. The first crop was estimated at 2 ½ Puttis, and therefore, the rate where only one crop could be raised was Madras Pagodas 6-29-20.

3. Those irrigated by hand (Cheyipotalu) principally "sandy soils near the sea-shore under high sand hills from which water oozes into pools cut for the purpose" These lands produced two crops amounting to 3 puttis. They were accordingly rated Madras Pagodas 5-47-10, the government share being taken at 6/20.

From this, we understand that the government's share and the Ryot's share were taken from the net produce after deducting the fee or village expenses etc. As mentioned already, the collector adhered to the rates established by custom under the former government.

Bilmakta system was adopted for assessing government share in the garden produce during this period in Northern Circars also and also in Telangana districts under Asafjahis where Rs. 2 to 4 per Beegah was collected depending on the nature of the soil-red black etc.[64]

But in Zamindari territories of Northern Circars before the Company's rule; the Bilmakta assessment was adopted for even poor ground or poor soils where small grain (pulses) was produced. A specific sum (per a measure of land) not liable to any other imposition was collected from the Ryots. In addition to that, an imposition called 'Sari', Zamindar's allowance was permitted by the Mughal government. It was 10 per cent of the collections in reward for maintaining order and encouraging cultivation. Ultimately, the Ryot got one third of the produce under this mode of assessment. [65] In some cases it ranged between one-fourth to one eighth of the total years gross produce. Here the government share was much less compared to that of wet crops and rainfed dry crops.

4. Concessional Assessment – Quit rent, Jodi, Shrotriyam

The last mode of assessment, under study, was the concessional quit rent called 'Shrotriyam' (Sanscrit) or Jodi (Tamil) imposed on 'Manyam' lands under Hindu rule and 'Inam' lands under Muslim governments. The holders of the Manyam or Inam lands enjoyed the whole produce of their assigned land by paying to the government a moderate fixed quit-rent called Jodi or Shrotriyam payable annually either in money or grain as stipulated. These lands were assigned both under the Charitable tenures and service and

Dasabandam – tenures. Villages and lands assigned to the temple (Devadaya) Mathas (Mathapura) and Masjids (Masjid Inams) Khanquas, Ashurkhanas and Dargas, learned Brahmans (Agraharas) all come under the Charitable tenures. Manyam or Inams given to village Ayagars, revenue and police officials like Deshmukh, Sthalakarnam, Deshpandia and Kattubadi and Amaram etc. and finally the Dasavanda Manyam granted for agricultural development; all belong to the service tenures. The holders of these Manyam/Inam lands were given tax concessions.

All these charitable and service Manyams/Inams were described as 'Sarvamanya' (tax-free). But in most cases the holders of these grants had to pay not only quit-rent but also other taxes indirectly.[66] Similarly, these grants though made in perpetuity (Achandrarca Sthayiga) and their quit rent fixed for ever, we have some instances of the confiscation of the lands of the Hindu religious institutions by the Qutbshahi government.[67] Even the Palegars also appear to have enroached upon the rights of the holders of the Manyams.[68]

Other Imposts on Agricultural Income

Besides the land revenue, the government also imposed other taxes on the cultivators on the following items.

1. Mamul Katnam:- Mamul Katnam was levied on Tirava on fixed money assessment. On every Pagoda or Varaha, the Ryot agreed to pay, a fixed sum was imposed by the Government. Similarly, in the case crop sharing (Varum) also a stated sum was imposed on every candy or Putti of the cultivator's share.

2. Ghair Mamool Katnams: or Putti was an oppressive tax imposed on both the Inamdars and also on Ryots. This was levied in Zamindaris and Palems on special occasions such as the marriage of the Zamindar etc.

The government also collected taxes on castes and professions, industries or trades, intoxicant liquors, drugs for temples and customs duties (sair).

Pullari: The government of the day also collected grazing tax called Pullari for grazing in the government waste lands.

(C) REVENUE RATES

During the period of Pallavas, Salankeyanas and Kakatiyas who ruled Andhra Desa or a part of it, the cultivator under all the tenures, got half of the gross produce, but bore the agricultural expenses himself. [69] During the pre-Muslim period or under Gajapatis, Vijayanagara etc. which ruled this area the government sharing of the produce was as follows. In the case of paddy produce (i. e. grain in the husk) which depended on periodical rains, the government share was one-half of gross produce. In the case of produce from dry-lands, but watered by artificial means such as tank, canal and wells, the government took only one third as its share. In the case of garden culture and plantations (fruits and vegetables) government demanded as its share only one-fourth to one eighth of the entire yield of the entire year. In raising these crops the cultivator had to incur extra expenses, trouble and time. And there was the hazard involved in carrying these items to the market and also in preserving them over a period. In view of these considerations, the Ryots were allowed to keep a major share in the case of those commercial and superior articles. And the governments assessed only a fixed money rent without fluctuations in the case of those garden produce.[70]

The Vijayanagara period temple epigraphs indicate the land revenue rates as prevailing in the temple villages called Devadana villages. These donees followed the same revenue rates as followed by the government in those village before their alienation to the temple. It appears that the same revenue rates were followed with minor deviations in the villages and lands alienated under all the categories and also in the crown/government villages. Ryots share remained the same. An inscription of 1550 A. D. from Chinna Ahobilam (Kurnool district) mentions these rates for both wet crops as well as garden produce of the temple lands in the village of Alamuru of the same district. According to this epigraph; the produce of paddy was to be shared equally by the cultivators (Kampulu) and the temple. But in the case of garden produce, (various fruits like areca, mango, plantain, orange etc.), the temple tenants were to get two thirds of the produce and the remaining one share was to go to the temple.[71] Veera Raghavacharya also is of the opinion that the tenants who cultivated the lands of Sri Venkateswara temple of Tirupati took half of the produce of the grain as their share.[72] But contrary to this opinion, Burton Stein, while discussing the tenure system of the villages of Tirupati Temple, states that the major share of the produce (Melvaram) went to the temple and the minor share (Kudivaram or Kulivaram) went to the cultivator. He further states that this system was prevalent in the villages under the government before their grant to the temple and the same system of sharing was retained by the temple. According to him, the major share (of the temple) varied between 51 percent and 75 per cent.[73] But either the epigraphs or the above authors do not indicate whether any village expenses (Meras to village artisans etc.) were defrayed from the gross produce before its division or whether the tenants had to bear them as was indicated in the sources of the post-Vijayanagara period. It is also very clear in the case of garden produce that, the major share went to the cultivator during the Vijayanagara period as was the case with the subsequent period. This system was intended, probably, to help the cultivator. The fruit trees took more time compared to the crops of grain to give the yield; and in the initial stages, the cultivator would get less income.

During the pre-Muslim period in Southern Coastal Andhra districts also almost the similar system of division existed. There, the Swatantrams (the term equivalent of Kalavasam used in Nellore district) or fees to the village officials/servants were usually first subtracted from the total crop and the remainder was then equally divided between the government and the Ryot.[74]

The Village fees or fees for village expenses meant for the Ayagars was paid even under the Hindu governments prior to the establishment of the Qutbshahi rule. *Athavanavyavaharatantram* (p. 5) which throws light on Vijayanagara revenue administration refers to 'Nijayam' of 2 Muntas and 'Arthayam' of 2 Muntas paid to village Ayagandlu by the cultivators from their produce. Besides these measures, the village servants also were getting their wages called 'Horohollu' and 'Morabatta' or Meras, a certain percentage collected on the number of ploughs. After deducting these measures from the gross produce, the share of the Ryot was taken out either one-half or two-thirds called 'Sangore' or 'Mungoru' respectively from the paddy crop raised under the tanks. If he was given half share, he was not to pay any additional tax in cash. But, in the case of two-thirds share given to the Ryot, he paid some additional cash (Motta Pakam – Paikam or money).[75] The 'Nijayam' and 'Arthayam' mentioned above were the equivalent of village expenses. It is, thus, clear that the Ryot under Vijayanagara was getting fifty percent of the net produce. Tradition also says that the land revenue was paid in kind in the proportion of half the produce, and this half was commuted for money.[76]

Revenue Rates under Mughals

During the Mughal period the system of division of the agricultural produce, as introduced by Murshid Quli Khan

(Diwan of Berar Balaghat) was followed in Andhra Desa also. For this three rates were followed:

1. Where the crop depended on rainfall, the state's share was one-half of the produce.
2. Where agriculture depended on well-irrigation, the share of the state was one-third in the case of grain and from one-ninth to one-fourth in the case of grape, sugarcane, plantain and other special and high-priced crops requiring laborious watering;
3. Where the field was irrigated from canals, the standard government share was one-fourth of the total produce whether grain, potherb, fruit, or seed. The revenue at the fixed rate of so many rupees per Bigha was assessed and collected after considering the quality and quantity of the crop from seed-time to harvest and its market price and actually measuring the sown area. Hence its name of Jarib (Survey). [77]

Under Asafjahis in the Telangana region, when he government and cultivator divided the produce (under Batai system where division of produce took place) equally (Adhenath and Adhemeans half). Before the division, the Six consoos on the candy (7 ½ percent) for the villege Ayagars or Bara balactedars (2 consoos for Patwari or accountant 1. consoo for Patel or Headman and remaining among others) were deducted. When the land was manured and irrigated from a well, the government share was one-third, two-thirds going to the Ryots with the usual deductions for Ayagars. In the Poonass (first dry crop sown in June) eleven parts go to the Ryots and nine to government and in the Rubee (second crop sown in October) eight parts to the Ryot and twelve to government with deductions as above. If the seed sown was advanced by Bania or sowcar, the produce was divided into three parts – one for the Ryot, one for the Bania and one for the government.[78]

Salarjung, the famous Diwn or Prime Minister of Hyderabad State also indicates the rates of government share of the produce prevailing before he took over the administrators in 1853. According to him 'Batai' system was prevailing in Telanga for wet crops. Here the government share under the tanks was 10 or 12 parts in 20. And for dry crops there was a fixed money assessment.[79]

Revenue Rates under Muslim Government not favourable to Ryots

The Revenue rates prevalent during the Muslim period, as found by the Company's officials, were less favourable to the cultivators and the share of the latter was reduced both in wet and dry land produce (they were unanimous in this regard). There were 'additional assessments' and many abuses and arbitrary demands and contributions by which the cultivators were reduced to unfavourable situation. It is reported in the Manual of Vizagapatam on the basis of the Circuit Committee that "... under the old Hindu government they (cultivator) paid half the produce in kind, but after Muhammadan conquest, the Zamindars employed in the management of the country imposed a Sist or fixed assessment on the land, to which extra assessment were afterwards added by which the share of the ryot was reduced nominally to one-third but actually to one fifth of the gross produce in rice lands which formed the chief cultivation of the country. In dry grain cultivation, the share of the ryots and the government was equal. These were the shares which prevailed in the Chicacole Circar. In the more Southern Circars of Rajamundry and Ellore, the ryots share was higher .... But he did not actually receive more than one-fourth or one-fifth and in dry grain it was half.... "[80] In the Krishna district area during the last quarter of the eighteenth century when it was under the company, the Ryots share was higher compared to that of the pre-company period. According to the report to the Board of Revenue the Ryot got 4/10th of the net produce. Out of every 10 Condis of the grain (probably paddy) the Ryot was to give 5 to government besides a tax of 1 pagoda on every Candy of the government's share. This tax and the allowances to Deshmukhs, Majumdar and Deshpandias reduced their proportion to 4 candies. By notification the collector of Masulipatam (dated 18-11-1789) proclaims that every body might cultivate as much as he could confident of government securing to him his proportion of 4/10th exclusive of Deshmukh's Savarams etc. [81] Mr. Travers, the Collector of Nellore District found in 1801 the following rates, prevailing in Western Poliams Venkatagiri and Kalahasti Zamindari estates and which was adopted by him in his settlement of 1801 A. D. The division of the crop which Mr. Traverse found to obtain for Paddy produce under the "Varapattu" or the system of division of crop which always prevailed for wet lands was.[82]

	In 9 Puttis			*In 20 Markals or Tumus*	*per cent*
	putti	*Markals*	*Seers*		
Ryot	3	14	14	8 - 14	41.25
Village fees	0	6	42	0 - 42	3.75
Government	4	19	0	11 – 0	55.00
	9	0	0	20 0	100

Mr. Travers, though does not state whether the division of produce for dry crops was the same, he adopted this division for both wet and dry crops in his 1801 settlement. But it seems, the division of produce in Puttis shown above was meant for produce of wet crops and that shown in

Marcals was for dry land produce. But in the dry crops, where the Ryot's share was 9 out of 20 Marcals, it included village expenses also.[83] Under both the measures mentioned, the ryots' share was 41. 25 percent and that of the government 55 per cent of the gross produce and the remaining 3. 75 per cent was towards village fees which were collectively described as "Kalavasam" or Swatantrams the perquisites granted to the village Ayagars – artisans, servants etc.

It appears by a comparison of the rates of revenue or the share of the government from the produce prevalent under the Hindu government and the Muslim governments given above that the ryots share was reduced and that of the government increased during the Muslim period in the case of wet produce.[84] There was an increase of 5 per cent in government share and decrease of 8.75 per cent in Ryot's share. Out of 8.75 per cent, 3.75 per cent is shown under Muslim governments as that of village fees. Under the Qutbshahis, the government collected half of the gross produce of the different sorts of dry and wet land. As all rents were paid in money during this period, the government share in kind was converted into money at the average price of preceding ten years.[85] It appears, the substitution of a money rent for a rent in kind seems to have been an important change introduced by the Muslim rulers. Regarding the Revenue rates followed in the Zamindari territories as well as the Haveli territories in Coastal Andhra before they were taken over by the company (i. e. Mughal-Asafjahi period) are indicated in the Circuit Committee Report, (p. 112). It records that the usual shares allowed to the cultivator in paddy are 8/20 to fixed cultivators, 10/12 and 12/20 to the Brahmins, Rachawar (Kshatriyas), Stranges and those favoured by the Zamindar and the dry grains ought to be divided equally between the Zamindar and the

Ryot. It also indicates that these shares were given before the deductions for village expenses were made.[86] These rates for the Haveli parganas of Northern Circars also are indicated by the Circuit Committee. It records thus ….. "It has been customary to receive government's share of the produce in specie, but the proportions have always been ascertained by an yearly valuation of the crop, one third being allowed to the fixed inhabitants, or resident hereditary cultivators, two fifths to strangers and one half to Telingas and those who cultivate the dry grain…"[87] Thus, it appears, the revenue rates or government share of the produce in both Zamindari as well as Haveli territories were almost same compared to the fixed or resident cultivator, the outside cultivators, the Brahmin owners and also those belonging to the ruling class – the Kshatriyas, Muslims, Velamas etc. were given more shares of the produce. Similarly, the cultivators from other villages who cultivated the land which the local Ryots were unable to cultivate themselves, were allowed a half share of the crop. But the local ordinary resident Ryot only received a third. In Nellore district under the Nawabs the resident hereditary Ryots were known as 'Kadim' who got only 36.75 per cent of the produce as his share and the non-resident – Ryot known as 'payakars' got 42.5 per cent. [88] This appears to have been the practice during the earlier periods. A Qutbshahi epigraph of 1577 A. D. from Malkapur village (Guntur district) states that the Kampus (Ryots) should pay the full assessment, the Brahmins, the Muhammadans and the Sukavasulu (dancing women) should pay the half the assessment. The later were also were exempted from paying the grazing tax.[89]

Thus, the share taken by the government from the Brahmins, Muslims and other ruling communities was less compared to that of resident hereditary cultivators because the former could not themselves cultivate lands and had to employ labour and had to incur more expenditure in that connection. The non-resident cultivator also had to incur more expenses in view of the fact that he had to get labour, manure, implements etc from outside. The government revenue rates sometimes were based on the nature of the soil. In Kurnool district under the Nawabs, the revenue settlement was made at the following rates depending on the nature and quality of the soil.

1. On Tuvva soil or soil mixed with sand – 1 to 1 1/16 Chalvani Rupees or 13 Annas 4 pies to 14 Annas (1 Rupees being equal to 13 Annas 4 pies) for a Munta (or about 2 ¼ acres) of land.
2. Red loamy lands 1 1/16 to 1 ¼ Chalvani Rupees or 14 Annas to Rs. 1-0-8 per Munta of land.
3. Regada (inferior black soil) 1 Rupees to 4 Rupees a Munta of land.
4. Black Regada (black alluvial soil) 10 or 12 Chalvani Rupees a Munta of land.[90]

This classification is in order of importance of the quality of the soil, the first one of least quality and the last one the best quality. The tax rates also depended on the quality of the soil; the best lands yielding more revenue and the least quality ones the minimum. Mr. Traverse, the Collector of Nellore district classified the arable lands, after survey and experiments, on the nature and quality of the soil into four classes or Tarams as given under in order of importance.[91]

Wet Yielding per Tum of Seed

Ist Class	(1)	Uttama (good), from 2 puttis to 1
IInd Class	(2)	Madhyama (medium) from 19 Tumus to 15 Tumus (1 putti=20 Tumus)
IIIrd Class	(3)	Kanisa from 14 Tumus to 10 Tumus
IVth Class	(4)	Inferior less than 10 Tumus

Dry Yielding per Gorru

Ist Class	From 30 Tumus to 20 Tumus
IInd Class	From 19 Tumus to 15 Tumus
IIIrd Class	From 14 Tumus to 10 Tumus
IVth Class	less than 10 Tumus.

On the basis of this classification, the collector fixed the rates of taxes. Probably similar classification was made in other regions for fixing the revenue during the earlier periods.

(D) MODE OF REVENUE COLLECTION

Two methods of revenue collections direct and indirect were followed in the government villages during the period. The direct mode was through, the government officials called Parupatyamvaru under the Vijayanagara and Amil and also Amin under Muslim government whether it was the Qutbshahi or Mughal and Asafjahi the direct mode was adopted mostly in the government villages which were not alienated to others. And indirect mode was by revenue farming system called Gutta under Vijayanagara and Izara under Muslim Governments.

During the Vijayanagara period, the crown villages are referred to as "Bandarawada Gramamulu, because the revenue in those villages were collected on behalf of the Bandaram or Government treasury by the central revenue officials such as Parupatyamvaru etc. They were assisted in this work by the local hereditary revenue officials like Nadagauda, Sthalakarnam, village headman and village accountant.

Similarly, in the crown territories under the Muslim governments called Khalsa and Haveli under Qutbshahi and Mughals, Haveli under Company and Diwani under Asafjahis, the government revenue officials such as Amins or Amils appearsome times to have performed the duty of collecting the revenue directly in those territories on behalf of the government. The hereditary revenue native Hindu officials such as Deshmukhs Deshpandias and village headmen and accountants continued to assist in the revenue collection.

This Amani system of revenue management was one of the two methods adopted in the Haveli districts in Coastal Andhra on the appointment of European Collectors under the immediate orders of Board of Revenue in 1787. The other system being revenue farming.

Amani system was considered as the best means of realising the land revenue then within their reach. This system was meant to remove the abuses and irregularities practiced by the revenue farmers, to ameliorate the condition of the cultivators and finally to increase the government revenue. But in practice, it was most open to abuse and frequently attended with great loss and inconvenience both to the government and to the ryots during this period. The government was compelled to engage a large establishment of native officers who by joining hands with the inhabitants defrauded the former. The Ryots also suffered a great inconvenience and loss. They had to keep the crop on the ground until their value was estimated by the government servants. The crops were often damaged and were prone to depredations. More over, the lack of adequate knowledge of the native language rendered it impracticable for the company's servants then employed in Havelis to collect the correct information on the subject. They were compelled to depend for this on the Dubashes who frequently indulged in fraud. Finally the company's officials also, due to their meagre salaries, indulged in corruption.[92]

Revenue Farming

The Second mode of revenue collection during the period in Andhra Desa was by Revenue Farming System which was wide-spread and was prevalent throughout the period of 17th and 18th centuries. This system of revenue collection was resorted to invariably in the territories belonging to the crown as well as those alienated to other under all the governments – Vijayanagara, Qutbshahi, Asafjahi and East India Company and to some extent the Mughal. Under the system, the highest bidders were given the job of collecting the land revenue and also the governments non-agricultural revenue.

Revenue farming system became an important mode of revenue collection during the Vijayanagara period. Epigraphs of Vijayanagara period contain references to the revenue contractors called "Guttaganlu". They are mentioned along with other government revenue officials like Parupatyamvaru, Adikamvaru and village revenue officials like Kapu and Karnam etc. in the inscriptions recording various grants 'Guttaganlu' are mentioned in the grants made by the kings and also the Nayakas in their respective territories indicating the prevalence of the system in the crown territories as well those alienated to the Nayakas. But the scanty information provided by the Vijayanagara sources do not help us to form any idea of the working of this system. The 16th century Portuguese travellers Domingo Paes and Ferneo Nuniz writing about the Vijayanagara Empire merely state that the common peasant suffered much hardship under the tyrannical assignees and the revenue farmers.[93]

Revenue Farming under Qutbshahis

We get more information regarding the working of the Revenue farming system for the Qutbshahi period and also for the succeeding periods. The three Relations, one by English Methwold, second by Dutch Schorer and the third by Anonymous writer, all of the first quarter of the 17th century throw much useful light on the system prevalent in the Qutbshahi kingdom of Golkonda.

For the revenue collection, the Qutbshahi government, according to these European accounts, farmed each district/ Sarkar annually and the revenue collection was entrusted to the highest bidders and the revenue collected was paid to the government by the contractors in three installments, every four months in a year.[94] Methwold states that the auctions were held every year in the month of July.[95] Anonymous Relation clearly states that the district of Nizampatnam was formed from the king for 55,000 Pagodas but its governer of that period paid 1,000 Pagodas a year more because he had to take it from another man.[96] This indicates that there was also the system of sub-letting of the farms in the Qutbshahi kingdom. Methwold gives further details regarding this. He states ... "the government is farmed immediately from the king by some eminent man, who to other inferiors farmeth out the lessor ones and they again to the country people".[97]

All these European writers give us the impression that the governers of the provinces or districts themselves held their posts on farming basis. We are told that the district of Masulipatnam yielded 180,000. Pagodas, Nizampatnam, 55,000 Pagodas and Kondavidu 40,000 Pagodas in money, chayroot, salt, cloth etc. For maintaining his position and his establishment, the governer cum revenue farmer was allowed by the king to deduct some amount. The governer of Masulipatnam was allowed to deduct 8,000 Pagodas and that of Nizampatnam 5,000. A very few of their subordinate officials like harbour master (Shah Bunder) the priest, the judge etc. were paid cash and others were paid in kind, paddy, salt etc.[98]

We do not know much about the establishment through which the Izaradars who were also called Hawaldars collected the revenue. They maintained a few Gumasthas for recording and maintaining accounts. They were helped and assisted by the hereditary native revenue officials like Deshmukh, Deshpandia of Pargana and village headman and the village accountant, all of whom got some percentage in the collection. Severe punishments were also given to the defaulting governers who held their posts on farming terms. Methwold relates that one Busbela Rao (probably Bujbal Rao), the Hindu governer of Masulipatnam at that time who failed to pay the farm money fully, was beaten with canes severely untill he died.[99] Anonymous Relation states that if the governers failed to make full payment in time, they were often flogged to such an extent that some times they could not recover their health during their whole life.[100] Schorer also states that the defaulting revenue farmers or governors were punished by trampling by elephants.[101] Corruption at the highest level also contributed to the greed of the governors who used to bribe the superior officers to get their positions.

The sub-lessees or sub-tax farmers called Izaradars and also Hawaldars were given full charge of Parganas and major towns having civil and criminal powers. As the chance of getting the area again in auction for the next year also was remote, they used to extract most by fair or foul means to amass huge amounts during their tenures. Under these circumstances, the cultivator's position became worse. The public cry never reached the royal Years as the officials surrounding the throne were under the obligation of Izaradars.

Amildars, the government revenue superintendents appear to have been more concerned with the punctual collection of the revenue than with the welfare of the peasantry. During the period, the revenue farmers were usually Brahmins or Banyas or Komatis according to

Anonymous relation who further states that a very few Muslims troubled themselves with revenue farming administration except as supervisors. [102] The tax oppression by the revenue farmers forced the peasants to flee the villages in many cases. Consequently, several village become deserted during the period.

Mughal Rule and Revenue Farming

Under the Mughal rule, Revenue farming was prohibited formally. The emperor Aurangzeb forbade the Diwan to give leases to anyone, especially subordinate revenue officials, on pain of imprisonment.[103] But as most of the Qutbshahi period intermediary local revenue officials like Deshmukh, Deshpande, Village headman and accountant continued, some as mansabdars, to function under the Mughals, who were used to the earlier system of revenue farming, there is every likelihood that in practice tax-farming continued indirectly under the Mughals atleast in remote places. The Mughal Jagirdars and the revenue collectors in the Khalisa territories could not resort to revenue farming now. Moreover the Mughal Diwan of Hyderabad also conducted now a systematic enquiry into the records kept by the Deshpandias and the tax collection was highly bureaucraticsed and made systematic. Now, paid Mughal tax officers with the help of village officials assessed and collected the land tax in cash on the basis of field surveys. The assessment of taxes was governed by written regulations and established rates per crop and measured unit of land.[104]

Asafjahi Period - Revenue Farming

Asafjahi rulers, though inherited much of the Mughal administration, could not do away with the Ijara or revenue farming in their dominions. The revenue and land revenue, customs; occupational tax, excise etc., of each district or

Sarkar was farmed out to one contractor who was called Ta-hah-hud-dar or Talukdar or Zilladar. The persons selected were generally wealthy and socially influential residents of Hyderabad city. Infact, the auction system was not practiced in the Nizam's state. The would be Talukdar approached the concerned minister and offered his services to collect the revenue of a particular Circar, the amount of which was to be higher than that of the previous year. This system was called 'Ta-ah-hud'. He was required to pay into the government treasury certain fixed sum to be collected from the district assigned to him with a deduction of two Annas (one rupee had 16 annas) on each Rupee for the payment of his subordinates and the defrayal of all the expenses strictly civil.

In the Kowlnama (the deed of contract) it was customarily mentioned that ".... in consequence of such and such a person's tender, government had granted him the following cowl with a view to ameliorate the condition of the Pargana. The Kowl included the details of Mal (revenue), Kalali or Abkari (excise) Moturpha (occupation tax) Baghat (tax on garden produce), Sar Darakhti (tax on trees) Amarai (tax on mango fruit) Kata (tax on cutting or reaping) Haq Naibana (Naib fee). Mahsuldari (villege collectors dues) Dumbaldari (free for permission to tread grain out of the husk).

These were made over to the Talukdar in return for a fixed amount named in the contract deed to be paid annually – Sayar revenues were generally excluded from the revenue contract.

All the state charges such as military expenditure, Mansab allowances etc. were to be disbursed by the Talukdar on receipt of Akham or order for each payment and these amounts were deducted from his cash remittances to government.

The Talukdar was instructed in the kowl "that he must bring together all the farmer and new Raits, give them assurances of fair treatment, bring the Taluka into a flourishing condition, pay to Raits all to which they were entitled and remit to government the annual payments as they became due".[105]

A *sanad* was issued to infavour of Talukdar announcing his appointment and instructing the Deshmukh, Kanungo, Deshpandia, Kulkarnis and cultivators of the concerned district to cooperate with him (Talukdar) in carrying the administration.[106]

The Talukdar was required to sign a *Kabuliat* (Deed of engagement) or *Ikrarnama* to the following effect .... "I do hereby declare that such and such a parganah has been entrusted to my care to manage the same departmentally (Ba Anwan Tashkhis Wa Tahsil Kham) and from the beginning of such year I do hereby promise that I will directly assess each cultivator honestly, and will realize the full amount due from him and will remit the same after deducting the charges for collection and according to the sanctioned scale, when each installment becomes due without raising any objections or causing any alteration. I also hereby engage to keep the Raiats contented and pleased by my statuary administration, and to do my utmost to increase the cultivation and population of the above, Mahals and to permit of no arrears.

I am also willing to be held responsible for any arrears of revenue, which may occur, as well as in the event of any cultivator obsconding, any villege becoming depopulated, or any field left waste, during the term of my administration. I undertake to guard the high road from the prevention of theft or highway robberys should such occur, I will arrest and punish the thieves and restore the stolen property to the owners.... I will forward all the prescribed statements to the government office i.e. Sarpatti (villege register of assessment giving particulars of each cultivator in each village) *Dowl* (register for each pargana giving details of each head of revenue for each village. *Jamabandi* (rent roll for whole Taluka giving details of each head of revenue). *Jama Kharch Kham* (detailed account of all the receipts and expenditure) duly counter signed by the Mukaddams, Kulkanis and Vasila (account of the revenue collected). etc. with the seal of the *Shariat Panah* (Kazi who administer law) duly attested counter signed by the Zamindars".[107]

Talukdar presented his *Nuzzar* (gift), often a good sum. He remained in his office as long as he paid his installments regularly. He was permitted to remain at Hyderabad. He inturn appointed a Naib (deputy) who had to collect the revenue. He again appointed Chotah Naibs, (equalent of Tahsildars under company), Peskars and other subordinates. It was the Naib who actually proceeded to his district and contacted the Zamindars and villege heads, so the Talukdar never visited his district and his Naib also never met the Ryots. The Talukdars led a luxurious life at Hyderabad and his concern was to make as much profit as possible from his farmed district. The remonstrations of the Ryots never reached beyond the bnoundaries of his villege but the government at Hyderabad was unaware of all this.[108]

The inferior revenue officers employed in the revenue collections were *Sheristadars,* usually Brahmins, accountants attached to the Chota or lesser Naibs, and Havildars who collected the revenue of one or more villages. The salary of the Circar Naib was Rs. 200 month, of the Deputy Naib Rs. 40 or Rs. 50, of the Peschar Rs. 20 to 25, and of the Sheristadars and Havildars Rs. 10 to Rs. 12.[109]

The Talukdar were both Hindu and Muslim – some of them were Arab and Pathan Jamedars who advanced money to Nizam now are allowed to farm Taluqs. After considerable amounts towards repayment of their debts and interest they remitted the balance of the revenue collected to the government. Similarly, the Hindu Sowcars who also were creditors to Nizam also became Talukdars. The Deputy Naibs were Muslims and some Hindus but the other inferior functionaries were Hindus. The functions of the Talookdar, Naib, Deputy Naibe and Havildar were those formerly exercised by Surdeshmukh, Deshmukh and Patel of Qutbshahi period and Surdaftar, Peshchas etc. were performing the duties of former Surdeshpandia and Deshpandia.

Sarbastu Cowle: The Talukdars of the Circar farmed in-turn, a certain number of villages to the principal Zamindars of the Circar for a fixed period to be renewed if the Zamindars performed their contract satisfactorily. This type of revenue farming was called Sarbastu Cowle or tenure. The sum to be paid by the Zamindar was fixed without any reference to favourable or unfavourable seasons and no remission were allowed. Zamindars often collected only land revenue and was excluded from collecting the Soyer (customs) which was usually left to the Talukdar who appointed separate people for its collection.[110]

Ijaru Cowle: When the villege revenue was farmed to the villege Headman or Patel – it was called the *Ijaru Cowle*. The villege headman sublet it and settled the revenue with government. An *Ijaru* Cowl was also granted to an individual who was willing to repopulate a deserted villege by repairing a ruined tank. This kind of farming villege revenue was common in Medak Circar. The Ijara of certain Mahals situated in Warangal and Malangur Sarkars for three years 1739-41 was given to one Nur Ali Khan. Similarly, one Udet Singh was assigned the Ijara for the collection of revenue for a period of three years (1734-36) for an amount of Huns

2869/8/4 of a few villages in the Pargana Oorder in Sarkar Murtuzanagar (Guntur).

How an Ijara cowl was granted for the restoration of a deserted villege under the Asafjahi government is indicated in an undated government sanad (Dhorwaghiri) issued to one Mahomed Ryam and his father Fakeer Mahomed. The Sanad was issued in the name of Surdeshmukh and surdeshpandega in the Haveli Chintapalli pargana. The villege Singavaram which had for a long-time been deserted was given to them for its restoration. According to this Sanad, the donees were to try to bring in the Ryots and make the villege flourishing by repairing the tanks, ponds and wells. They were to be punctual in paying the government dues, presents to Brahmins, temples etc. according to custom and dues to every one in the village (probably village Ayagars). The Donors were to receive their due as follows – 2 ½ Maunds sowing in the Poonass (rainy season dry crop) and 1 ½ Maunds sowing of pady in the Tabee (wet and second crop) near the Chintala tank (land having that seed capacity) besides 4 Pylees in the Khandy from the produce of the village and in cash one Anna in the Rupee from the rents paid by toddy drawers, Banias etc. and also two Beegas of land for dry crops, marriage tax, one bundle of common straw from every field and a Consoo of unhusked grain; and one quarter of a pice for every bullockload of grain passing through the village.[111]

The revenue farming system under the Asafjahi was much abused and contributed to the oppression of the peasants. The system of assessment was Ryotwari (peasant-wise) but only in name but in reality Mouzawar (village assessment). Each village was separately assessed as a whole. Any deficiency in the revenue that arose owing to the relinquishment of the fields or desertion by the cultivators was made up by taxing the other cultivators proportionately.

The revenue farmer or their agents used to do their utmost to extort excessive dues from Ryots.

There was much oppression in the collection of revenue. The standing crops were not allowed to be removed from the field until government demand had first been satisfied. This was done either by a cash payment or by providing a letter of credit from the money lender who was the local trader (sowcar).[112]

The system of revenue farming, whatever be the government, gave rise to the misery and woes of the cultivators. The ordinary peasant was unable to identify the real master to whom he should pay the dues. There was no connection between the Revenue contractors and the peasants. The middlemen, the agents of the contractor and also the government hereditary revenue officials exploited them. The cultivators had to satisfy the excessive demands of the depraved and corrupt officials who had meager official salaries.

The methods of torture adopted during this period for non-payment of revenue dues by the peasants in Hyderabad state were similar to those followed in the fifteenth century as described by the famous Telugu poet Srinatha.[113] If money could not be realized by the disposing of the produce of peasant, his cattle and household articles were attached. Stones were placed on his back and head and pincers (made of elastic wood) were tied in most cruel manner and chameleons were forced into his dhoti etc.[114]

Some of the methods of torture of earlier period were continued even under the company's rule. In fact the company's revenue officials justified their continuance. The Ryots and Curnoms sent anonymous petitions dated 25-11-1791 addressed to the Board of Revenue complaining against Mr. Cochrane Basil, the member of Guntur Committee about the methods of revenue settlement and torture adopted by him Cochrane justified the methods of torture such as making revenue defaulters stand in the sun with stones on their shoulders etc. on the ground that those practices had already been made use of. He further argued that the revenue could not be realized with out resorting to such methods.[115]

The system Revenue farming resulted in splendour at the headquarters and squalor in the countryside. Wealth accumulated in the hands of very few and the producer were left with bare minimum and had a hand to mouth existence. Unable to bear the oppression some of them migrated to more hospitable places. And as a result many villages in all the three sub-regions became depopulated and deserted and land became barren due to lack of repair of irrigation works during the period.

Revenue Farming under the English East India Company

The revenue farming system was prevalent in both the Zamindari territories as well as Haveli/government Parganas in coastal Andhra region when it came under the Company's rule in 1765. The Company also did not disturb that system till 1802 when the Permanent Zamindari Settlement was made.

Revenue Farming in Zamindari Territories under Company

When the English company took over the Northern Circars in 1766, that area was given on a three years rental to the Nizam's Fouzdar, Hasan Ali Khan. After 1769, an attempt was made to make separate arrangement with each Zamindar.

The Zamindars were allowed to appropriate the revenues of their respective territories for themselves in consideration of paying a certain sum to the government stipulated in the written engagements they entered into. This sum was denominated 'Jumma' or rent (later tribute or Peshkash). This amount they realised from the cultivators either in kind or cash. But the universal practice was that they resorted to revenue farming.... " to persons, on annual or longer leases; the contracts including one or more villages, districts, or larger portions, and some times entire Zamindaries ...".[116]

This view is endorsed by the report of the committee of circuit about northern circars dated 1784. It found that since the decline of the Musalman government the Zamindars, experiencing a greater liberty than before have indulged themselves in indolence, and entrusting their parganas to renters have delegated the full extent of their own authority to them".[117]

In 1795 Shobanadri Rao, Zamindar of Mailavaram in Masulipatam Circar appointed two new renters one Zeevan Rao to pay a rent of 18,000 Madras Pagodas for Gudivada parganah and second Tauloory Jogaiah to pay 12,000 m. p for the rent of the Vinnakota Pargana including the Soyer (customs) of Charmahal. Both agreed to pay the amount according to the Zamindar's Kistbundy (installment Agreement) to the company's treasury. The balance of his Cabooleat amount 1782-18 Pagodas for the remaining territories for which he could not get a new Renter he agreed to pay himself by providing responsible Sowcar Security. Now company government issued Sanads to the new Renters assuring them the government protection as long as they observed punctuality in fulfilling their obligation to the company.

Necessary government orders also were given to Choudaries, Despandias, Curnums etc. and revenue sepoys belonging to those Parganahs to obey and assist the new renters.[118]

More over, the Renters delivered the agreements they settled with the Zamindar and one of them also promised to provide the security of a Sowcar at Madras as insisted by company for the punctual payment of the revenue to the company's treasury. The other Renter Jogaiah being a responsible Sowcar and security was not insisted. The company government was requested to issue Sanads to that effect. [119] The above renters were while being informed of the irregularities of the late or a previous Renters directed not to deviate from what is Mamool (tradition) and use their exertions for the peace and tranquility of the Parganas and to objserve punctuality in payment.[120] This record indicates the functioning of Revenue farming system in Zamindari territories under East India Company.

It is interesting to note that there were a few Muslim Renters Cojah Satur farming Dia and 6 islands for 26,000-8 per annuam for five years. He sends a letter dated Oct. 1795 requesting a remission of 5000 pagodas per annuam on the ground that he incurred a loss of 9000 pagodas inconsequence of the river not overflowing and tanks not getting filled. But his plea was rejected as misleading.[121] Similarly, Puchasaib was the renter of a part of Kondapally Pargana.[122]

Thus each Zamindar was required to submit either himself or through his Vakil a Cabooliat or an undertaking for every year and also a sowcars security for the punctual payment of his (Kistrabundy) installment.[123] The Zamindars usually, as mentioned already, farmed the revenue of their territories to rentors.

Some of the Zamindars failed to pay the balances of their tribute in time. In those cases the company government took harsh measure to collect it. When the Zamindar of Munagala (Masulipatam Circar) failed to pay 300 pagodas on Punasa crop (rabi) which was ready for harvest, government appointed its Gumasta Buddirazu Veeraraju to secure that crop till the above sum was paid and for the due payment of current years (1795) payment the Gumasta was to secure the other crops till the Zamindar had complied then with and attends government office (Huzoor) for adjusting the Jamabandy. Collector also issued orders to the Choudaries, Deshpandias and inhabitants of Munagala Zamindari not to pay any amount till the Zamindar discharged his balances and gave security for the current years Kistbundy.[124]

Renters and Zamindars allowances

Name of the Renter	*Name of the Parganaha*	*Cist or gross Revenue as stated by Zamindar*	*Renters Remiss-ions Allowa-nces*	*The amount of the Rent*	*Deduct the Zamin-dars charges*	*Revenue to be paid to the Company*
Chalraly Panakalu	Neddadole, Pentapadu, Bahharzully Gondapole Umborepally Cuddadaly	80,078	4368-27	75,709.9	5,709-9	70,000
Nandoori Laxmin-arsoo & Purvaluna Subarauzu	Nunnastalam	25,383-18	1150	24,933-18	3,933-18	21,000
Basvaraju Moortiraju	Chavendralu Aumony villages	11,900	262	11,638	638	11,000
Vinnakota Kondanna	Whyore, Madoor, Soyera and Munna-russum	38,492	1250	37,222	12,222	25,000
Total		1,55,853-18	6,330-27	14,950-27	22,502-27	1,27,000

The chart showing the Dowle Account of Paraganas of Nuzividu district dated November 1790 indicates the allowances of Rentes, Zamindars and government share.

In the Havelis

In the Haveli Parganas which constituted a large part of the Northern Sarkars under Company's government during the period of provincial chiefs and councils (1765 to 1787), the revenue collection was farmed out to renters for certain periods. The Haveli territories under the chiefs and council of Masulipatanam were farmed out to a Dubashe (interpreter) for ten years.[125] Similarly, the Havelis dependent on the chief and council of Vizagapatam and situated in the southern division of Cicacole were let out in 1777 for ten years to Sitarama Raju, the brother of Zamindar of Vijayanagaram. [126] The renters in both Haveli and Zamindari territories collected government share of the crop in kind and paid to Zamindar its equivalent in cash.

After the appointment of collectors in the Havelis in 1787 also the revenue farming system was resorted to by the collectors in many of the cases in Coastal Andhra districts. Now, instead of letting out the whole Sarkar to one individual as was done under provincial chiefs and councils, only Parganas or even lessor divisions were farmed out for stipulated rent, besides also following Amani system.[127]

For the most part it was let out annually village by village to the headmen, the government share of the produce being commuted into money at current or average prices. As this system was not based on survey it was therefore imperfect. And there was little provision to protect the cultivators from the oppression of the headman.[128]

The mode of land revenue collection in the Haveli Parganas of Northern Circars adopted by the Company's government was, thus, by revenue farming. These renters were mostly Dubashes (interpreters) who were also the agents belonging to the different chiefships and councils of the company itself. Most of them were Soucars or traders some Muslims some Niyogi Brahmins, a few Velamas and Rajus and Reddi, who could advance money and made revenue farming their profession. The Company's government conferred upon these speculating renters many of its powers which became most ample means of oppression.[129]

For example, the names of Renters in the Nizam Patam Circar, names of their forms and amount paid by them as December kist 1795 are mentioned in the District Collectorate Records.[130]

1. Valapoody Butchaiah Renter, of Valaty Pollom.
2. Puddalsemboodoo, renter of Surepoody
3. Jumala Shaloo, renter of Cauvoor
4. Cundurthy narsaiah, renter of Palapallah
5. Lamacca Venkaiah, renter of Mondradoo
6. Putre Srinivassa Row, renter of Nizampatam
7. Sadasiva Naik & Nagabhusham Row, renter of Ventapollam
8. Body Pau Panah renter of Alooar

The names of Renters of some other farms in the same Nizampatam Circar mentioned alongwith their form and their installments of revenue on another occasion. They include[131]

1. Bagotula Ganapathy renter of Chandole.
2. Turpacca Dharma Lingam, renter of Cadacudur
3. Komati Vekiah, renter of Pedda Ganjam
4. Muppala Ramaiah, renter of Baupatla
5 Turgah Nagannah, renter of Peddamutlapadu

Armed with unrestricted power of collection, the renters and sub-renters practiced every type oppression on the ryots. These contractor disregarded, according to their convenience, the engagement they entered into with the Ryots. Regarding the nature of this oppression, Fifth Report from the Select Committee on the Affairs of the East India Company reports thus "... If they (revenue farmers) agreed with the cultivators at the commencement of the year, for a rent in money, and the season proved an abundant one, they then insisted on receiving their dues in kind. When they did take their rents in specie, they hardly ever failed to collect a part of them, before the harvest time had arrived and the crops were cut, which reduced the ryots to the necessity of borrowing from money leaders, at a very heavy interest of 3,4 and 5 per cent per month, the sums requisite to make good the anticipated payments that were demanded of them. If from calamity or other cause, the ryots were the least remiss in the discharge of their rents, the officers of the renters were instantly quartered upon them, and these officers they were obliged to maintain, until they might be recalled on the demand being satisfied. It was also a frequent practice with the renters to remove the inhabitants from fertile lands, in order to bestow them on their friends and favourities; and to oblige the ryots to assist them, when they happened to be farmers in the tilling of their lands, and to furnish them gratuitously with labourers, bullocks, carts and straw..."[132].

In Nellore district which constituted a part of the Carnatic under the Nawabs, also the Fauzdar farmed out to renters. Talukas or Parganas were farmed out to the highest bidders whose hope of profit lay in what he could extort from the people. In the last quarter of the 18th century the whole provinces in Karnatic were leased and the provincial Fauzdar or governor himself became the head renter.[133]

There were three chief renters in Nellore district, before it was taken over by the British in 1780. They were (1) Seshagiri Ravu, who had the greater part of Nellore and paid 2,02,000 Madras Pagodas for 3 years as rent and land customs; (2) Narasimha Reddi who had Kandukur and northern Parganas of the same district for Madras Pagodas1,29,698 for three years (3) and Nizam Ahmad Khan in Ongole for Madras Pagodas 71,610 (Nellore Manual, p. 497). Similarly in Chicacole Sircar, the revenue renters in 1768 were Sitarama Raju renter for Vijayanagaram paying a rent of 2,74,059 Rupees; same renter for Vurutla paying a rent of Rs. 10,000; Payaka Rao for Satyavaram paying Rs. 75,000 and Akkaji and Jagannatha Raju for Chicacole Haveli paying Rs. 1,52,500. [134]

These persons sub-rented to others. We are told, the Deshmukhs continued to collect their Rusooms and enjoy their Inam villages, though no longer responsible for the collection of the land revenue. Sthalakarnams whose function was to check irregularities in revenue collection frequently themselves became renters not only of villages but of whole parganas and the office of the village Karnam fell into disuse.[135]

Even after the assumption of Carnatic by the Company (in 1780) the region was placed under the charge of the Committee of assigned revenue. This committee in 1783 let-out the Carnatic territory including Nellore, in fourteen large farms of leases of nine years, at increasing rents. But these renters who were men of very low origin and ignorant of their business had, with a few exceptions failed in their payments. Their estates were sequestrated and several of them were put into confinement. And, finally the Collectors who were made incharge of the region in 1788, let out the area in smaller portions to the inhabitants.[136] Even in Guntur district which came under the company, the Zamindars were renting out the villages to contractors.[137]

It is clear, thus, that the mode of revenue collection by revenue farming was widely prevalent Andhra Desa during the period under study. It was practiced in all the three regions and almost under all the dynasties and also in the territories belonging to the crown/government and also under Nayakas, Zamindars and Zagirdars and probably Palegars in Rayalaseema also resorted to it. The revenue renters got a profit of one-sixth of the collection.[138]

Revenue Collection in Installments

The government, it appears, collected its due from the cultivators in several installments, spread over several months of the year. We do not have information regarding this practice during the Vijayanagara period. We have evidence for the prevalence of this practice of collecting revenue in installments in Rayalasima under the Palegars and Nawabs and in the Zamindari territories of Coastal Andhra before those regions came under the English. Thomas Munroe also instructed his subordinate collectors to collect revenue of the first year (1800) in six Kists or installments beginning in January and ending in June, the first and the last Kists were to be each 10 percent and the four intermediate ones each 20 percent of the whole.[139]

In Zamindari territories, it was usual practice to collect the revenue in four Kists in June, September, December and February months so that the whole is received by the end of harvest. Regarding this arrangement prevalent in Northern Circars, the Manual of the District of Vizagapatam (p. 230) reports "…. It was proposed to take the first payment after cutting the small grain in September in money; one half of the paddy in kind in December and February, when a sufficient time will have lapsed for the disposal of the remainder, the other half in specie…" Thus, the installments were collected partly in cash and partly in kind.

Under this system, the cultivator started paying the installments of revenue from the time of sowing the crop and was obliged to advance the amount of three Kists before he harvested his major crop. Most of them, who were poor, had to borrow that money from Soucars or moneylender paying heavy interest. The Zamindars were not under this disadvantage. He was not obliged to go to the moneylender because, he paid the tribute to his overlord only after the harvesting season was over that too in several installments.[140]

In Kurnool district, under the Nawabs, the government revenue was collected in four Kists in the case of division of crop, (paddy etc). In the case of garden produce where fixed money rent was assessed, it was collected in three Kists viz. 30th Jesththa (May-June), 30th Asvija (September-October) and 30th Makha (Jan-Feb.)[141]

Zamindars paid the tribute to company in several installments or kists, sometimes even six kists. But in the case of tribute payment by Zamindars also the Sowcar came into the picture. As a security for the payment of kists in time, the Zamindar was required to provide the security or Teeps of an influencial Sowcar. Zamindar's own security or Teeps were not accepted by the company government. The Teeps were some-kind of promissory notes. In that case the Zamindars incurred extra expenditure in the shape of interest to the sowcar.[142]

The chief and council of Masulipatam transmited to the governor and council at Madras in on 9-2-1784 the accounts relating to the current revenue, old balances, ready money and Teeps (securities from Sowcars) received each year from 1772 to 1782.[143] This shows the widely prevalent practice of providing sowcar Teeps or securities by the Zamindars in paying their tribute to the company. In 1784 Sowcar Latchmadoss and Narasimha Naik complained to the company government that the Zamindars to whom they gave Teeps were still in arrears to them, though they have discharged their arrears to the company as per the terms of the contract in the Teeps.[144] In the same year 1784 another Sowcar Madura Doss represented to the governer and council at Madras that Appa Rao, the Zamindar of Nuziveedu owned him 5 to 6 lakhs of Rupees and the Zamindar was obsconding. Madura Doss requested the government that certain parganas should be placed in his charge so that he could recover his amount. The governer and the council transmitted this representation to chief and council at Masulipatam for an enquiry.[145] Similarly in 1786, the Nuziveed Zamindar and his son agreed to the chief and council at Masulipatam that they would produce a bill of Giridara Doss Sowcar payble to company within 10 days for Madras Pagodas 40,000-00, their tribute.[146] It appears, these Sowcars were rich Marwadi traders as their names indicate. Alongwith these Latchmadoss and Madura doss and Giridara doss we also came across the names of sowcars like above mentioned Narasimha Naik and Sadasiva Naik who were are also providing security to the Zamindars for tribute payment and acting as company contractors for procuring cloth. As mentioned already they were are also providing security to the Zamindars for tribute payment and acting as company contractors for procuring cloth. As mentioned already they were collecting interest on the amount they were advancing on behalf of the Zamindars. We donot know their social background, whether they were Banjara Naiks or local Baliza Nayudus.

Tribute Paid by the Feudatories

Tribute, meaning 'Kappamu' in Telugu and 'Peshkash' in Persian, was paid by the feudatories, hereditary military chiefs holding certain territories on military service tenure. As mentioned in the chapter on Land Tenures, the

Amaranayakas, Palegars, Mokasadars, the Rajas of Samsthanams in Telangana and also the tribal chiefs of the Agency/forest areas north of Godavari river belonged to this category. They were under obligation to supply armed forces to the suzerain wherever required and pay a fixed amount annually as tribute. In fixing the quota of armed men and the amount of tribute to be supplied by these chiefs, the government must have followed some criteria. The overall productive capacity of the territory and the number of villages or the density of the population of that territory or additional responsibilities performed by the chief must have been taken into consideration. The variation in this regard found in the case of some of the sixteenth century Nayakas of Vijayanagara Empire provided by Nuniz clearly indicates this criteria.[147] This is also indicated in Chart I of the chapter on Tenures. The remnants of these chiefs along with the revenue officials like Deshmukhs, Deshpandias etc. came to be designated as Zamindars during the eighteenth century and the amount paid by them was known as Paishkash as mentioned already. The territories of military chiefs of the pre-Mughal period and the Zamindars of the later period were not subject to the detailed assessment of land revenue actually under cultivation. The cultivated lands in their villages were measured and assessed by the government officials as was done in the case of crown villages where the Deshmukhs were held responsible for revenue collection. These Zamindars paying tribute are mentioned in the Mughal and Asafjahi period sources as 'Peshkashi-Zamindars. This term 'Zamindar' was also applied to Deshmukhs, Deshpandias etc, who were also made responsible for collection of the Peshkash for the area assigned to each of them. They were scattered all over the State.[148] Under the permanent Zamindari settlement of 1802 also, the amount fixed as due from each Zamindar in Coastal

Andhra was termed as 'Peshkash', which was approximately one-third of the total gross revenue collected by the Zamindars in their territories. This gave them one-sixth of the total agricultural produce for their maintenance including their establishment. The shares of the Zamindars and the Ryots from the produce, the amount of Zamindar's Rusoom and finally the amount of tribute paid by Zamindars to the overlord at the end of the Mughal period are indicated in the representation given to the Collector of the Masulipatam district and also the later's account, both of 1795 A. D. According to these sources, the Zamindar's share of the produce from the Ryots was divided into 3 parts – one part was deducted on account of Grama Kurch (village expenses) and Zamindar's Rusoom and the remaining 2 parts as rent (tribute) to the Circar (government). Regarding the division of the produce, the native inhabitants (local cultivators) got 10 parts out of 20 parts. To strangers 11 parts out of 20 parts and to respectable people. Viz. , Brahmins, Cammavaru, Velamavaru and Rachavaru 12 parts out of 20 parts.[149]

Excessive Tax Burden and the oppression of Peasants

Excessive tax burden and the consequent oppression of the peasant, was the characteristic feature of Medieval Indian economic life and also that of this region. Regarding this, Thomas Munroe in one of his letters observes "However light the Indian revenue may be in the books of their sages, only a sixth or a fifth, in practice it has always been heavy". He further maintains "I could not ever discover the least foundation for the assumption that the Hindu assessment had been raised by the Muhammadan conquest...".[150] Epigraphic evidence shows that during certain periods of Vijayanagara history, the tax burden on the peasant was heavy. Unable to bear the tax-burden, the peasants had to resort to sell their lands.[151] This excessive tax burden and the oppression of the ryots continued unabated during the entire period under consideration.

Revenue farming, an important methods of tax collection of the period, was one of the factors that contributed considerably to the tax oppression, both under the Vijayanagara and Qutbshahi rulers. Revenue farming was resorted to invariably in all the territories belonging to crown as well as those alienated to others under both the states mentioned above. There are references in the Vijayanagara epigraphs to the revenue contractors called 'Guttaganlu'.[152] The Sixteenth century Portuguese travelers Domingo Paes and Fernao Nuniz who visited the Vijayanagara Empire in the first part of the sixteenth century, States that the common peasant suffered much hardship both under the tyrannical assignees and revenue farmers.[152]

The glaring oppressive nature of the revenue collection from the revenue contractors called Izaradars by the Qutbshahi government and in turn by these lessees from the peasants and the distressing condition of the latter during the first quarter of the 17th century is amply attested to by Methwold, Schorer and anonymous relation in unmistakable terms.[154] The revenue collection of the divisions called Sarkars, Parganas and Simths were auctioned annually and the successful bidders, the Izaradars were given full possession of the area including civil and criminal powers. As the chance of getting the area again in the auction for the next year also was remote, they used to extract most by fair or foul means to amass huge amounts during their tenure. Under these circumstances, the cultivator's position became worst. Their cry never reached royal ears as the officials surrounding the throne were under the obligation of the Izaradars. This oppression combined with the unrestrained plundering of villages by decoits (Pindaris) forced the peasants to flee the villages and consequently several villages became deserted.

This oppression might not have been continuous and universal. The epigraphis of Vijayanagara period which refer to the oppression of the peasants and their protest by silent migration to better places also refer to the measures taken by the government to redress those grievances. During the reign of last Qutbshahi ruler Abul Hasan Tanasa when Madanna was the prime minister (1674-77), remedial measures such as the abolition of the practice of annual auctioning and appointment of remunerated revenue officers and the rehabilitation of deserted villages by giving tax concessions were taken.[155]

Under the Mughal rule, the auctioning of revenue was prohibited and revenue was collected through officials. But strict assessment of revenue and the fresh imposition of capitation tax (Jazia, abolished in only 1722) at the rate of 4 per cent of assessment, considerably increased the tax burden on the peasants.

The nature of revenue collection was no better and the oppression of the cultivator was not less severe under the Asafjahis and the English East India Company. The revenue auctioning system was followed under Asafjahis and territories were farmed out to contractors who were required to advance a considerable portion of the anticipated revenue. These contractors were mostly Afgan chiefs, Arab and Marawari Shahukars and gay merchants whose only concern was to get maximum profits out of the transaction. There was neither a court of justice nor revenue tribunal before which the cultivators could give their complaints against the revenue farmers. Several Talukas, which were farmed out, became depopulated and were left uncultivated due to the maladaministration of the revenue farmers. The government also did not get information about the sufferings of the inhabitants.[156]

Similarly, the petty government officials also were currupt and exacted many illegal payments. If the Ryots were not in a position to pay the revenue, his personal belongings were auctioned by Mahsuldar (bailiff) and he and his family were frequently subjected to torture to induce them to disclose their hidden money or ornaments etc.[157]

The East India Company also did not alter the existing agrarian structure in Coastal Andhra districts during the early period, from the date of their acquisition in 1765 to 1802 when the permanent settlement was made. The existing Zamindars/revenue farmers were allowed to continue to collect the revenue in their areas while the Khalisa/Haveli parganas were parceled out into estates/divisions and sold to the highest bidders who were also treated as Zamindars.

Revenue farming contributed to the oppression of the Peasants even under the Nawabs of Carnatic which comprised the Nellore and Chittoor districts also. The Fouzdar who was the chief officer and representative of the Nawab in Nellore district and who was stationed at Nellore gave out the revenue collection of the districts to several renters. The oppression of the cultivator is described vividly in the Nellore District Manual thus "... The Fouzdar, whose power was the only check on the renters, lent to their side as being those who could pay best, so that the inhabitants got scant justice. Even the slight check disappeared in the last quarter of the eighteenth century when the misgovernment of the Carnatic reached its height under Mahomed Ali and Oomdat-ul-Oomrah. The whole provinces were leased out, and the Fouzdar and head renter were often the same person. This was repeatedly the case in Nellore. Under these circumstances the last resource of the inhabitants was flight. Large numbers were thus driven from their villages and took refuge either in Ceded Districts, Madras or the Company's territory in the Northern

Circars...".[158] This Manual further states "The oppression of the under-renters (usually heads of villages) principally consisted in levying private contributions on frivolous pretences; in under-assessing the lands in the occupation of themselves, their relations, and friends and making up the difference by an over-assessment of the other village cultivators, more especially those who were the poorest, and therefore, unable to protect themselves; in forcing the poorer ryots to cultivate their lands and perform for them, free of charge, various other services; in monopolizing the produce of the several villages which they afterwards disposed of at an advanced price......".[159]

The revenue policy of the Nawabs of Kurnool also was characterized by the same type oppression as that of Nellore. The revenue administration of the Kurnool under the Nawabs before its take over by the British was in the greatest disorder and was carried on without any system. The amount to be paid by each village was changed according to the caprice of the Nawab who used to increase his revenue demand without any valid reason. We are told that in one village Nannur, the Nawab added 500 rupees to the demand, because a horse of that value died there. The inhabitants fled the place unable to pay it.[160]

In the Zamindaris of Coastal Andhra also the cultivators were under similar oppression. It is reported in a letter addressed to the District Collector of Guntur Mr. Hudson from the assistant Collector thus .... "Another kind of oppression by the Zamindars is the renting of a small portion of ground to an inhabitant, who pays the most exhorbitant price and even of this, he is often deprived. He is compelled to work for the Zamindar and the head-inhabitants. The same thing happens during the harvest season. The inhabitants harvest is postponed and his crop spoiled. The Zamindar sits up on him for the rent. He sells his own private property, pays the rent and leaves the village for good..... ".[161] This type of oppression must have prevailed in most of the Zamindaris of all the three regions of Andhra Desa. The above mentioned assistant collectors letter further observes that several acres of land in the Zamindari villages were lying waste. This he attributes to the want of population and the harsh treatment meted out by the Zamindar to the cultivators.[162]

The agricultural labourers were treated in the same manner in the Zamindari villages. We are told that a Cooly (labourer) was made to work in the heat of the sun from morning till night and was often sent away with out paying the wages for his labour.[163]

Ryots Opression – Protest Migration

The Ryots when there was tax oppression obsconded or migrated enmass to the neighbouring Parganas where there was less oppression. This they were resorting to even during the Vijayanagara period. We get evidence for this for the sixteenth century Rayalasima region. During the period of English Company also, they were adopting some of these methods of protest. As any government's revenue depended on cultivation, it had to persuade them to return to their villages for cultivating. In 1795 the cultivators of 5 villeges in Kondapally, territory, obconded enmass when they were pressed for the payment of balance amount (probably of previous installment) and refused to come back till they were given cowls for the relief). The concerned Renters were directed to encourage them and recall them by adjusting the Jamabandy A cowl was immediately issued to the Curnums and ryots of there villages to return immediately to their respective villages and carry on the cultivation assuring them that their just claims will be allowed them.[164]

On 15-6-1795, the Renter of Vinnakota Pargana (Machilipatam Circar) wrote to the concerned district Collector that the Ryots of his pargana were going to other districts without obeying the Collector's orders and requested that the order was to be enforced.[165] And on 19-6-1795, the Ryots of those above Vinnakota pargana requested the Collector that the renter might be ordered to adjust their accounts before they returned to their villages. At the same time they were warned against disobedience of orders.[166] This is a clear case of villeger's protesting against Renters oppression by giving up cultivation and migrating to the neighbouring districts. And it appears, the collectors had to issue special orders to prevent the Ryots migration during this period. Similar situation arose in Zamindaris also where tax oppression forced the Ryots to migrate enmass to other benevolent places. As some of the Zamindars of Guntur circar were collecting oppressive taxes immediately after the district came under company's rule, many Ryots migrated to the neighbouring districts and took up cultivation there. As very few cultivators were left in the Guntur District to start the cultivation in time and on full-scale, the company government could not get full revenue that year (1789). Government was compelled to take certain measures like stopping collection of taxes on provisions and ensuring just division of produce etc. to induce Ryots to come back and resume cultivation.[167]

Ryots Oppression (in Zamindaris) by Army

The Ryots were required to provide bullocks and other things for the army when it was on the move. A petition from Mahepati Rao, Zamindar of Pithapur complains to the company that one captain Chesshyre had in several instances interfered in his Zamindari by pressing for bullocks sending sepoys into the villages who bet the inhabilants and extorted Batta from the.[168]

(E) REVENUE ORGANISATION/ADMINISTRATION

Under every government, there was a separate Department to took after the revenue administration. Revenue being the most important aspect of the administration of the period, this department must have been a very important one among the government departments. In the Vijayanagara Empire, the revenue department was known as 'Athavana' and it had under its jurisdiction the administration of the entire revenue of the empire. This department was probably headed by a minister and consisted of officials, like secretaries or record keepers (Sampratis) writers (Rayasam or Lekhakulu) and accountants (Karnams). *Athavanavyavaharatantram* (p. 8) mentions Vijayanagara revenue officials like Sarvadhikari, Athavanam and Parupatyam along with Nadagera (Nadu Gaudu) and village Gavudu and Sanabhog. It states that the Gavudu and sanabhog were village headman and accountant and Nadigera (probably Nadu Gauvudu) and the counter part of Deshmukh of Muslim period) was in-charge of revenue collection of Hezali, a revenue division consisting of 10 or 12 or 20 or 40 villages equivalent of a Sthala in the Telugu region. Parupatyagadu was superior government officer incharge of revenue collection of Gadi, a higher revenue division consisting of 4 or 5 Hezalis. It further states that 10 to 20 Gadis made one sima. He was to submit the revenue accounts in the office of Athavanam (Kacheri). Even the revenue contractors (Gutta) were also to settle their accounts in the office. Athavanam was probably the central revenue department in the Vijayanagara Empire and Sarvadhikari was probably the principal secretary incharge of revenue department. Vijayanagara epigraphs mention various officials associated with the land revenue collection like Parupatyamvaru, Rachakarnam, Sthalakarnam and Gramakarnam or Urakarnam, Nad Gaud and village Headman.

Parupatyamvaru, it appears were the chief revenue collectors or superintendents appointed by Vijayanagara government to supervise the revenue collection at the level of Gadi (equalent of a Taluka). They must have supervised the work of the Sthalakarnams and village Karnams or accountants. He is mentioned along wth Rachakarnam, Sthalakarnam and Urakarnam in many Vijayanagara epigraphs recording land grants and revenue remissions.[169] Similarly, Venkatadri, the governor of Kandanavolu Rajya (Kurnool) of the Vijayanagara Empire, under Sadasiva Raya, who exempted the Mahajanas of several Agraharas from the payment of certain taxes, issued an order to the Doras (Amaranayakas) Parupatyagaras, Rayasamvaru, Avasaramvaru and Rachakarmalu connected with the revenue administration of that Sima, prohibiting them from collecting those dues. N. Venkataramanayya, an authority on Vijayanagara history, gives the opinion that these Sima-Parupatyagar in their capacity as Sima's revenue officers, also acted as the executive officers of the Temples in their jurisdiction. This is confirmed by an epigraph of Krishnadevaraya from Karnataka which refers to Parupatyagar having the authority to enquire into the affairs of a particular temple in that region.[170] The same epigraph records the orders of above monarch relieving Parupatyagar from temple duties.

The epigraphs which mention the Parupatyamvaru, do not throw any light on their duties, emoluments etc. Probably they supervised the revenue collection of a Sima, the equalent of Gadi of Athavanatantram and they were assigned Manyam lands and other perquisities for the maintenance of their establishment *Athavanavyavaharatantram* (p. 20) mentions the slary of Parupatyagara as 10 varahas, that of Gumasta 2 varahas, Sirastha (accountant) 5 Varahas. Probably these were monthly salaries during the later Vijayanagara period.

In Golkonda Kingdom also there was a revenue department headed by a Revenue Minister. It had control over the collection of land tax. There was also a central treasury, Kazana where all revenues were paid.

Amildar: These were Revenue Supervisors or Superintendents called Amildars one in each district/Sarkar. Amildar was a Muslim officer. He supervised the revenue collection and it was his duty to see that the governors who were appointed in Golkonda kingdom on farming terms (revenue contract) revenue farmers and probably also the Zamindars and the other revenue collectors Deshmukhs, and Accountants/Deshpandias fulfilled duly their obligations. He can be described as the counter-part of Vijayanagara period *Parapatyagara* to some extent.

We do not have information on Amildar's salary emoluments. Most probably he was assigned revenue of a certain territory or Muqasa towards his emoluments. *Athavanavyavaharathantram* mentions 10 varahas as the salary of Amildar, along with that of Gumasta (clerk) and Sirastadar (accountant) (p. 20).

It was also the duty of the Amildar to stop the Izaradars from making illegal collections from the holders of Inams etc. For example, in 1638 when the caretaker and public crier of the mosque at Lonkher village in Rajamundry Sarkar complained to the Qutbshahi king Abdulla Qutbshah that the local Ijaradar-Balas Venkatadri had seized the produce of the endowed lands of the mosque and was making other demands, the king ordered, by a Farman, the Amildars to recover the grain from the Ijaradar and to put an end to all illegal demands on the *Mosque's* Inam Lands.[171]

Qanungo of Hyderabad Province

During the Mughal period, a Qanungo was appointed for Hyderabad province. He was revenue recorder for

Hyderabad and Hyderabad Karnatic. The first Qanungo was Babu Pandit (1690-1702). His successor Shaik Sadulla held the post from 1702-1707, and again, Babu Pandit was re-appointed as Qanungo in 1708. Babu Pandit was made a Mansabdar of 200 Zat and 70 Sawar, and he held a Jagir towards his emoluments.[172] Qanungo and his staff were responsible for obtaining accurate figures on assessments and collection of revenue in the Parganas and for keeping this information current in the office registers. Qanungo played the role of an operator of an intelligence or reporting arm of the revenue system. Reports from his agents scattered throughout the two provinces of Hyderabad and Karnatic furnished information on agricultural produce and revenue collections in every Pargana. Qanungo's work threatened to expose the dishonest Jagirdars or their agents and other tax collectors who under-reported their receipts. Qanungo reported directly to the Diwan of the Deccan Subah and provided a check on the activities of the provincial Diwan.

The Amildar, during the Asafjahi period combined in himself the military (Fouzdar), financial (Shakdar or Shiqdar?) and also majesterial (Ziladar) powers. As Majistrate, he was assisted by a Daroga, Mufti or Molavi, Kazi and Kotwal. In his capacity as Fouzdar or head of the troops, the Amildar held the Jagirs or military fief, which was personal, under obligation to maintain a certain number of cavalry and infantry for the protection of the area under his jurisdiction and assist his master in times of foreign war. All lesser Jagirdars/Mansabadars with their respective quotas of soldiers were under his command. But the most important of his functions was as Shakdar or Shiqdar. He did the management of the collection of revenue.

Two types of officials assisted him in the revenue collection. The first category were the native hereditary revenue officials and included Deshmukhs, Deshpandias,

Patels, Karnams, who held their appointments, rights, privileges by a Sanad from the government and with the goodwill of the Ryots. The second category included Amins, Majumdars or Sheristadars, Tahseldars with their Moharries or Writers/accountants, who were more the immediate dependents of Amildar.

Diwan (Asafjahi Period)

At the top of the Revenue Administration, there was the Diwan at Hyderabad, the head-quarters of the Nizam's dominions. The Diwan occupied the second position to the Asafjahi king in hierarchy. Diwan was responsible primarily for revenue administration.

Amalguzar and Amil

There was a revenue official at the level of a Sarkar/district called Amalguzar during the Asafjahi period. He, probably supervised the work of Amils, the revenue officials at Taluqa level. Several Parganas/Mahals were grouped together and were called as Taluqa. As Amil was the revenue official and made the revenue settlement of the Khalisa parganas and also incharge of the Collection of Sair or Sayer (non-agricultural taxes) at the Mahal and the other divisions. he was responsible for revenue administration of Taluqa (other than Khalisa parganas). He was the chief officer for the assessment and fixation of land revenue of the Taluqa.[173] Nayeem has prepared a table showing the territorial jurisdiction of some20 of the Amils for the year 1747 A. D. Six of them were Hindus and the remaining were Muslims.[174] From this information, it is clear that the post of Amil of Qutbshahi period was retained under Mughals and Asafjahis and they became Mansabadars holding Jagirs.

During the Asafjahi period, the Amildar, when appointed, had to give an undertaking called 'Ta' ahud' indicating the amount to be collected by him and also a deed of acceptance called 'Qa'buliat', accepting the responsibility of revenue collection and to deposit the amount in treasury. When Anwar-ud-din Khan was appointed as Amil of the Sikakul Sarkar, he executed Qabuliat stating that the accepted the responsibility of revenue collection and that he would deposit the amount of Rs. 35,000 revenue from all sources which was only fifty percent of the revenue to be collected. The remaining half he promised to spend towards the deployment of Sibbandi troops. [175] It was also his duty to promote agriculture and increase the population in the area of his jurisdiction.

Amin: Amin of Mughal period was almost the counterpart of Amildar of Qutbshahi period. He was a revenue assessment officer at the Pargana and some times at a Sarkar or district level. He was appointed in Hyderabad province during the Mughal period. He was answerable for the collection of revenue from crown lands or Khalisa Parganas. Forty or fifty Parganas in Telangana region which were reserved for Khalisa were administered by the Amin of Elgandal who was also its Fauzdar. Amin of Khalisa in Telangana had large staff to help him administer those Parganas. Some times, the posts of Amin and Fauzdar were given to the same person. In 1696-97, the Amin of Khalisa Parganas of Telangana was one Kar Talab Khan who was also its Fauzdar. In 1690, he became the Diwan of Hyderabad province, besides retaining for himself the above two posts. [176] For all the Khalisa Parganas situated in the coastal Andhra districts, the Fauzdar of Sikakul or Srikakulam, who was the general administrator of those districts, was appointed as their Amin during the period of Aurangzeb. [177] Similarly, in the year 1697, one Hasan Quli Khan was made the Fauzdar of Khammam, Mustafanagar and Eluru. He was also made the Amin of all Khalisa lands in those three districts.[178] Amin was a Mansabdar. There were Amins who were responsible to collect Sair of divisions like Mahal.

Hereditary Revenue Officer

The hereditary revenue officials connected with the land revenue administration and also the entire agrarian life included Sardeshmuk and sardeshpandia at the Sarkar/ district level, Deshmukh and Deshpandia or Sthalakarnam at the level of pargana or Sthalam, and the village head and village accountant. The origin of these offices, their functions and their emoluments have been already discussed in the chapter on land-tenures.

All these officials were the Hindus and people of some influence and local standing in the areas of their jurisdiction. The Sardeshmukh, the Deshmukh and the village headman were mostly non-brahmin and of agricultural communities, like those of Reddi, Velama, Kamma, Raju, Balija etc. , while the Sardeshpandia, Deshpandia and *Sthalakarnam* and the village accountant were invariably Brahmins of Niyogi sect. All of them had their establishments comprising of Gumasthas, peons etc for the performance of their duties.

These hereditary revenue officials were common to all the governments, whether Hindu or Muslims. These positions were native institutions and their origin can be traced to the pre-Muslim period. As the revenue administration was very complicated and as the alien governments were least interested in these matters, these hereditary officials became indispensable and were continued under all the succeeding governments.

European District Collectors under East India Company

In 1794, after the abolition of the provincial chiefs and councils, European Collectors were appointed over each district by the Board of Revenue in the Northern Sarkars.

Their emoluments consisted of a commission in the collection. Mr. Robert Hughes who was appointed the collector of Guntur district in the year 1789 was to get a commission of 5 per cent which should not however exceed Rs. 8,000/0 from the Board of Revenue.[179]

However, the Board of Revenue observed in this regard in 1803 that "the allowances to the Collector of Zillahs were regulated by a uniform scale confining to the receipts of the Collectors of Zillahs to a salary of Pagodas 200 a month and a commission of one percent on the revenue. Subsequently it was determined to limit the receipts of the collectors of Zillahs on account of salary and commission to the sum of St. Pagodas 4,800 per annum....... ".[180]

The duties of the Collectors were to form an estimate of the produce of each division under their control from the Anchana accounts. They had to force the Zamindars in the district to pay one-fourth of the estimated produce and take bonds for another one-fourth before he was allowed to take the produce. He also was to take proposals from the Zamindars for the revenue of the next year. The Collectors also were not to allow the Zamindars to keep a large number of armed followers than was necessary for the collection of revenue.[181]

The Board of Revenue furnished clear instructions for his guidance. He was to be administered the revenue oath by the President at Madras or the Mayor. He was also provided with an assistant with allowances equal to Captain's pay and Batta per annum. He was instructed to send the necessary accounts and reports to the Board of Revenue. The Collector, on his arrival in the district was to form an abstract of the Dowle or an estimate of the produce of each Division of the Circar based on the Anchanas or Account of Appraisment. He was to call up on all the Zamindars of the Circar for the immediate payment of one fourth of the amount of the government share of the estimated produce as stated in the Anchana accounts of the District. Then, he was to take obligation for fourth Kist payable within two months of issueing orders for the Dumbala (Dumbalas indicated the share of the Ryots), relinquishing them the present crops. The collector was directed to keep soyer or government duties or any other source of revenue under his own management. After issuing orders for dumbala, he should proceed for the settlement with the Zamindars for the present year.

As the company government could not allow the zamindars to have armed followers more than necessary for their rank and situation, the collector was to insist on their reduction and allow to maintain only the necessary Sibbandy for the collection of revenue.[182]

Notes & References

1. The British administrators estimated that the land revenue represented ten elevenths of the net rental of the country.
2. European travellers in their accounts of India of this period commonly described the king as the owner of all land in India and therefore he appropriated the rent of the soil.
3. See P. V. Parabrahma Sastri, *Rural Studies in Early Andhra*, p. 123.
4. *South Indian Inscriptions*, Vol. X, No. 748.
5. *Anantapur District Gazetteer*, p. 131.
6. *SII*, VoL. X No. 772.
7. Besides three types of cultivable land (Sagubadi Polamu) there was Beedu (Wastland), Gobhumi (grazing land) Pandubhumi (meaning not known) See Cuddapah Inscriptions, p. 79; and, District Records, Godavari, Vol. No. 908, A. P. State Archives and Research Institute, Tarnaka, p. 186.
8. The grain measures in Andhradesa till the introduction of metric system were as follows – One putti consisted of 20

Tumus, one Tumu of 4 Kunchams, one Kuncham of 16 Solas-so-one putti was equalent to 80 Kunchams. A Kunchamu was roughly the equalent of 10 Kg. During the period of Mughal rule, the north Indian grain measures like Mauns and seers appear to have been introduced.

9. See M. Somasekara Sarma. , *History of the Reddi Kingdoms*, pp. 363-367.

10. *Ibid*; and also see the epigraphs of 1313-14 and 1429-30 A. D. from Darsi village, one of Kakatiya Prataparudra's period and the other of Vijayanagara period – Butterworth and V. G. Setti, *Inscriptions in the Nellore District*, pp. 294-352.

11. *Fifth Report*, pp. 150-151

12. DCR, 2990, p. 42.

13. Guide to the Records of Masulipatam District, p. 25-26.

14. *Anantapur District Gazetteer*, 1905, p. 130.

15. taken from W. Francis, *Vizagapatam District Gazetteer*, p. 164.

16. J. F. Richards, p. 21;

17. *Ibid*.

18. *Ibid*.

19. Doc. S. A. H. nos 101 to 120, taken from Nayeem. , *Administration of Deccan under Nizam-ul-mulk*, p. 134.

20. *Ibid*. , pp. 134-135.

21. *Kurnool Manual*, p. 58.

22. *Ibid*. , p. 158.

23. *Guide to Masulipatam District Records*, II, p. 22.

24. *Ibid*. , p. 18.

25. *Ibid*. , p. 20

26. *Ibid*. , p. 19.

27. *Nellore Manual*, p. 271.

28. Ibid. , p. 272.

29. S. H. Bilgrami, *A Memoir of Sir Salar Jung*, Bombay, 1883, p. 31.

30. Hyderabad Affairs, I, p. 464.

31. *Ibid.*
32. Rupee was a Mughal Silver Coin adopted by the Qutbshahis after 1636.
33. N. Venkataramanayya, *Cuddapah Inscriptions*, pp. 268-9
34. *Ibid.* , pp. 414-5
35. *Kurnool Manual*, p. 57
36. *Vizagapatam Manual*, p. 124
37. *Fifth Report*, p. 303
38. John William Kaye, *The Administration of the East India Company*, 1966, Alhabad, p. 224
39. *Fifth Report from the Select Committee on the Affairs of the East India Company*, p. 303.
40. *Nellore Manual*, p. 270
41. *Vizagapatam Manual*, p. 124
42. *Kurnool Manual*, p. 58
43. *Ibid.*
44. *District Records Godavari*, Vol. No. 4639, A. P. State Archives and Research Institute, Tarnaka, p. 55
45. *Godavari District Manual*, p. 314.
46. *Kurnool Manual*, pp. 60 & 61.
47. *Nellore District Gazetteer*, p. 262.
48. Jamabadi Settlement Report, Godavari, dated 30-3-1825, *Guide to the Records of Godavari District*, II, p. 263.
49. *Kurnool Manual*, p. 61.
50. *Guide to the Records of the Godavari District*, Vol. I, p. 162.
51. *Nellore District Gazetteer*, p. 261.
52. *Guide to the Records of the Godavari District* Vol. I, p. 162.
53. Garce in this part of the country was probably a grain measure, like putti.
54. taken from W. Francis, *Vizagapatnam District Gazetteer*, p. 165.
55. *Ibid.*
56. Soma Reddy, R., *Studies in the Socio-economic History of Medieval Andhra Desa*, New Delhi, 2007, pp. 116-122.
57. Hyderabad Affairs, Vol. I, p. 464.

58. S. H. Bilgrami, *A Memoir of Sir Salarjung*, p. 318.
59. *Cambridge Economic History of Medieval India*, II, p.
60. *Nellore Manual*, p. 510.
61. *Kurnool Manual*, pp. 58 & 59.
62. *Athavanavyavaharantram*, p. 9; *Circuit Committee Report*, p. 111.
63. *Nellore Manual*, pp. 509-510.
64. *Circuit Committee Report*, p. 111; Hyderabad Affairs, I, p. 464; Ibid. , II, p. 677.
65. W. Francis, *Vizagapatam District Gazetteer*, p. 165.
66. See my article "Taxation and Hindu Temples in the Telugu Districts under the Vijayanagara Empire", *Proceedings of the Indian History Congress*, 1978.
67. See my book *Hindu and Muslim Religious Institutions – Andhra Desa 1300-1600*, New Era Publications, 1984, Madras, pp. 28-30, 41.
68. *Nellore Manual*, p. 274.
69. See P. V. Parabrahmasastri, *Rural Studies in Early Andhra*, pp. 125-26.
70. *Fifth Report*, p. 151.
71. *S. I. I.* , Vol. XVI, no. 174.
72. T. K. T. Veeraraghavacharya, *History of Tirupati*, 1976, f. n. p. 21.
73. Burton Stein, *All the King's Mana: Papers on Medieval South Indian History*, Madras, 1984, pp. 68-69.
74. W. Francis, *Vizagapatam District Gazetteer*, p. 164.
75. *Athavanathantram*, p. 10.
76. *Anantapur District Gazetteer*, 1905, p. 130.
77. Nayeem, *Administration of Deccan under Nizam-ul-mulk*, p. 99.
78. Compiled by Maulvi Syed Mehdi Ali, Hyderabad Affairs, VIII, 1886, Hyderabad, p. 464-464.
79. Compiled by Maulvi Syed Mehdi Ali, Hyderabad Affairs, VIII, 1886, Hyderabad, p. 6.
80. *Manual f Vizagapatam*, p. 222; and also see *Fifth Report*, pp. 151-152.

81. *Guide to Masulipatam District Records*, II, pp. 141 & 146.
82. *Nellore Manual*, 476-477. (56 pukka seers = 1 Marcal or Tum; 20 Marcals = 1 putty or candy).
83. *Nellore Manual*, p. 477, foot notes.
84. Even in the case of produce of the dry crops, the government share was increased from 10 Marcals to 11 Marcals in 20 during the Muslim Period in Nellore District (see foot note and on p. 476 of Nellore Manual)
85. *Anantapur District Gazetteer* 1905, p. 131.
86. also see *Guide to Masulipatam District Records*, III, p. 197.
87. taken from W. Francis, *Vizagapatam District Gazetteer*, p. 165.
88. *Nellore Manual*, p. 478.
89. *SII* X No. 748.
90. *Kurnool Manual*, p. 58.
91. *Nellore Manual*, p. 507.
92. *Fifth Report*, pp. 174-177.
93. Robert Sewell, *Forgotten Empire*, p. 354.
94. *Anonymous Relations, Relations of Golkonda*, p. 81.
95. *Ibid.*, p. 11.
96. *Ibid.*, p. 81.
97. *Ibid.*
98. *Relations of Golkonda*, p. 81.
99. *Ibid.*, p. 11.
100. *Ibid.*, p. 81.
101. *Ibid.*, p. 57.
102. *Relations of Golkonda*, p. 82.
103. I. J. Collection, 1/9/36, (taken from *Mughal Administration in Golkonda-Richards*), p. 169.
104. *J. F. Richards*, p. 171-172..
105. Moulavi Chiragh Ali, *Hyderabad (Deccan) Under Sir Salar Jung*, Vol. II, p. 157.
106. *Ibid.*, p. 158.
107. *Ibid.*, pp. 158-160.

108. *Hyderabad Affairs*-I, p. 577.
109. *Ibid.* , Vol. II, p. 482.
110. *Ibid.* , Vol. I, p. 578.
111. *Hyderabad Affairs*, Vol. II, p. 488.
112. Moulavi Chirag Ali., *Hyderabad (Deccan) under Sir Salarjung*, Vol. II, p. 161.
113. S. Pratapareddi, *Andhrula Sanghika Charitra*, p. 100.
114. Syed Mahdi Ali. , *Hyderabad Affairs*, VII, p.
115. *District Collectorate Records*, 3006, pp. 667 to 681.
116. *Fifth Report*, p. 150.
117. W. Francis. , *Vizagapatam District Gazetteer*, p. 166.
118. District Collectorate Records, 2992, pp. 24 & 25.
119. *Ibid.* , p. 11.
120. *Ibid.* , p. 25.
121. *Ibid.* , p. 25a and 25b.
122. *Ibid.* , p. 2992, p. 3.
123. *Ibid.* , 2992. p. 19.
124. *Ibid.* , 2992, p. 20.
125. *Fifth Report*, p. 176
126. *Ibid*.
127. *Ibid.* , p. 174.
128. W. Franciz. , *Vizagapatam District Gazetteer*, p. 169.
129. *Fifth Report*, p. 154.
130. District Collectorate Records, 2992, p. 164.
131. *Ibid.* , p. 55a.
132. *Fifth Report*, p. 152.
133. *Nellore Manual*, pp. 481-482.
134. Lanka Sundaram, "Revenue Administration of Northern Circars", *Journal of Andhra Historical Research Society*, XI, p. 168.
135. *Guide to the Records of the Nellore District 1801-1835*, p. 2.
136. *Fifth Committee*, pp. 192-93.
137. *Kistna District Manual*, p. 347.

138. *Manual of Vizagapatam*, p. 230.
139. *Cuddapah Manual*, p. 150.
140. *Circuit Committee Report*, p. 112
141. *Kurnool Manual*, pp. 58 & 59.
142. District Collectorate Records, 2774A, pp. 115, 161, 162, 16
143. Guide to the Records of Masulipatam District, I, p. 84; DCR, 2781, p. 124.
144. *Ibid*.
145. *Ibid*.
146. Guide to the Records of Masulipatam District, p. 85; D. C. R., 2781, pp. 196-200.
147. *Forgotten Empire*, pp. 365-370.
148. Nayeem, *Administration of Deccan under Nizam-ul-mulk*, pp. 203-04; Nayeem also furnished on the basis of Archival material, the amount of Peshkash collected by each Deshmukh/Deshpandia from the Zamindars Parganawise.
149. *Masulipatam District Records*, III, p. 197.
150. Minutes of Sir Thomas Munro. pp. 237-38. ; quoted from T. V. Mahalingam, *Administration and Social Life under Vijayanagaram* Part-I, 1969, Madras, p. 91.
151. *Ibid*.
152. Inscriptions of Nellore District, Part-I, no. 109, pp. 149-150; Ibid II, pp. 747-757, 711, 788 and 7\820, Ibid III, pp. 120, 1215, 1240, 1242, 1247, 1261, 1262, 1274, 1276, 1277 & 1278.
152. Robert Sewell, *Forgotten Empire*, p. 354.
154. Moreland. , *Relations of Golkonda*, pp. 11, 54, 79 & 81.
155. *Cuddapah Inscriptions*, pp. 1915, 1013 & 1014; SII X, 771; SII, XVI, no. 333.
156. Moulavi Chirag Ali, *Hyderabad under Sir Salar Jung-II*, pp. 162-63.
157. S. H. Bilgrami, *A Memoir of Sir Salarjung*, p. 32.
158. *Nellore Manual*, pp. 482-83.
159. *Ibid*., pp. 483-84.
160. *Kurnool Manual*, pp. 59460.

161. *Guide to Masulipatam District Records*, II, p. 285.
162. *Ibid.*
163. *Ibid.*
164. D. C. R. , 2991, pp. 61-62.
165. *Ibid.*, p. 47; D. C. R. , 2991, pp. 30-31.
166. *Ibid.*, p. 47; DCR, 2991, pp. 30-31.
167. D. C. R., 2996, pp. 54-59.
168. D. C. R., 2779, p. 116.
169. *South Indian Inscriptions*, XVI, no. 33.
170. *Epigrahic Carnatika*, IV, ch. 99.
171. taken from J. F. Rciahrds. , *Mughal Administration in Golkonda*, p. 26.
172. *Mughal Administration in Golkonda*, pp. 162-167.
173. Nayeem. , *Administration of Deccan under Nizam-ul-mulk*, pp. 47-48.
174. *Ibid.*
175. Nayeem, M. A. , *Administration of Deccan under Nizam-ul-mulk*, p. 155.
176. In 1701 Kar Talab Khan became the Diwan of Bengal, later its governor and eventually its independent ruler (see *Mughal Administration in Golkonda*, p. 182.)
177. *Ibid.*, p. 183.
178. *Ibid.*
179. *Guide to the Masulipatam District Records*, part-II, p. 129.
180. *Guide to Masulipatam District Records*, III, p. 215.
181. *Ibid.*
182. D. C. R., 2996, pp. 5-12.

CHAPTER – IV

AGRICULTURAL DEVELOPMENT

This chapter is designed to describe the agricultural development that include the founding of new agrarian settlements and bringing new land under cultivation, revival of deserted villages and agriculture, augmentation of irrigation facilities to the lands already under cultivation, and crop pattern. An account of related aspects like famines, agricultural communities, land survey etc also will be attempted in this chapter. Many of these aspects underwent considerable changes during this period due to contemporary political and economic changes that were taking place at the regional, national and global levels.

Land Reclamation

Land and human resource were most important among the agents of production and also most important sources of revenue to the state. This applies also to Telugu region of the period under study. Contemporary sources testify to the flourishing agriculture in large tracts of land, and abundant sources of irrigation in this region. The French traveller Tavernier writing in the second part of the Seventeenth century writes thus ... "The kingdom of Golkonda, speaking generally is a rich country, abounding in corn, rice, cattle, sheep, fouls and other commodities necessary to life. And there are numerous tanks, there is also abundance of good fish...... Nature has contributed more than art to make these tanks, of which the country is full".[1]

We have evidence to show that during the period of the Kakatiyas and Vijayanagara which ruled this region during the earlier periods, large extent of land was brought under cultivation in Telangana and the Rayalasima regions respectively. But there were, still extensive forests and uncultivated waste lands to be brought under cultivation during the period under consideration. Moreover, during certain periods, villages were depopulated and much land fell out of cultivation due to causes like famines, floods, pestilences and also the oppressive taxation policy of the rulers. Land reclamation was necessitated to cope up with the problem of the pressure of growing population and also the government's need for more revenue.

The land reclamation in this region during the period of study was not as extensive as that of the earlier period due to the political uncertainty of the period. However, we have some scanty information to form some idea of the same.

Foundation of new villages and also the revival of deserted villages was an essential part of the government effort for extension of cultivation. During this period, it appears, many villages were founded and deserted villages were repopulated and great patches of land were brought under cultivation. The endeavours of the contemporary governments in this direction are indicated by the records of the period. The government besides undertaking the reclamation work itself, also encouraged private initiative in that direction. And there are many instances of land reclamation by private investment.

The establishment of new villages in the forest clearings proved to be a hard task fraught with many difficulties. It was not always easy to find suitable settlers who would consent to be transplanted to form the new communities. It was usually left to the efforts of enterprising private individuals chartered by the state who would visit the old villages in their neighbourhood and gather together bands of people eager to break loose from the entanglements of the joint family and to set themselves up in independent home steads.

Dasavandam for Founding of Villages

The government encouraged the founding of new villages by offering various inducements to the founders and the settlers. They were rewarded, for undertaking this work, with lands under various tenures under the 'Dasavanda' system, depending on the nature of the work. For example, for the establishment of a new village, land was granted under 'Pallekattu Manyam' tenure. Lands were granted under 'Achchukattu-Manyam' tenure to the investors for bringing new lands under cultivation by clearing jungles and leveling the land. For providing irrigation facilities such as a canal and a well, they were granted lands under "Kaluva Dasavandam' and "Bavikattu Manyam" tenures respectively. An epigraph of first quarter of the Seventeenth century from Nandaluru village (Cuddapah district) refers to :Pallekattu Manyam" "Bavi Dasavandam" and "Kaluva Dasavandam" granted by a certain Matli Venkatramaraju, a feudatory chief to one Appalaraju who undertook the work of establishing a new village called Anantarajupeta, digging an irrigation well and a canal. For establishing the village, he was granted 8 Kuntas of dry and wet land as "Pallekattu Manyam" and half of the land brought under cultivation under the well and canal excavated by him as "Dasavanda Manyam". Further, for cultivating the remaining half of the land reclaimed by him by cutting trees and leveling it, he was given tax concession for three years. He was to pay to the owner at the rate of 1 Ruka per kunta of the land first year, 2 Rukas second year, and 5 Rukas third year onwards.[2] Another 'Kavulu' deed from the same place i.e. Nandaluru (Cuddapah district) and of the same period, which also records the grant of "Pallekattu Manyam" and 'Dasavanda Manyam' to an investor for founding a new village and bringing new land under cultivation, states that the latter was given half of the land brought under cultivation by leveling and providing irrigation with canal water as 'Dasavanda'. For cultivating the remaining half, he was given tax concession for three years at the rate a bit different from above mentioned, of 1 Ruka for 1 Kunta of land for the first year, 2 Rukas second year and 3 Rukas third year onwards.[3]

While the tax concessions at the above rate were given for reclaimed wet-lands, whether irrigated by a well or a canal, different rates of concessions appear to have been followed for cultivating dry lands brought under cultivation and which were rain-fed. Another Kaul deed of the same period and place as mentioned above, states that for the remaining half of the land, after giving half of it to the investor under Dasavanda and the total of which was dry land, the tax was to be paid at the rate of quarter Ruka per kunta first year, half a Ruka second year and one Ruka third year onwards.[4]

Different rates of tax concessions were followed depending on the nature of the work involved in the reclamation, i.e. the amount of the investment and labour involved in the work. For example, a Kaul deed of the first part of the Seventeenth Century from Nandaluru Village (Cuddapah district) states that the investor was to undertake the reclamation of the land under an irrigation tank which remained idle for a number of years. For cultivating the already leveled old fields under the tank, he was to pay tax at normal rates, i.e. 3 Rukas per year for each Kunta of wet land (rice field) and for cultivating dry land already leveled, he was asked to pay different rates of tax for different crops like that of Ragi, Aruka and Pulses. Ofcourse, these were at the rates applicable for the dry crops normally. They varied from a quarter Ruka to one Ruka per Kunta of land. For bringing some more land under the tank under cultivation for the first time by clearing jungle and by leveling it, he was granted half of it as "Dasavanda". And for cultivating the remaining of this land, he was given tax concession to be raised gradually over a period of 5 years, that too crop-wise.[5]

Different rates of tax-concessions for crops of different duration and value to be cultivated in the reclaimed land are mentioned in an epigraph from a village of Cuddapah district. According to this, the investor was to get 2 Kuntas of land to be irrigated under the well dug by him as "Bavi Manyam" and for cultivating the remaining land, he had to pay to the local ruler a quarter Ruka per Kunta first year, half Ruka second year and 3 Rukas from third year onwards for raising long duration crops (Peddapairu) and for garden crop.[6] The latter crops were of short duration. Finally, another Kaul deed of the same place and date recording the grant of some land under "Dasavanda" and "Bavi Manyam" tenures for leveling the land and digging a well, mentions higher rates for cultivating the remaining state land brought under cultivation. Under this arrangement, the investor was to pay tax on dry crops at the rate of 2 Rukas fourth year onwards. Probably, these lands compared to those mentioned in other cases, were of superior quality. According to the same record, for cultivating Tobacco under well irrigation, the cultivator had to pay still higher rate i.e. 4 Rukas first year, 8 Rukas second year, 12 Rukas third year and 16 Rukas fourth year onwards.[7] This was probably due to the high commercial value of Tobacco. Thus, the government gave tax concessions on these lands only for the first few years and then for the following years, it collected taxes at normal rates under the graded taxation system.

Revival of depopulated village is indicated in an inscription of 1656 A.D. from Gangavaram village (Anantapur district). It records the Kowl or Kavulu granted to several individuals such as Appana Devana, Hanumappa Nayudu, Nama Reddi, Nagi Reddi of Ayidukallu village and Sadaya Kaduraya of Pedakallu villege, by Dalavayi Dachappanayaka, the agent of the king in appreciation of their having settled the farmers in the village of Gangavaram which had become depopulated and as a result gone follow. The new settlers including those who undertook to settle them were given certain privileges and tax concessions.[8] Similarly, a epigraph of 1691 A.D. from Pulivendula, (Cuddapah district) records the terms offered by the order of Muhammad Jafar, an officer of Golkonda government, to induce the merchants and oil-pressers to come and settle down in that village which had been deserted. The terms included the exemption of obligations to supply certain articles by them to the palace and also certain taxes.[9]

The extent of the land granted to the investors under the Dasavanda tenures was not always uniform. It was some times half of the land reclaimed, some times one-fourth and some times a fixed measure. On these lands, they paid tax at concessional rates. And for cultivating the new lands that remained with the state after granting it under various tenures, tax concessions were given to the investors for the first few years under the system of graded taxation. They were allowed to cultivate the land for the first few years free from the payment of any rent or fiscal charges; from the fourth year taxes were fixed at low rates which were gradually raised year by year until they came up to the level of those obtaining in the old established villages of the vicinity. The quantum of land and the rate of tax concessions given, depended on the nature of the work, the soil, the crop etc.

The establishment of a village called Eklaskhanpuram near Dharmavaram town in Addanki Sima (Kurnool district) by a Qutbshahi governor Eklaskhan is known from an epigraph of 1600 A.D. from that place. It records tax concessions on the lands newly brought under cultivation in that villege.[10]

Regarding the procedures followed when a new village was founded, some interesting details are furnished in an epigraph dated 1775 A.D. from Gandikota village (Cuddapah district). According to this epigraph, when the village Kottalapalle was founded by one Subbadasari at the instance of local Qutbshahi officer, a small fortress was built, the Ayagars or village officials and servants were appointed and the bufalloes and sheep were sacrificed at the site.[11] That, all the important communities to be settled in the new village were also involved in the foundation ceremony of the village, is recorded in the Teruvulapuri Kaifiyat. It states that when the new village Teruvulapuri was founded, each of the communities laid the foundation stone or "Shankusthapana" in one of the eight corners of the village site. Carpenter laid the foundation stone in north-west, barber in the Centre, Malas and Madigas in the two sub-corners (Upashankulu).[12] This particular evidence also indicates the special importance attached to the important communities and particularly the artisans in the village life.

Irrigation – Construction of Irrigation Works

The paramount importance of irrigation for agriculture in this region was realized from very ancient times. The prosperity of state depended on the provision of irrigation facilities for agricultural development. Contemporary literature and inscriptions extol the religious merits of construction and maintenance of irrigation works. It was considered as one of the 'Saptasantanams' (seven acts of religious merit). The construction of many tanks and canals was undertaken not only by the rulers, their feudatories and their ladies but also by the rich private entrepreneurs and also religious institutions like temples and Mathas during the preceding period. As Telangana region contains a large number of irrigation works provided by the Kakatiya rulers, the Southern Andhra districts especially the Ceded districts and Nellore district abound with tanks and canals provided mostly during Vijayanagara period. Thomas Munro, writing about Cuddapah district in 1801, says that he had never come across a district in which there were so many tanks.[13] There were 4,194 tanks in Cuddapah district alone of which 1,314 or less than one-third belonged to the government, 2,646 were of Dasabandam category 15 Shrotriem, and 209 private tanks.[14]

The existence of large number of irrigation works in the Rayalasima region and especially in Cuddapah district is indicated by the remarks of Munro made in July 1801. He remarks... "for there is scarcely any place where a tank can be made to advantage that has not already been applied to this purpose by the inhabitants...".[15]

Following in the foot steps of their predecessors, the Qutbshahi rulers also took considerable interest in providing irrigational fecilities in this region. Many of the tanks in and around Hyderabad and some in Southern Telangana districts like Nalgonda are of Qutbshahi period origin. The famous tanks like Hussain Sagar tank, Masab tank, Mirjumla tank, Ibrahimbagh tank, Durg tank in Hyderabad area and Ibrahim patnam tank in Ranga Reddi district are some of the famous Qutbshahi period tanks.[16] In an epigraph of Qutbshahi period dated 1529 A.D. from Rachapeta, (Nalgonda district) it is recorded that one Masanad Yeli Kutuban Muluk Odeyalu permitted his son-in-law Kemana Muluk to construct a tank at Empuru villege.[17] An inscription from Panugallu (Nalgonda district) dated 1554 A.D. states that Rahmatulla, an officer under Ibrahim Qutbshah, got repaired the dam across the river Musi near the villege of Namali in Indrapura Sima (Ramannapet and Nalgonda Talukas) and also brought into use the old canal to feed the tank named Uday Sumudram near Panugallu. Again that water was led through channels upto the river Krishna filling other tanks on the way between Namali village and the River Krishna.[18]

The fall of the Qutbshahi dynasty appears to have given a setback to the agricultural development. There is no evidence to the provision of any major irrigation facilities under the succeeding dynasties i.e. the Mughals, the Asafjahis and the East India Company. Only the existing works were maintained for which arrangements were made by the grants of the earlier period. There are some stray references to their repair by those governments. For example, a epigraph from Gandikota (Cuddapah district) dated 1696 A.D. records the construction of a canal called Murneti Kaluva by cutting through a hillock Motikonda by Inatkhan Bittani, the Mughal Fouzdar. It is also stated that the old canal was damaged due to floods and as the Dasavandikas could not repair the canal, the above Fouzdar had to reconstruct it. At that time, Hazi Khan Bittani was administering the region of Gurramkonda under Mohammad Safi, the Diwan of entire Karnatic region while Julpikar Khan was the subedar of Dewan and Aurangzeb Padshah was ruling the country.[19]

Maintenance and Repair of Irrigation Works

The maintenance and repair of irrigation works was atleast as important as the construction of new ones. Maintenance involved the guarding of dams and proper upkeep of supply channels, removal of silt or deposits from tank beds and the river canals, repairs of distribution channels and sluices to prevent the irrigation works becoming useless. Owing to heavy floods in the rainy season, the tank-bunds breached, the feeder channels got silted up and the level of tank-beds rose rendering them useless for irrigation purpose. We find from contemporary sources, that sufficient care was taken for the proper upkeep of the irrigation works during the period. In these records we notice measures like annual repairs of tank-bunds, removal of silt deposits in the tank-beds and repairs of canals and sluices. Various measures were adopted for the purpose.

Dasavandam for Maintenance

At the time of the construction of a new irrigation work itself, many a time, separate and permanent provision was made for its upkeep under the Dasavanda system. This system which became popular for agricultural development through private enterprenuership was continued throughout the period under study. For example, an epigraph of Achyutaraya's period (Vijayanagara) from Dondapadu villege (Cuddapah district) states that a certain, Obulayyadeva Maharaja granted 'Dasabandam' land to two persons Singamareddi Timmaya and Kanchena Timmaya for having built a tank and also for the maintenance.[20] Similarly, in 1597 A.D., an edict, issued by a certain Aubalaraja, a Nayaka to the Reddis of Reddicherla village (Cuddapah district), states that the income from the 'Dasabanda Manyam' of 3 puttis of land given to them, should be spent for the repairs of the village tank. This record specifically states that those Reddis should enjoy the income from that Dasabandam land also should maintain and undertake repairs, if any, for the tank every year. It also further states that if some of them were absent or left the place, the remaining Reddis should enjoy those 'Manyam' lands and look after the tank repair.[21]

The Qutbshahi rulers also followed this method for the maintenance of irrigation works. They appear to have continued it which was followed under the earlier dynasties. The inscription of 1554 A.D. from Panugallu which records the repairing of the dam across the river Musi near the village Namali (Nalgonda and Ramannapet Talukas) by Rahmatulla, a Qutbshahi official, also states that he arranged for the regular maintenance of the dam, canals and tanks by granting 'Dasavanda Manya' out of the irrigated land under the Panuganti tank.[22] Similarly, Abdulla Qutbshah, the Sultan of Golkonda, granted a land of 50 Kuntas as 'Dasabandam Manya' in 1653 A.D. for the maintenance and repairs of the tank Peddavoorapati Cheruvu at Venubaka village according to the Venubaka Kaifiyat.[23]

Even during the Mughal period, this Dasavanda system was followed. An epigraph of 1696 A.D. from Gandikota (Cuddapah district) mentions the grant of one-sixth of the irrigated land as Dasavanda for the maintenance of Murneti Kaluva by Inatkhan Bittani, the Mughal Fouzdar who got it repaired. This epigraph clearly states that the 'Dasavandikas' or the holders of the Dasavanda Manyam lands under this irrigation work under an earlier period arrangement failed to repair it.[24]

In all the above cases, a part of the land brought under cultivation under the new irrigation work was given to the persons who undertook the work of construction or excavation under the Dasavanda or Dasabanda tenure. The granting of those lands was meant as a reward for the construction as well as the regular maintenance of the work in future.

Dasavanda for Revival and Repair

Not only for the construction of new irrigation works and their regular yearly maintenance, but also for revival and repair of old and ruined ones, the 'Dasavanda Manyam' lands were granted. This is indicated in a number of epigraphs. For example, it is stated in an inscription of 1691 A.D. that the bund of a certain Sanitank (Chittoor district) had breached at three places in that year and the farmers (Kampulu) who repaired the bund were granted $1/4^{th}$ of the land under that tank under Dasavanda tenure, remaining $3/4^{th}$ land under that tank being with the state from that year onwards.[25] A similar epigraph from the same area but dated 1692 A.D. state that the persons who repaired a breached tank, were to get half of the land as 'Dasavanda' under the tank and the remaining half to be retained by the government from that year onwards.[26]

These above two records belonging to consecutive years, hail from almost the same area. The nature and purpose of both are same. Probably the tanks were different. But the Dasavanda portion of the land given in the case of the first grant being only $1/4^{th}$ is far less than that of the second which is ½. The reason for the difference was probably due to the difference in the extent of the repairs work. But in both the cases, the persons who repaired the tank did it collectively by investing their money and also personal labour. There were a number of farmers involved in the work but not a single entrepreneur. These farmers who also undertook to cultivate the government land under those tanks repaired by them were to get $1/4^{th}$ of the produce as their share and ¾ of the yield being the government share. And, finally, the holders of these Dasabanda Manyam lands as it was the case with other service and charitable tenures, paied only quit rent or tax at a concessional rate as they are described as 'Sarvamanya' (tax-free).

Some times, a separate arrangement was made, besides for the repair, for removing the silt deposited in the tank bed to maintain its storing capacity. This is indicated in the epigraphs of Vijayanagara as well as the Asafjahi period indicating the prevalence of the system during the entire period under study. For example, an epigraph of Vijayanagara period dated 1548 A.D. from the village Kalchapadu (Cuddapah district) states that, along with the grant of land as 'Dasavanda Manyam' for repairing a ruined and breached tank, 'Pellettu Manyam" of 3 Tumus of land was granted to several persons by a certain Nayaka for the purpose of removing the silt from the tank-bed to increase its depth.[27] The "Gaddettu Manyam" tenure under which land was given for similar purpose mentioned in another epigraph dated 1788 A.D. from the village Majakur (Cuddapah district) also is same as "Pellettu Manyam" tenure.[28] Since a permanent provision was made for this purpose in both the cases, it appears that the work of removing the silt from the tank-bed was undertaken every year during the summer months when the tank was dry, and the silt removed was used to strengthen the earthen part of the tank-bund. It was also probably used for manuring the fields.

Kattu Kodage System

From Anantapur district we come across another tenure of land granted for the upkeep and repair of irrigation works. For example an epigraph of 1541 A.D. from Tirumadihalli village states that when the residents of that village repaired three breaches of the tank-bund of that village the Government granted them one 'Kattukodage' tenure for that purpose[29]. Similarly, the gift of land under 'Kattukodage' tenure to two persons Maliganda and Parusaganda for repairing the tank at Doddakatta village is referred to in an epigraph of 1551 A.D. from Halukur village[30]. The term 'Kattukodage' and its tenure, it appears, is of Kannada origin but it is almost same as 'Dasavanda' tenure. It's usage in Anantapur district area was probably due to its proximity to the Kannada area of the Vijayanagara empire and its influence.

Cheruvu Mera System

In many cases, the farmers cultivating the land under the tank were made responsible for its regular maintenance. Under this system they contributed a small portion of their produce under that irrigation work and spent it for the upkeep of the tank and the distribution – canals. This contribution is generally referred to as 'Cheruva Mera' and usually consisted of one 'Kuncham' (about 10 Kg.) on every 'Putti' measure (80 kunchams) of grain produced from the land irrigated by the tank to be maintained. Therefore it's provision is also referred to as 'Kuncha Mera'. We have much evidence for this type of arrangement. For example an epigraph of 1582 A.D. from a village of the Nellore district refers to this 'Kuncha Mera' collected on all the lands including those of government and 'Manyam' tenures under the tank for its maintenance[31].

Some times this 'Kuncha Mera' was collected from the produce of all the dry fields of the village for the maintenance of the village tank. This is indicated in an inscription of 1579 A.D. from Valluru village (Nellore district) which refers clearly to the levy of 'Kuncha Mera' on all kinds of grain raised in the dry fields within the four boundaries of that village[32].

Some times the 'Mera' grain was collected from the produce of both the dry lands of the village and the wetlands under the tank to be maintained. For example, an epigraph of 1638 A.D. mentions the collection of one 'Kuncha' for every 'Putti' of produce on all the lands under the tank and dry lands including the Manyam lands[33]. But an epigraph of 1678 A.D. from a village in Rapur Taluq, Nellore district refers to two different rates for the dry and wet lands. It mentions the collection of one 'Kuncha' for every 'Putti' on dry land and Tumu (4 Kunchams) for every 'Puti' on wetlands under the Potuganti tank for its maintenance[34].

The quantity of 'Mera' grain was raised when it was felt that the existing quantity was not sufficient for the maintenance of the work. This is referred to in an edict dated 1625 A.D. from Bhojapatiraju village (Nellore district). It states that the 'Meras' collected formerly for the maintenance of the local tank was at the rate of one 'Kuncha' per 'Putti' of all kinds of grain and it was raised from that year to two 'Kunchas'[35].

Irrespective of the nature of tenure to which the village belonged, this 'Cheruvu Mera' arrangement was the same. This is indicated in an epigraph of 1638 A.D. from Akupalle village (Nellore district). It records a request that the system of 'Cheruvu Meras' should be continued for the upkeep and repair of that village tank whether that village came under military tenure (Amaram) or that of a revenue farmer (Guttagani Vasana) in future[36]. And no body including the 'Manyam' holder, or Inamdars were exempted from this as is indicated from some of the above epigraphs.

At times, the Government remitted the revenue payable to it to help in the repair of the tanks. An epigraph from Ongole of the period under study states that the Government's share of the produce under a tank of that place should be utilized for the repairs and maintenance of the tank[37].

In some cases, the farmers whose lands were irrigated by a particular tank or a river channel were expected to contribute free labour service or work without receiving wages for the upkeep of that irrigation work. This is indicated in an epigraph of 1570 A.D. from a village in Nellore district, which records exemptions of temple lands from the bonded service of river-channel (Etikaluva Vetti)[38]. In some cases all the villagers were made responsible for the upkeep of the tank. An interesting epigraph dated 1602 A.D. from a village in Nellore district records this arrangement. According to it the villagers including the Vettimadigas (bonded) were to keep a constant vigil for the safety of the village tank particularly in rainy season when it was full[39].

For the maintenance and repair of the irrigation works during the period, the people of particular communities like Upparas (masons) and Vodderas (earth digger) appear to have been employed. An epigraph of Nellore district dated 1635-36 A.D. and issued under the orders of Velugoti Venkatapati Nayudu, a Vijayanagara Nayaka, states that the 'Meras' collected from all the fields of a particular tank should be entrusted by the cultivators, the headman and accountant of the village to the 'Upparas' for the repair of that tank[40].

The Vadderas (Vodde Boyeelu) getting some land as Manyam for the construction of tank is referred to in an inscription of 1788 A.D. from the village Majukur (Cuddapah district)[41]. Even under the Qutbshahi rule also these people appear to have been employed for the purpose[42]. As it is the practice even now these people appear to have specialised in digging, stone-cutting and masonary work during the period under study.

Finally, the responsibility to execute 'Mera' grants and to see that the tanks were properly maintained, was fixed on the persons who were in-charge of revenue collection in those villages. That include the 'Sandata' the 'Amaram' and the 'Gutta' officials (The meaning of the first is probably revenue officials but the second means – military tenure holder and the third revenue farmer) and also the village headman (Kapu) and accountant (Karnam). They were also warned not to covet and misappropriate the 'Mera' income. This is indicated in several epigraphs of Nellore district dated between 1635-36 A.D. and 1638-39 issued under the orders of the local Vijayanagara Nayaka Velugoti Venkatapati Nayudu[43].

It appears from the above records that, during this period in that area the irrigation works were neglected and agriculture was affected probably due to the misappropriation of 'Mera' income by the local officials. This was again the result of the unsettled political conditions in Vijayanagara Empire due to Civil Wars after the death of Venkata-II in 1614 A.D. The above mentioned Venkatapati Nayudu must have tried to revive those tanks to improve agriculture in his Nayankara territory. Some of the records of the earlier period also indicate how the tank 'Mera' system was discontinued in this area without giving any specific reason for it. An epigraph of 1582-83 A.D. from the village Vidavaluru (Nellore district) states that the old grant of 'Meras' at one 'Kuncha' per 'Putti' for the maintenance of the tank in that village has been discontinued. Therefore, Koneti China Timmanayudu, Nayaka of Udayagiri sima, again granted 'Meras' at the same rate on all the lands under the tank and also 100 'Kuntas' of land under that tank for the tank maintenance[44].

Thus, the importance of not only providing irrigation facilities but also of their proper maintenance and repair for the development of agriculture was very much realised in Andhra during the Vijayanagara period. It is found that sufficient care was taken for the upkeep of those works by undertaking annual repairs of tank-bunds, removal of silt deposits in the tank-beds, river channels and repairs of canals and sluices. Various measures were adopted for this purpose. First of all, at the time of construction of an irrigation work itself, a separate provision was made where some lands was granted under 'Dasavanda' or 'Kattu Kodage' tenure for its regular maintenance. Many a time, the cultivators themselves were made to contribute for its financing through a system called 'Cheruvu Mera' and some times they had to contribute free labour called 'Vetti' for this. Finally, the local revenue officials were made responsible for the implementation of those provisions for the upkeep of the works, while the people of stone-cutters/ masan communities were engaged for the actual work. These arrangements for the maintenance of irrigation works appear to have continued during the subsequent periods.

The system of Dasabandam Inams was followed even under Company. As late as 1834 we find the collector of Nellore district appreciating this system and suggesting its continuation to the Board of Revenue.

The Collector states that "the grant of Inams for constructing tanks etc is well calculated to meet the object in view and that one fourth of the land brought under cultivation is a sufficient inducement. But in cases where the construction etc. is attended with very great expense as by clearing jungles etc, the Collector may be at liberty to recommend ½ or 1/3 of land as Inam. In the event of the Dasabandam Inamdar being unable to make the requisite repairs to the tanks etc., it should be ascertained wether this results from his inability or negligence. If the former, one third of the produce should be allowed to him and the remainder taken to make good the advance made by the Circar for the repairs, provided that the outlay can be recovered in three years. If on the other hand, the person is unwilling to undertake the work, a small portion, say one fifth of the produce, should be allowed to him and the remainder attached for the first time of his failure and should be still found negligent, the collector should be authorized to take a such measure as may suit his case....".[45]

Famines

Till the improvements in the means of transport and communications by roads and railways rendered the transport of food grains in large quantities and for long distances feasible, the famines were a recurring phenomenon in Andhra Desa as it was the case with the other regions of India. A large number of famines occurred in this region not only during the period of study but also during earlier periods resulting in heavy loss of life, migrations and loss of revenue to the government. Regarding the famines that occurred during the pre-colonial period, not enough is known to enable us to make out a correct list of the years of the famines and the causes of their occurrence. the exact extent of the area affected by them and their intensity. Only some of the famines because of their severity are described in detail in the contemporary sources. Regarding the frequency of the famines during the Company's period it is truly said "The unfortunate ryot had hardly emerged from one famine before he is submerged under another.[46] This applies also to the period under consideration.

The famines of the period had been due to three causes viz. drought, war and excess rain and floods. The cause for the vast majority of the famines was drought which was the result of the failure of the customary rainfall and consequent failure of the food crops on which the subsistence of the population depended. Some of these famines were due to war. For example, Madras Presidency witnessed in 1781-82 a severe scarcity caused mainly by the devastation of the company's war with Hyder Ali of Mysore.[47]

Famines and scarcities of 1792 and 1800, in this region were due to excess rainfall and floods.[48] In July 1791, a tidal wave washed away many cattle and much of the produce in coastal and river villages of Guntur district. The tidal water which remained knee deep for weeks ruined the food grains stored in underground pits. (Pataras) leading to scarcity of food. Next year i.e. 1792, there was a severe drought in that area.[49] Similarly, a gale of wind accompanied with much rain on 20th October, 1800 had done great deal of damage to the Coastal villages of Bapatla, Cherkur, Motupally etc of Guntur district. Several villages have been swept away, tanks breached, crops and grain stocks destroyed many people and a large number of cattle perished.[50] In the serious floods canals and wells had been either destroyed or greatly damaged. Several villages with considerable number of their inhabitants with their properties have been swept away.[51] Cattle in thousands perished in the rain and many houses have been washed down.

Nature, Effects and Extent of Famines

The famines, whether long-term or short-term, were disastrous in their nature and resulted in the loss of life, migrations and loss of revenue to the government. We get more information about some of the famines because of their severity and long period effects on the region.

In 1629-30, during the reign of Mughal Emperor Shah Jahan, there was a severe drought that affected entire Deccan along with Guzarat. The consequent famine was so acute that starving people fed on cats and dogs and even on human flesh. Backers are said to have prepared bread with the floor adulterated with powerdered bones. There were instances of giving up their own children for bread by the hungry mothers. Many thousands of people migrated to the north-western provinces and almost the whole of Deccan was desolated.[52]

The Famine of 1685-86 is referred to in several village Kaifiyats from Chintapalli, Vinukonda, Sattenapalli and Repalle Parganas of Murtuzanagar Sarkar (Guntur district).[53] It appears that this famine was quite widespread and its effects long-lasting. It affected the worship in the local temples. In fact the Vangipuram Kaifiyat (Repalle Taluq and Guntur District) described it as twelve years famine.[54]

The Famine of 1792-93 that affected the Telengana region and particularly the districts of Mahboobnagar and Hyderabad along with Raichur and Gulbarga of Karnataka was very severe in its nature. Thousands of people are said to have perished in this area due to this famine. In Hyderabad city itself, 9000 people died. We are told that the affected area came to be dotted all around with human skulls to such an extent that the devastating famine was remembered for a long time as the "Doi Barra" or "Purrelakaruvu" (skull famine).[55] This 1792 famine was so severe in Guntur district area that a sixth of the poorer labouring people died of starvation there[56]. The settlement Report dated 19-12-1792 also states that the cultivation in the Nizampatam Circar was badly affected for want of inhabitants and cattle. The decrease in population during that year was very alarming 4874 people died and 5625 cattle perished.[57]

Rise of Prices

In times of drought, floods and scarcity, the prices of food grains rise of several times to their ordinary amount. If in ordinary years the prices of food grains of the common people was from 20 to 30 seers (equivalent of a kilo gram) per rupee, in times of great scarcity they rose to 8 or 10 seers per rupee. As there was no quick means of transporting of grains from one place to another during the period, it further aggravated the scarcity.

During the famine of 1792 which affected Hyderabad and Nagarkurnool district, Jowari was sold at the rate of two and half to three seers per rupee.[58] In 1800 cyclone in Coastal belt of the Guntur district, though there was Jowar (Jonnalu) available within three coss of Guntur town the people experienced a temporary scarcity in Guntur.[59] In consequence of the scanty supply of rice in Masulipatnam district, the prices have gone up so high as to cause a great distress.[60]

Epidemics

The seasons of severe scarcity were followed invariably by great epidemics because famine and pestilence were considered the twin off springs of the drought. While the drought withered the crops, the diminished water supply got polluted. The failure of the rains and the consequent abnormal conditions of temperature and humidity proved favourable to the spread of malignant diseases such as Cholera, small fax, dysentery and fever which also took a heavy toll of human lives.

Migration of people was another important consequence of the famines. The migrations affected the cultivation and other production activity.

Classes of People Affected

No doubt the frequent and severe famines directly affected the Ryots and also the government land revenue. But the classes of people that suffered most in these famines and who were in need of relief were the land-less labourers, smallest land holders, artisans, small traders, infirm persons and beggars and finally the dependants who could not support themselves or were incapable of labour.

The scarcity of food some times induced the poor-parents to get rid of their children owing to the impossibility of feeding them. The company government directed the collector of Masulipatam in 1791 to pay particular attention to the relief of children at public charge and convey them to places where they can be taken care of.[61]

Famine Relief

No information is available about the relief measures undertaken during the period of either Vijayanagara or Qutbshahi or Mughal rule. During the early decades of colonial rule when the position of the English East India Company was not so secure, the latter did not feel any sense of general obligation to extend relief to its subjects affected by famine. As a result, the company's government did not take the direct responsibility to give famine relief during that period. During the famine of 1782 in Northern Circars when the persons depending on public charity had increased, the company's government felt that it was expedient to distribute affected people among the various Zamindars in Chicacole Sarkar in particular where grains were very cheap. It proposed that the Zamindars might also be directed to make arrangements for their maintenance.[62] Once its position became stable and its administration improved, the Company's government began to feel a sense of obligation to give relief to its famine stricken subjects. These relief measures, though meager, compared to that given in contemporary England, mitigated, to some extent, the suffering of the local population.[63]

As early as 1790, we find the Madras Government undertaking famine relief measures when the distress of the poor inhabitants at Masulipatam was too alarming. The Collector of Masulipatam made arrangements in that year for the supply of foodgrains to the public of Masulipatam town and issued strict orders to the adjoining villages to spare the grain in excess of their own requirement and restricted the export of grain to other places.[64]

The Board of Revenue also directed the Masulipatam District Collector to search for the hoarded food grains and compel the owners to dispose of it among the inhabitants at reasonable prices.[65] There was a general tendency among the rich farmers and traders to hoard or conceal the food grains with the hope of getting a better price in future. The Revenue Board also directed that the surplus grain from Tanjor district should be exported only to the Northern Sarkars which were affected by famine.[66]

Some times the movement of food grains was hampered by the levying of customs duties at too many places in Zamindari territories affecting the famine relief work by the company's government. In 1791 the Collector of Masulipatam reported that hundreds of people were perishing daily by famine and all the attempted relief had failed as the Zamindars continued to levy heavy duties on all articles passing through their territories.[67]

During the early period, the government gave gratuitous relief by giving food to the affected people at those place where the immigrants assembled. Food was given in the relief camps which were opened for the poor people in need of food.

Agricultural Process and Crop Pattern

The process of agriculture during the period was same as it is today except the mechanization part of it. This statement applies to ploughing, manuring, sowing, transplanting, weeding, harvesting etc. The agricultural implements included plough (Nagali or Madaka) Weeder or grubber (Guntaka) seed drill (Gorru) hand-rake (Dante) Axe (Guddali) pick axe (Monaguddali) Sickle (Kodavali) pitch fork (Ragola) etc.[68] *Sukasaptati* a seventeenth century Telugu literary work, while describing the duwellings of the Peasants (Reddis) in the Rayalasima region mentions various agricultural implements such as 'Gorru', (an implement pulled by bullocks for leveling land before and after sowing) Gurugadi, Edikola (for puparing the field and Weeding) 'Kadi' (wooden pole for fastening bullocks to the plough) and 'Palugulu' (ropes for fastening bullocks to various implements) all of which were kept in their compound.[69]

Rotation of crops and raising mixed crops were known. The methods of agriculture followed in this part of India were in no way inferior to those followed in other parts of contemporary India and the globe. The day when Jowar seed-sowing commenced was also a festive occasion. *Sukasaptati* (a.2) mentions this as 'Vintati Panduga' and describes how the village priest fixed the auspicious day and time for that purpose and collected his fees from the farmers. Thomas Munro is said to have complemented the agricultural and industrial skills of the Indians in an enquiry conducted in British Parliament about India in 1813. He argued that the Indians were no way inferior to the Europeans in this respect.[70] He must have kept the Andhra Peasants on mind while making this statement, since he worked in Ceded districts. There were no fundamental changes either in the process of agriculture or the agricultural implements during the period. Andhra Desa was, as it still is, predominantly agricultural country and it is described by the contemporary European travelers as exceedingly rich country as far as its agricultural produce was concerned.

Crops

The abundance of food crops, specially in coastal Andhra districts, is attested to by the Anonymous Relations of Golkonda in the first quarter of the Seventeenth Century.

He also mentions that the surplus food grains from Coastal Andhra region were exported to Southern Coromandal and Malabar country. He reports thus.... "The Coastal Country for ten or twelve leagues in land abounds in provisions, the abudance increasing as one goes north, so that every year many Sampans, carrying rice, millet, pulse and other grain, butter and oil are dispatched from the whole Coast to Doraspatnam, Arianagom, Pulicot, Mylapur, Contany Connemont, Tegnampatam, Portonovo, Altegenampatam. The Portuguese used formerly to come for these provisions ... and carried much merchandise to Cochin.......".[71] As mentioned already, Tavernier the French traveller of second part of seventeenth century, States that the Golkonda kingdom was a very rich and fruitfull country abounding in corn, rice, cattle, sheep, fowls etc.[72] Methwold, the English traveler of first quarter of Seventeenth century also gives similar picture. He writes thus ... "the earth in some places affords two crops of rice in a yeere, rare three croppes, and in most places but one, yet there with very great increase; they sow other sort of Pulse, different from ours and fare up into the country they have good wheat, but not much, for it is little eaten by the Gentiles; roots they have of most sorts which have here and good store of Potatoes......"[73] It appears that large variety of crops were rised in this region during the period of study.

It appears that paddy was grown in abundance in many parts of this region and it was the principal crop. It was a crop grown under wet cultivation, under the tanks, canals and also under lift irrigation. It was staple food of the middle and upper classes. Where as Millet or corn called Jonna, (Jowar) and Sajja (Bajra) was the staple food of the lower middle class and poor people.

There are references to several varieties of paddy grown. Some of them were of long duration of 6 months crops and were of finer varieties and some of coarse variety and short duration crop. While a two or even three crops of paddy were raised, the millet and pulses were mainly grown as Karif crops.

Wheat was grown as Rabi crop. As wheat was consumed mostly by the Muslims, it was not produced in large quantities. Wheat of good quality was grown only in the interior[74] but not in coastal areas. It appears that the Hindus did not prefer wheat consumption and it was rare.

Potatoes mentioned by Methwold were probably some tubers of native variety but not those which now bear the name. Potatoes did not appear in this region by our time. We do not have evidence to the introduction of Maize (Makka Jonna) in this region by this time. This crop from the new world, was already introduced in Rajasthan and Maharastra even before 1620 A.D.[75] Among the various types of corn grown in the Gandikota area (Cuddapah district) the Gandikota Kaifiyat mentions Thota Jonna, Pachcha Jonna, Chitta Jonna and Yarra Jonna. The other cereals mentioned in this source include Chama, Ragi, Korra, Sajja (Bajra) and Arika.[76] These constituted the staple food of the poor. We do not know whether the Thota Jonna mentioned here was Makkajonna or Maize. Among the pulses grown in the region, the Guntur Kaifiyat mentions Bobbarlu, Anumulu, Vuluvalu (horse gram) Senagalu, Pesalu (Bengal gram green gram) and Minumulu (black gram).[77] Gandikota Kaifyat which includes all cereals and pulses, oil seeds and also cotton under the category of "Kaya danyamulu", also mentions other pulses like Kandulu (pulses) and Alasandalu.[78]

The spices grown in the Cuddapah district area include Jeelakarra (cummin seed) Pasupu (turmeric) Menthi (Fenugreek) Tellagaddalu (white onions) Omam (the seed of Bishop's weed or sisonammi) Daniya (coriander seeds)

Yarragaddalu (Red Onions), Bangi (?) Mirapakayalu, (Chillis) Tamalapakula (betal leaves) and also (Pogaku) Tobacco.[79]

It is interesting to note that 'Pachchimirapakayalu' or green chillis also mentioned above among the garden crops like fruits and vegitable,[80] was grown widely in the Cuddapah district area. We do not have evidence to indicate as to when exactly this crop whose origin is from the new world, was introduced here. Chillies are mentioned along with other agricultural produce in an epigraph dated 1516 A.D.[81] It appears that this was introduced here within a short period after the arrival of Portuguese on the West Coast of India. Thevenot of Seventeenth Century mentions chillis among the agricultural produce of the Golkonda kingdom.[82] Pepper called 'Miriyam'continued to be raised and used in this region even after the introduction of Chillis. A Kowl deed of first part of Seventeenth century from Cuddapah district mentions the raising of the crop of Pepper (Miriyam) in that area.[83] From this type of evidence, it is not possible to know the extent of pepper cultivation in the region and also the type of soils suitable for its cultivation.

Sesamum: or gingelly, important edible oil seeds and also a cash product was produced quite widely in Andhra Desa during this period. North Coastal Andhra produced this item on a large scale and Sesamum oil was an important item of export from this region. It was because of this reason that it's coast was known as Gingelly Coast. Oil seeds were one of the important agricultural produce in the Peddapur and Pitthapur Zamindaris and Rajahmundry Circar.[84] There is no evidence of groundnut cultivation which appears to have been introduced here much later.

Kusumalu:, another edible oil seeds grown under well irrigation as a garden crop is mentioned in the Guntur Kaifiyat.[85]

Similarly Castor seeds are also referred in some of the Kaifiyats.[86] Probably, this crop was also grown widely throughout the region and its oil was used for lighting lamps and also for greasing the wheels of the Bullock carts etc.

Mustard along with Sesamum and castor are mentioned in several contemporary sources.[87] But Mustard must not have been used as oil seed in this region as it is not popular source of edible oil here even now.

The Vegetables and fruits were produced as garden crops. Among the fruits grown were Arati (Plantain), Nimma (lime), Kittali (orange) Sitapandlu (custard apple), Panasa (Jack fruit).[88] and mango, myrobolam, elephant apple and tamarind.[89] The vegetables grown in this region included Kakara (bittar guard), Bendakayalu (ladies fingers) Potlakayalu (snake guard). Beerakayalu (vegetable sharp angled guard) Chikkudu (beans) Chamakura (leaf) Rajagiri (pulses) Pachchimirapa (green chillis) Vankayalu (Brinjals), Gummadi (Pumpkin) Sorakayalu) Bottle guard), Pendelam (a root) Mullangi (radish) and Dosakaya (Cucumber).[90]

Anonymous Relations of Golkonda adds to this list fruits like Pomegranates, Pine-apple, Jamoon (black cherri or Allaneradu) grapes and says that they were abundant in the entire region.[91]

Regarding the grapes, the Anonymous Relations states that in April great quantities of that fruit were brought from Golkonda to the low country (coastal districts) where they could not be grown owing to the brackishness and bitterness of the soil.[92]

Betel leaf was another cash crop grown and consumed in this region from very early period.[93] Circuit Committee Report refers to white betel leaf grown in Ellore (Godavari district) Haveli Parganas. It further informs that it was much priced and large quantities of it were sold to great profit at Hyderabad, where the cultivation of it was unknown before its introduction in recent times in the neighbourhood of Hyderabad.[94] Similarly, Betelnut was also grown in some of the coastal areas like Peddapur Zamindari (Godavari District).[95]

Chay root (Chiliveru in Telugu), another cash crop used as dye and much of which was produced in Masulipatnam and Guntur, Nizampatnam and Rajamundry Circars and Kondapally during the period. Digging for Chay root was an exclusive right of the government. The digging for Chay root was done under the supervision of the government revenue servants. Some of the Chay root was also produced by the peasants as a garden crop paying Bilmakta or fixed rent to the government. Wild Chay root or that which was grown in jungles was the most esteemed. The Chay root produced in Nizampatnam also was in great demand for its strong beautiful dye.[96]

Indigo (Neeli in Telugu), an important raw material for dying industry, and so a cash crop was produced widely both in the coastal region and also in the interior. Anonymos Relations of Golkonda States that most of the indigo was produced in the villages around Kondapalli, Masulipatnam, Nagulavancha (Khammam district) Sandrapatla, Game, Golpudy and Ecour (Ellore).[97] The Dutch Shorer also confirms this. He says that plenty of best indigo comparable in quality to that of Lahore indiga was produced in this area and particularly at a place called Nagalwensa (same as above).[98] Tavernier states that Golkonda kingdom was one of the producers of the best variety indigo sold in the form of cake.[99] Thevenot saw many indigo gardens on his way from Hyderabad to Kollur in Guntur district.[100] Indigo was raised as a dry crop mostly in red and sandy soils in Punasa or rainy season sowing in June. It was harvested only once. Sometimes, it was grown with irrigation and sown in October and its leaves were harvested several times in an year.

Tobacco an important cash crop introduced in India by the Portuguese at the beginning of the sixteenth century, was grown considerably in this part of the country during the period of study. It appears to have spread very rapidly. Irfan Habib rightly describes the introduction and rapid extension of the cultivation of tobacco as a notable feature of the agricultural history of the seventeenth century.[101] It's consumption became so widespread and popular with the rich as well as poor in India that Aurangzeb had to forbid its cultivation.[102] And it appears that the peasants of Andhra Desa, as in other parts of Mughal India, took to the tobacco cultivation with enthusiasm and it was grown for export as well as for local consumption.

Regarding the export potential of tobacco of this region, Methwold relates thus .... "They have within few years planted store of tobacco, and much of it is exported to Mocha, Arrecan and not a little drunke (smooked) amongst themselves....". About its quality, he further describes thus... "It is but weak, yet sure more care in curing and making it up would help that fault; they only dry the leaves in the sun, and use it so, with out further sophistication.....".[103]

The commercial value of tobacco is indicated by the high rates of taxes imposed on its crop. According to an epigraph of the first part of Seventeenth century from Cuddapah district, for cultivating tobacco in the garden land brought under well irrigation, the cultivator had to pay 4 Rukas first year, 8 Rukas second year, 12 Rukas third year and 16 Rukas on each kunta of land fourth year onwards.[104] These rates were much higher than those obtaining in the case of other food crops which ranged between a quarter Ruka to 3 Rukas per kunta under graded taxation system. This was definitely due to the high commercial value of tobacco. This is further confirmed by Tavernier who states that when a stranger came at the gates of Golkonda fort, the police searched him carefully to see if he had any tobacco or salt because they yielded principal revenue to the king.[105] Regarding the popularity of its consumption, Tavernier noticed even women providing tobacco, besides, food to the needy travellers on the public roads in this region in the later half of the Seventeenth century.[106] Similarly, it is reported in the *Circuit Committee Report* (p.80.) that Tobacco was cultivated in the Haveli parganas of Masulipatnam and the tobacco snuff of Bandamurulanka and Masulipatnam were in great repute. This report mentions tobacco among the principal agricultural products of Peddapur and Pitthapur Zamindaries and Rajamundry Circar (pp.95, 97 & 108.) These evidences indicate the widespread cultivation of tobacco in Coastal Andhra and Rayala Sima districts. Gandikota Kaifiyat mentions Tobacco as one of the crops grown in that place.[107]

Cotton, another cash crop was grown on a large scale in this region. It was grown almost in every village. Sugarcane was grown wherever the soil was suitable and water was available. These crops are mentioned in many contemporary sources. It was estimated that the quantity of cotton grown in the year 1806 was between 2,17,700 and 2,27,570 maunds in Cuddapah district alone. The total extent of land under Cotton cultivation throughout the Ceded districts was 163, 258 acres.[108]

Cotton

Towards the end of the Eighteenth Century, the English East India Company government appears to have encouraged the cotton cultivation in Andhra. Probably the government realised that the non-availability of sufficient cotton would result in rise of prices of textiles which the company had to procure for export. The resolution of Board of Revenue of

1795 was intimated to the Ryots of every description in the Fourth Division of Masulipatam Circar that every reasonable encouragement would be afforded to all such Ryots who were willing to extend Cotton cultivation. Advances to Cotton Ryots were also provided.[109] The Board of Revenue calls upon the Collectors in a letter dated 17-6-1795 to send a report regarding the best means of encouraging the Cotton cultivation.[110]The Revenue Board's letter dated 27-7-1795 approving the proposals of collectors to give out advances for cultivating Cotton was widely published. All those who apply for advances were required to furnish security.[111]

In the letter from Commercial resident, Vizagapatam dated 26-6-1796 written to government and copy of which was sent to collectors, it is stated that the growth of cotton had diminished beyond all expectations in Vizagapatam District and Banjaras brought cotton only from other districts. This letter pleads that the concerned officers should explain to the Ryots about the advantages of raising cotton crop. They were to be told that cotton would yield Rs.25 against Rs.18 yielded by other crops on dry land. It required very little attention and care when once sown, was less dependant on rain and less subject to the depredations of animals. Once planted cotton plants could yield cotton for several years without additional labour. The Commercial Resident was infavour of introducing Maritious Cotton and wanted the government to grant cowls to cotton Ryots for longer period which would be advantageous to Ryots.[112]

Podu Cultivation

Besides the regular cultivation another method of cultivation in vogue in this region was Podu, the method of cultivating lands in the hilly jungle tracts by the tribals. An interesting account regarding this method of cultivation is furnished by Godavari District Gazetteer thus... "... The Koyas in the

Agency carry on shifting cultivation called podu by burning and clearings in the forests.... Two methods prevail; the ordinary (or calaka) Podu and the hill (or Konda) Podu. The former consists in cultivating certain recognized clearings for a year or two at a time allowing the forest to grow again for a few years, and then again burning and cultivating them; while under the latter, the clearing is not returned to for a much longer period and is some times deserted for ever. The latter is fashion in the more hilly and wilder parts, while the former is a step towards civilization. Regarding the process of cultivation and crops, it is further recorded thus... "In February or March, the jungle trees and bushes are cut down and spread evenly over the portions to be cultivated, and when the hot weather comes on, they are burnt, the ashes serve as manure and the cultivators also think that the mere heat of the burning makes the ground productive. The land is ploughed once or twice in Calaka podu before and after sowing, but not at all in Kondapodu. The seed is sown in June in the Margasira Karte, Hill Colam and Sama are the commonest crops. The former is dibbled into the ground".[114] Similar account is given in the Vizagapatam district Gazetteer.[115] In view of this it may be assumed that some of tribals like Chenchus, Gonds etc living in the forest and hilly tracts of Rayalasima and Telangana sub-regions also followed this method of cultivation during this period. The forest tribes must have been following this method for the past many centuries.

AGRICULTURAL COMMUNITIES

Peasants and Labour

Agriculture was carried on by peasants living in villages. While the entire village community was based on the agriculture, was associated with it either directly or indirectly and depended on it for subsistence, it was the peasants and the agriculture labour who were directly involved in its process. While the peasants were the holders of the land and cultivation was based on individual peasant farming, the labourers did the work in the field either on monthly or daily wages. The peasants in this part of the country are referred to as 'Krishivalulu' but more commonly as 'Kampulu' or 'Kapulu'.[116] The Peasants are referred to during the Mughal and Asafjahi period as in north India as 'Riaya' or 'Raiyat'[117] and "Combee" (Kapu).[118]

Two Classes of Cultivators

There were two distinct classes of cultivators in Andhra Desa of the period. They were the resident cultivators and the outside cultivators. In Nellore district, these two classes were the 'Kadims' and the 'Payakaries', respectively. The term Kadim means ancient or old, therefore the Kadim was resident Ryot having no property in the land. His counterpart in Mughal north India was known as 'Khudkhast' (which means sower on his own account and Vatandari peasant in Western Deccan.[119] He was the fixed inhabitant of the village where he had lands. The Payakaries (the term Payakari is a Persian word means a sower on account of another) were the outside cultivators. His counterpart in Tamil country was 'Parakudi' and was called 'Upari' in contemporary western Deccan. The Upari were the Peasants who were employed by the village community without being bestowed any Vatan of the village. As village tenants, they cultivated the lands which lapsed to possession of the village community by reason of dying out or wandering away of the original owners.[120]

The Kadim Ryots, were the hereditary and permanent farmers of their villages and could not be ousted as long as they paid the government dues. But they had no proprietary right on the land and could not sell it. They were responsible for cultivation, and it was with them that the government made the revenue settlement. Any advantage resulting there from accrued to them as a right and they were liable for the whole assessment. The Payakari Ryots on the other hand, cultivated the lands under the Kadims with whom they made agreements and from whom they received their share of the crop. The Kadim Ryots did not get any 'Swamybhogam' or 'Tonduvaram' as enjoyed by the Mirasidars who got it as landlords' share. The share of the Kadim cultivator also was less favourable and was less than that of the Payakaris. While the Kadims received 6, 7 or 8 shares in 20, the Payakaris 9 to 10 shares. The average share of the Kadims was 36.75 percent of the produce, that of the Payakaris 42.5 percent. The latter, thus, got a favourable treatment like the Muslims, Brahmins and cultivators belonging to the ruling communities like Kshatriyas and Velamas who got50 per cent share.[121] In the North Coastal Andhra, north of Godavari river, Rajputs, Velamas and Cultivators from other parts (same as Payakaris) who took over land which the inhabitants of any village were unable to cultivate themselves, were allowed a half share of the crop, but the ordinary, resident Ryot only received a third of the produce.[122] And in the Haveli territories, one third was allowed to the fixed inhabitants (same as Kadim) and two-fifths to strangers (outside cultivators).[123]

The reason for the Payakaris getting more shares was due to the disadvantageous place he was placed in as non-resident cultivator. In obtaining manure, labour, implements etc from outside he had the disadvantage of incurring additional expenditure and labour. The Kadim Ryots were under the necessity of employing the Payakaris because of their responsibility to the government to keep up the cultivation in the village, and also because of their limited means to cultivate the entire land themselves. This was also inspite of the fact that they were receiving less share compared to that of the Payakaris. In Andhradesa, during this period considerable land appears to have been under the cultivation of the Payakaris. In 1801 one-sixth of the land in Nellore district was cultivated by the Payakaris, while two-thirds of the cultivation was carried by the Kadims.[124] The term 'Sukavasi' met with in some of the epigraphs also stands for there payakari Ryots.

The exact cast-composition of these two classes of cultivators is difficult to indicate. The bulk of the peasant land holders of this period belonged to the Sudra communities like the Reddy, Kammas, Balija, Velama, Telika, Boya etc and also Kshatriya, Brahmin castes. But the bulk of the agricultural communities of the period – Peasants or labourers, belonged to the fourth caste i.e. the Sudras and also the Panchamas – Malas and Madigas.

The Brahmins were precluded from taking to agriculture by the Dharma Sastras. The Brahmins in the Agraharas do not appear to have themselves taken up cultivation of their lands. They were cultivated by the Kapus who lived in the hamlets called 'Pundis' or 'Gramagrasapu Pallelu' attached to the main Agraharas. But there are instances to show that some of the Brahmins took to agriculture during the period. *Sukasaptati* describing the residences of some rich Brahmin landlords mentions the groves, crops, stores of grain, cattle sheds sugar cane mills, cattle etc. owned by them.[125]

The Sudras belonging to the lower strata like the Gollas (shepherds), Tenugu or Boya (shepherds), toddy-tappers etc. and the untouchables like Malas and Madigas formed the bulk of the agricultural labour. They might have some times worked as agricultural labour on part-time and seasonal basis, besides attending to their own caste professions and some times as full time employees on year-wise basis with monthly wages. And the bulk of this labour was undoubtedly supplied by the untouchables. Irfan Habib has rightly pointed out that "the existence of 'untouchables' was thus a pillar of Indian peasant agriculture from very early times, ever since, that is the food gatherers and the forest folk were humbled and subjugated by settled agricultural communities. It would not, indeed, be surprising if the actual status of many of them in Mughal India too was semi-servile, implying some kind of bondage, including the obligation to render forced labour (begar) to Zamindars and upper caste peasants".[126] This description can be aptly be applied to these communities not only of the period of study in Andhra Desa but to the period till we got our independence for the country.

Live Stock

Cattle rearing and dairy farming was an important occupation allied to agriculture during the period. Though much information is not available on this aspect of agrarian system, some picture of it can be formed from the scanty information available. It is probable that the kings, nobles and the rich people had maintained large cattle heards for their own use-cows and she-bufalloes to cater to their dairy needs and also for a regular supply of bulls for ploughing and weeding their fields, for water lifting, for transport of their produce home and also to the market. The frequent mention of plough and the water lifts like Mota and Ratnamu naturally leads one to infer that abundant livestock was available in the area.[127] This inference gets confirmed to some extent, by the European eye witnesses accounts. Coromandal is mentioned as one of the cattle-breeding places including those of sheep and goats of south India, by Paes, Nuniz, Verthema and Barbosa.[128] The Anonymous Relation of Golkonda States "... innumerable quantities of tame animals, oxen, cows, buffaloes, sheep, goats of three kinds...... but they give nothing like so much milk as those of our country. All the horses of the country are of small size, but they are better for traveling than large horses, because here large horses may not be ridden but they are imported from Petane. Horses from Arabia or Ormuz are very highly esteemed".[129]

The imprecatory passages in the earlier and contemporary period epigraphs indicate the sin and the religious merit attached to the killing and protecting, respectively, of the cows besides that of violating and protecting land grants. One of them says "He who imposes taxes on lands free from tax incurs sin of killing 1000 cows but who removes taxes on them obtains the merit of protecting crores of cows".[130]

The temples of the time might have maintained their own dairy in which, the cows, sheep and she-buffaloes donated by the devotees were kept in the custody of the shepherds referred to as 'kilari' and 'Boyas'.[131] Besides ensuring a perpetual supply of the dairy products to the temples, the male calves and bulls appear to have been used for transporting temple goods and ploughging temple lands.[132]

Reference to 'Gobumi', 'Gocaram'[133] and 'Gramopakantam'[134] meaning[135] grazing grounds; and 'Pasuvula Pullari'[136] and 'Sulavari' (both meaning, grazing tax in several stone records and also to 'Bandelu' meaning fines collected on stray cattle for destroying crops, indicate that in every village there were government waste lands (Banjarabhumi) for grazing cattle and in some cases government forest land for grazing cattle. The government collected grazing tax and also collected fine on stray cattle if they destroyed the crops etc. Rich farmers might have maintained their own grazing lands. The farmers appear to have had their cattle sheds situated in their back-yards. Sukasaptati refers to these sheds and also cattle, the bullocks, cows, sheep etc. in the compounds of the Brahmin and Reddi cultivators of Rayalasima region. This work also refers to the cattle-feed like hay, straw of millet and Jute stored in heaps in the backyards of the farmers.[137] It was estimated, on the basis of Survey (1802-1807) in Ceded districts that the total number of cattle (all categories) was 16,92,519, sheep was 1,147,492 and goats 694,533.[138] This gives some idea of the cattle wealth of the region.

Peasants in South Coastal Andhra region maintained a very good breed of cattle-cows and bullocks. Towards the end of the eighteenth century some of them appear to have preferred cattle breeding due to excessive land revenue, instead of cultivation. This region particularly the present Prakasam district, even now famous for Ongole breed of cattle, had during this period of study, this variety. Enugula Veeraswamy writing in 1830 about this region in his *Kasiyatracharitra*, refers to this breed. He writes that the cattle beyond Krishna river was healthy and robust. He saw big herds of such healthy cattle grazing in the fields here. He writes "…. I have never seen so far during my wide travel from Kanyakumari onwards such bulky and tall animals. Kapus of this place will not care even for their cultivation before their service to these cattle. They grow grass on medows, pay a tax at the fixed rate for waste land and feed their cattle and thus they keep them in fine condition. Cattle wealth is common in these parts…".[139] Thus Veeraswami is referring to the Ongole breed of cattle, which the peasants preferred to raise in preference to cultivation.

The famous tall and short horned cattle of Ongole were wide-spread in Prakasam, Nellore, Guntur district areas. The Ryots of Nellore appears to have found cattle rearing more profitable than cultivation. Mr. Travers, the first Collector of the Nellore District attributed the importance attached to cattle-breading to the insecurity of cultivators rights during the pre-British period in this area. He says, in his settlement Report for the year 1801-02: "Having been repeatedly deprived of their cultivation when brought to maturity, experience pointed out to the inhabitants of these districts the want of security for the fruits of their labour. As a substitute affording them this advantage, their attention and labour have been given to the rearing of large herds of black cattle of a superior breed much in demand which they secured from the grasp of the renters by moving from their villages to those neighbouring…"..[140]

Even the cows of this breed were known for their milk-yield. This cattle found good market even outside this region. Rich peasants maintained their own pasture lands and for grazing in the government lands, grazing tax called 'pullari' was paid.

Finally, it is not possible to estimate as to how much of the cattle manure was utilized for cultivation during the period. It is quite likely that some of it was left in the grazing lands and some used as fuel leaving only a part of it to be used as manure. It is also quite possible that the method of manuring with the help of flocking of sheep and goats was also widespread.

Notes & References

1. *Tavernier*, Vol. II, p. 121.
2. *Cuddapah Inscriptions*, pp.1-13, 1014; For similar information also see *Ibid*, pp. 1015, 1016 & 1017.
3. *Cuddapah Inscriptions*, p. 1915.
4. *Ibid.*, pp. 1016 & 1071.
5. *Ibid.*, p. 1019
6. *Ibid.*
7. *Ibid.*, p. 865.
8. *SII* .XVI, No. 333, p. 338.
9. *SII*, X, no. 770, p. 404.

10. SII X no.753.
11. N. Venkataramanayya, *Cuddapah Inscriptions*, p.103.
12. *Mack Mss*. Book No. 17, Vol.100, p.330-32.
13. *Cuddapah Manual*, p.113.
14. *Ibid*., p. 12.
15. *Cuddapah Manual*, p. 12.
16. These tanks are still extant.
17. *Inscriptions of A.P. Nalgonda District*, II, Hyderabad, 1994, II, no.36. hereafter IAP.
18. *Inscriptions of A.P. Nalgonda District*, II, Hyderabad, 1994, No. 84 and 82.
19. *Inscriptions of A.P. Cuddapah District* III, no 208.
20. *Annual Report on South Indian Epigraphy for the year 1938*, nos 224, 225, p. 230.
21. Venkataramanayya, N., *Cuddapah Inscriptions*, pp.356-357.
22. I. A. P. Nalgonda District II, Hyderabad, 1994, no.84, and 82.
23. *Mack. Mss*., Vol. 103, p. 192-93.
24. *I.A.P. Cuddapah District*, III, no. 208.
25. *SII*, Vol.X, p. 769.
26. *Ibid*., p. 771.
27. *Cuddapah Inscriptions*, p. 374.
28. *Ibid*., p. 248.
29. *Annual Report, Anantapur District*, 49 of 1917.
30. *South Indian Inscriptions*, Vol.IX, Part No.643, p. 640.
31. *A Collection of Inscriptions or Copper Plates and Stone in the Nellore District, Nellore*, 124.
32. *Inscriptions of Nellore District* (I.N.D.) Part-I, No.109, pp.449-450.
33. *Ibid*., III Part No.28, pp. 1240-41.
34. *Ibid*., III Part No.54, p. 1278.
35. *Ibid*., III, No.6, pp.763-764.
36. *Ibid*., Rapur, 3.
37. *N.I*., Ongole, 79.

38. *Ibid.*, Nellore, 105.
39. *Ibid.*, Kandukuru, 48.
40. *Inscriptions of Nellore District*, II, p.820.
41. *Cuddapah Inscriptions*, p.248.
42. Sec.(a) *Inscriptions of Nellore District*, pp.569-570 (b) *N.I. Kandukur*, 48.
43. *Ibid.*, II, pp747, 757, 711, 788 and 820; *Ibid.*, III, pp.120, 1215, 1240, 1242, 1247, 1261, 1262, 1274, 1276, 1277 and 1278.
44. *Inscriptions of Nellore District*, II, 892 and 893.
45. *Guide to the Records of the Nellore District* 1801-1835, Vol.323, p. 239.
46. Moulvie Mahdi, *Replies to Questions contained in Chapter I of the Memorundum of the Famine Commission*, Bombay, 1879, p.6; hereafter Moulvi Mahdi; *Report of the Indian Famine Commission Part I Famine Relief*, London, 1880, p.9; Suravaram Pratapa Reddy, *Andhrula Sanghika Charitra*, p.415; hereafter Pratapa Reddy, S.; *Anantapur District Gazetteer* 1905, pp.100-121.
47. *Ibid*.
48. *Ibid*; *Guide to District Records Masulipatam District*, Vol.III, pp. 272-274.
49. *Elliot Report*, Para 10.
50. *Index Volume to District Record Masulipatam District*, Vol.III, pp. 272-274.
51. *Ananthapur District Gazetteer*, 1905, p.120.
52. *Moulvi Mahdi Ali*, p. 7.
53. *Grama Kaifiyattulu, Guntur Taluka*, I, p.21, 38 & 74; Ibid, III, p. 67.
54. *Ibid.*, I, p. 74.
55. *Moulvi Mahdi Ali*, p.8; *S. Prataparedddi*, p. 415.
56. Gordon Mackenzie., *Manual of the Krishna District*, 1833, Madras, p. 113.
57. *Index Volume to District Records of Masulipatam*, Vol.III, p.108.
58. *Moulvi Mahdi Ali*, p. 8.
59. *Guide to District Records Masulipatam District* Vol.III, p. 274.

60. *Ibid.*, p. 442.
61. *Guide to District Records Masulipatam District*, p. 341.
62. *Guide to District Records Masulipatam District*, p. 173.
63. *Reports of the Famine Commission*, Part-I, p. 27.
64. *Guide to District Records Masulipatam District*, p. 352.
65. *Ibid.*, p. 341.
66. *Ibid.*
67. *Ibid.*, II, p. 99.
68. *Kurnool Manual*, pp. 212-213.
69. *Sukasaptati*, 2, p. 416.
70. S. Pratapa Reddi, *Andhrula Sanghika Charitra*, pp. 390-91.
71. *Relations of Golkonda*, pp. 68-69.
72. *Tavernier*, p. 121.
73. *Relations of Golkonda*, p. 8.
74. Schorer, the Dutch Relations also states that good wheat was produced in interior but was sold at Masulipatam (*Relations of Golkonda*), p. 63.
75. Irfan Habib., *Agrarian System of Mughal India 1556-1707*, pp.42-43.
76. *Cuddapah Inscriptions*, p. 138.
77. *Grama Kaifiyattulu*, Guntur Taluka, II, p. 72.
78. *Cuddapah Inscriptions*, p.138, 1019 & 1012.
79. *Ibid.*
80. *Ibid.*, p. 105.
81. *Mack. Mss*, vol. 106, pp. 199-200.
82. *Thevenot*, p. 144.
83. *Cuddapah Inscriptions*, p. 847.
84. *Circuit Committee Report*, p. 95, 97, 108.
85. *Grama Kafiyattulu*, Guntur Taluka II, p. 72.
86. *Ibid.*
87. *Epigraphia Indica*, V, 27, 55, 56; *Mack. Mss.*, 26, pp. 117 and 118.
88. *Gandikota Kaifiyat, Cuddapah Inscriptions*, p. 105.

89. *Chennur Kaifiyat, Mac. Mss.* 140, p. 98; *TTDE* II, No. 97.
90. *Gandikota Kaifiyat, Cuddapah Inscriptions*, p. 105.
91. *Relations of Golkonda*, p. 85.
92. *Ibid*.
93. There is a mention of Akuthotavaru or the persons who grew betel in the temple service as early as 1319 A.D. (*SII* X,), p. 528.
94. *Circuit Committee Report*, p. 52.
95. *Ibid*., p. 95 & 108.
96. *Circuit Committee Report*, pp. 61_62 and 80.
97. *Relations of Golkonda*., p. 79.
98. *Relations of Golkonda*., p. 61.
99. *Tavernier*, (ii) p. 17.
100. *Thevenot*, p. 145.
101. Iraf Habib, *The Agrarian system of Mughal India*, p. 50.
102. *Ibid*.
103. *Relations of Golkonda*, p. 36.
104. *Cuddapah Inscriptions*, p. 1019.
105. *Tavernier*, p. 125.
106. *Tavernier*, p. 225.
107. *Cuddapah Inscriptions*, p. 138.
108. *Cuddapah Manual*, p. 257.
109. D.C.R., 2991, p. 130.
110. D.C.R., 2991, p. 28.
111. D.C.R., 2991, p. 129-30.
112. D.C.R. 962, pp.315-327; Guide to the Records of Guntur District 1795-1835, p. 14.
114. *District Gazetteer - Godavari*, I, Ch. IV, pp. 78-79.
115. *District Gazetteer – Vizagapatam*-I, pp. 111 & 103.
116. *SII*, X, p. 769.
117. Irfan Habib, *The Agrarian System of Mughal India 1556-1707*, p. 137.
118. Hyderabad Affairs-I, pp. 461-463.

119. *Ibid*.
120. Hiroyuki Kotani, *Western India in Historical Transition*, 2002, Manohar Publishers, p. 2.
121. We find similar favourable treatment given to the Payakaris compared to Kadims also in the salt production during this period. For this see *Nellore District Manual*, p. 488.
122. W. Francis *Vizagapatam District Gazetteer*, p. 170.
123. *Ibid*., p.166; also see the epigraph of 1577 A.D. (*SII* X No.748) for the favourable treatment shown to Muslim and Brahmins etc.
124. *Nellore Manual*, pp. 477-478.
125. *Sukasaptati*, 2, 145.
126. Irfan Habib, *The Agrarian System of Mughal India, 1556-1707*, Second Edition, pp.143-144.
127. *Godavari Manual*, p. 509.
128. *Forgotten Empire*, *op.cit*., p.386; Varthema, *Travells*, pp.114 and 122; Barbosa, I, pp. 166 and 200.
129. *Relations of Golkonda*, p. 86.
130. Iswara Dutt, *Inscriptional Glossary*, Introduction, p. xxviii.
131. *SII*, VI, no.70 and 760.
132. *SII*, XVI, no.227; *TTDE* V. no.154.
133. *SII*, VI, 814; *Ibid*., V, 1157; Cuddapah Inscriptions, p. 679.
134. K. Iswaradutt, *Inscriptional Glossary*, p. 101.
135. *SII*, X no.509; *AR*, 1926, B.no.38; *Ibid*, 1943, B. no. 131.
136. *Krishna District Manual*, p. 357.
137. Quoted from S. Pratapareddy, *Andhrula Sanghika Charitra*, pp. 305-308.
138. *Appendix to Fifth Report*, pp. 271-272.
139. Eenagula Veeraswamy., *Kasiyatracharitra*, p. 223.
140. Proceedings of the Board, 15th July, 1802, Travers Settlement Report for Fasli 1212.

CHAPTER – V

SUMMARY AND CONCLUSIONS

It is an accepted fact that the economic backwardness of independent India was a consequence of colonial rule of the British for nearly two centuries. It was its agricultural economy that was most acutely affected by the colonial rule. Andhra Pradesh, the Telugu linguistic region of Independent India is no exception to this phenomena. The agrarian exploitation and the consequent crisis of the colonial period however is more truly the vestige of the agrarian system prevalent in this region during the pre-colonial period. The roots to the malady of the Colonial period are, thus, to be traced to the pre-colonial agrarian system. The British and their subordinate Asafjahi rulers mostly borrowed it from the earlier rulers and made it more oppressive because of their colonial demands. Therefore, a thorough probe into the agrarian system of Andhra Desa during the crucial period of two centuries preceding the colonial rule (A.D.1600-1800) is attempted in the present study. This study is essential for understanding the economic history of the region and also for a proper understanding of the nature of colonial exploitation in its proper perspective.

Pre-colonial Andhra Desa, like other parts of India was predominantly an agricultural region where the agriculture provided livelihood, either directly or indirectly, to an immense majority of its people. The period of Seventeenth and Eighteenth centuries, A.D. constitutes an important epoch in the history of Andhra Desa. It witnessed enormously varied and complex agrarian situation different in many respects from that of the preceding and succeeding periods. This situation was mainly due to the political instability and confusion that prevailed under the rule of miscellany of political powers-Vijayanagara, Qutbshahi, Mughal, Mysore, Asafjahi, French and English.

The changes at the national level and global changes like the extension of Mughal rule over the region, emergence of the European Companies on the Indian horizon, establishment of direct trade with Europe and other parts of globe and the consequent growth of the agro-based industries such as textiles etc. all had their impact on the agrarian life of the region. They left a major imprint on many of its basic aspects such as the land tenures, land revenue system, agricultural development, crop pattern etc.

The agrarian relations of the pre-colonial India have drawn the attention of scholars like W.H. Moreland and Irfan Habib who have indicated in their studies, the complex nature of land tenures, revenue assessment and collection, agrarian oppression, the dominance of certain classes of people as intermediaries and their control over agricultural resources. They paved way for undertaking the systematic agrarian studies at the micro-regional level. In fact, there are a few writings of this type. The works of Burton Stein and Noboru Karashima, though fascinating and penetrating studies on these aspects are confined to the Tamil region of South Indian during the Chola and Vijayanagara period only. The interesting studies by J.F.Richards and Jaya Sree are confined to Mughal and Vijayanagara periods respectively. Similarly the works of M.P.R Reddy and A. Satyanarayana are confined to Andhra region under Madras

Presidency during the Colonial period. Thus, there is no thorough and comprehensive work on the agrarian system of pre-colonial Andhra Desa of those two centuries, i.e. Seventeenth and Eighteenth covering all its aspects. Andhra Desa denotes all the three sub-regions of modern Andhra Pradesh, namely Telangan, Coastal Andhra and Rayalasima.

During the period of two centuries under study whatever be the governments whether Hindu, Muslim or Christian the land tenures in this region have been studied under two main categories (1) Government or crown villages (2) and villages and lands alienated to others for some purpose.

The first category i.e. the government of crown villages/ lands were held and managed by the government. Their revenue went to defray the costs of building ad maintaining strategic fortresses and garrisons under royal control. The number of villages belonging to this category was very small compared to the second category. These villages were referred to as Bhandarawada Gramas or Simahasananikichella Gramalu under Vijayanagara, Haveli under Qutbshahi, Khalisa under the Mughals and Diwani under Asafjahis. In 1690 A.D., out of the total 87 Khalisa Parganas, 53 were in Telangana and 34 in Coastal Andhra and all of them yielding revenue of Rs.64, 41,217. And because of proximity to the capital city Hyderabad the concentration of Haveli Parganas in Telangana was more. The term Haveli of the Qutbshahi period became more popular comared to that the Mughal-Khalisa. It was still in use in the English Company's records when the northern Sarkars came under them.

The second of the main categories of land tenures i.e. the villages ad lands alienated to others admits again two-fold classification based on the purpose of alienation (a) Service tenures (b) and beneficiary or charitable tenures. The service tenures again consisted of military and civil service tenures.

The military service tenures were held by the Amaranayakas under Vijayanagara and Qutbshahis, Muqasa under Qutbshahis, Chieftains/Zamindars/ Mansabdars under Mughals and Surfkhas and Paiga Jagirdars under Asafjahis. The number of villages held by each of them depended on his importance, the number of troops maintained by him and the amount of tribute paid by him. The military tenures except those of Mughal Mansabdars/ Jagirdars were held on hereditary basis. The military Chieftains/Zamindars of Coastal Andhra and Telangana and also the Polegars of Rayalasima were of different origins. Amaram, Muqasa and Kattubadi soldiers also belonged to this category. Similarly the Mannewar and Kavalgars performing police duties also were military service tenure holders. Throughout the period under the study, nearlty three fourths of the agricultural resources were under the control of the military tenure holders. While majority of them were Hindus belonging to the communities like Velama, Reddi, Kamma, Balija, Boya, Golla etc. during the Vijayanagara period some of them were replaced by Muslims during the Qutbshahi, Mughal and Asafjahi periods. These military tenure holders were not subject to the detailed assessment of land revenue actually under cultivation. Their Peshkash/ tribute was fixed on ad-hoc basis through negotiations between them and the suzerain power. Only the Mughal Manansabdars holding Jagirs did not pay any tribute.

The Civil Service tenures were held by all the hereditary revenue officials from the district level to that of village. They included Sardeshmukh, Sardeshpandia at Sarkar/district level; Chaudari/Deshmukh and Deshpandia/ Sthalakarnam/Majumdar at Pargana level; Reddi/ Muqaddam and Patwari/Kulkarni at the village level. All of them were assigned tax-free villages/lands on hereditary basis and enjoyed some perquisites.

Through nomenclature changed under different dynasties all of them were found to be so indispensable by all the governments that they were continued through out the period. All these tenure holders were invariably the local Hindus. While the revenue collectors belonged to the dominant peasant communities the Brahmins of Niyogi sect were the accountants and registrars. Another interesting thing is that some of the hereditary revenue collectors and Registrars at the Pargana level slowly transformed themselves into revenue farmers and finally became Zamindars in Coastal Andhra during the eighteenth century. They came to maintain armed forces and were paying Peshkash.

Similarly, the village officials/servants, including the head and accountant, all called 'Panniddaru Ayagandlu' also held the civil service tenures. They were assingned land-manyam/Inam, with tax concessions and other perquisites on hereditary basis for undertaking service to the village agricultural community. The Ayagar system an important institution of medieval India became so useful in this region that even the British administrators could not dispense with it. It continued to function till the Andhra Pradesh government abolished the hereditary aspect of the village headman and accountant during the tenure of N.T.Rama Rao as Chief Minister.

The specific service tenures like Dasavandam under which lands were assingned with tax concessions to private entrepreneurs for agricultural development also come under this category. These tenures were granted by all the governments including the British Company of the period.

Finally hundreds of villages and thousands of acres of land were assigned under charitable tenures to all the religious institutions both Hindu and Muslim, feeding houses and learned persons. These charitable tenures were assigned by all the states on perpetual basis with tax concessions. The extent of lands assigned to each of them depended on their influence.

The government of the period which considered itself as the proprietor of the soil collected a share of the produce of the soil which was the principal source of its revenue. The land revenue system which was in vogue in this region during the period was an important and extensive subject. It has been studied under the following heads – Revenue assessment, Rates, mode of collection and the organization.

Different revenue assessment methods followed depended on the nature of crop, irrigation facility etc.

The basic system of assessment or ascertaining the crop before its harvest and fixing the government share was almost common through out the region under all the governments with minor changes in procedure. It was based on some kind of land survey and measurement and the assessment figures of the earlier period maintained by the local revenue accountants. The only difference is that from Muslim period onwards the assessment and collection of land revenue was made in cash rather than in kind which was the system prevalent under the Hindu government. Throughout the period we find corruption on the parts of revenue officials involved in the assessment.

Several different modes of revenue assessments were followed. The fixed money assessment under which all arable lands in every village had a fixed money valuation registered in village registers. The Visabadi system, under which the village revenue was fixed in lump sum per annum and divided into shares and distributed among the Ryots periodically, also comes under this category. This system was widely prevalent during the period in all the three sub-regions. Though convenient to the government, Visabadi system proved to be more advantageous to the chief Ryots of the village and disadvantageous to the poor Ryots. Sist and Malvati system of Assessment prevalent mostly in zamindari territories of north Coastal Andhra also belonged to the fixed money assessment. Gutta or Bilmakta fixed money rent per so much of crop adopted in the case of garden produce was another method of assessment.

The sharing system or division of crop was grain assessment. It was called variously as Bhagam, Varun, Gallabakshi and Battai. Under this the government and the Ryot shared the produce after the harvest. Most of the land was assessed on the basis of this system during the period. Finally the government adopted concessional assessment on villages and lands granted under charitable tenures, service tenures and also those granted for agricultural development. But at the same time additional imposts like Katnams/ Nazars, Pullari or grazing tax were also levied.

The revenue fates depended on the nature of irrigation, soil and also the crop. The government share ranged between one half to one-fourth under the Hindu governments. This was done after deducting the fees to the villages officials/ servants. The revenue rates prevalent during the Muslim period, as found by the Company's officials were less favourable to the cultivatior whose share was reduced considerably in all types of crops. There were also 'additional assessments', abuses and arbitrary demands. The substitution of money rent for a rent in kind was an important change introduced by the Muslim governments.

Two methods of revenue collection direct and indirect were followed during the period. The direct mode was through central government revenue officials like Parupatyamvaru and Amils who supervised the Collection with the assistance of hereditary revenue officials. This mode of collection was resorted to both in crown villages and also in the villages alienated to others. It was called 'Amani' and was meant to remove the abuses and irregularities associated with Revenue farming. But it was also open to abuses by the revenue officials and was attended with loss to both the government and the cultivatior. The second method, i.e. the Revenue farming system called Gutta or Ijara was widespread and prevalent throughout the period in all the territories belonging to crown as well as those alienated to others. The Europeans travellers of eighteenth century who give many details about the working of the system also highlight the glaring oppression perpetuated on the peasants and also on the revenue farmers during the Qutbshahi period. This oppression was not less sever under Asafjahis and the English.

The system on the whole, is characterized by excessive tax burden and the consequent oppression of the peasant due to revenue farming system and the corruption on the part of officials through out the period and in all the sub-regions.

Regarding the machinery of the government for revenue collection; while the central government revenue officials or Revenue farmers supervised the revenue collection the hereditary revenue officials at Sarkar, Pargana and village level, like Deshmukhs, Despandias, village headmen and accountants did the actual collection. They enjoyed Manyam/Inam, villages/lands and other perquisities.

The agricultural development in the region during the period took the form of founding of new agricultural settlements and bringing new lands under cultivation; revival of deserted Villages and augmentation of irrigation facilities to the lands already under cultivation, most of which were undertaken by private entrepreneurs. The latter were rewarded by grant of lands under Dasavanda system and tax concessions for their investment. The agricultural development during the period of study was not as extensive as that of the preceeding period, due to political uncertainty of the period. But the scanty information available prove that the above Dasavanda system was followed throughout the period in the region. While much of the agricultural developments in Rayalasima and southern Telangana sub-regions was undertaken during the Vijayanagara and Qutbshahi periods respectively the subsequent period did not witness much activity in this respect. The above 'Dasavanda' and also 'Cheruvu Mera' system followed by all the governments ensured the maintenance of irrigation works not only during the period but also subsequently.

The recurring famines and the accompanying epidemics in the regions, as in other parts of India, resulted in heavy loss of life and migrations. They had a disastrous effect on the agrarian life. They affected all the sub-regions. The severity of the famines was accentuated by the lack of speedy transport system and also by the lack of enough concern on the part of the Governments for the suffering of the people.

The process of agriculture of the period was same as that of today except the mechanization part of it. No dramatic changes took place in the process. But, this period witnessed some changes in the crop pattern due to the influence of global changes. Rotation of crops and raising of mixed crops were known and the European travelers who describe this process and abundance of crops of the region and English administrators like Thomas Munroe attest to the Superior methods of cultivation followed by the local Ryots. We understand from contemporary evidence that Andhra Desa was an agriculturally surplus region exporting it to the neighbouring regions in India and also abroad. While paddy and various types of corn and pulses were grown in plenty, wheat was grown in a limited way. While some of the indigenous crops like cotton, chayroot and indigo and also spices got an impetus due to the increased trade in items like textiles because of the European Companies. This period saw the introduction of new crops like tobacco, chillies in this region which became important cash crops soon.

The agriculture methods followed by the tribals living in the forest tracts have not been influenced by the outside changes in the plains and they continued to follow the old Podu cultivation blissfully.

While the entire village community was based on agriculture, it was the peasants and the agriculture labour who were directly involved in its process. While the peasants were the holders of the land and cultivation was based on individual peasant farming. The labourers did the work in the field either on monthly or daily wages. The Peasants are referred to as 'Krishivalulu' but more commonly as 'Kampulu' or 'Kapulu'. There were two distinct classes among them the 'Kadim' and 'Payakari; the resident and outside cultivators respectively. The Kadim whose counter part in Mughal India was 'Khudkhast' was the fixed inhabitant of the village where he had lands. The payakari whose counterpart in Tamil region was 'Parakudi' and in Western Deccan 'Upari' were the tenents from outside. The share off 'Kadim' peasants was less favourable compared to that of payakari. The exact caste composition of these classes of cultivators is difficult to indicate. While the bulk of the peasant land holders of this period belonged to the communities like the Reddi, Kamma, Balija, Velama, Kshatriya, Brahmin etc., the agricultural labourers were drawn from Boya, Golla and the bulk of them from Mala and Madiga communities.

Cattle rearing and dairy farming was an important occupation allied to agriculture during the period. Peasants maintained cattle heards to cater to their dairy needs and also for a regular supply of bullocks and he-buffaloes for plugging their fields for water lifting and for transporting their produce. There are references in the contemporary literature to grazing land, grazing tax, and cattle sheds and cattle manure.

BIBLIOGRAPHY

ORIGINAL SOURCES

Inscriptions

Andhra Pradesh Annual Reports on Epigraphy, 1965, onwards.

Annual Reports of the Archaeological Department of H.E.H. the Nizam's Government from 1914-15 to 1940-41.

Annual Reports of the Archaeological Department, Southern Circle, Madras.

Annual Reports of the Archaeological Survey of India.

Annual Reports on Indian Epigraphy.

Butterworth and Venugopala Chetty, *A Collection of the Inscriptions on Copper Plates in Nellore District.*

Copper Plate Inscriptions of Andhra Pradesh Government Museum, Volume I & II, (ed.) N. Ramesan, 1962, 1970.

Corpus of Telingana Inscriptions, (ed.) Hyderabad, I, II and III by Dr. P. Srinivasachari, 1940, 1958 & IV by M. Somasekhara Sarma, 1973.

Cuddapah Inscriptions, (ed.) N. Venkataramanayya, Madras, 1972.

Epigraphia Andhrica, Volumes I to IV.

Epigraphia Carnatica.

Epigraphic- Indo Moselmica.

Epigraphia Indica.

Inscriptions of Andhra Pradesh, Hyderabad.

Karimnagar District by P.V. Parabrahma Sastry, 1974.

Nalgonda District.

South Indian Inscriptions Vols. (Archaeological Survey of India, New Imperial Series).

Tirumala Tirupathi Devasthanam Epigraphical Series Vols. Madras.

Topographical List of *Inscriptions from the Madras Presidency*, 3 Vols. Madras, 1919, V. Rangacharya.

Warangal District by N.Venkataramanayya, 1974.

Manuscripts

Anonymous Author, *Tuzuk-e-Qutbshahi* (Persian), No.412 in the Salarjung Museum Catalogue of Persian MSS I (Written probably during the period of First Nizam of Hyderabad), Vol. I.

Anonymous Historian, *Tarikh-i-Qutbshahi* (Persian), A.P. Government State Archives Copy.

Brown, *Local Records*, Government Oriental Manuscript Library, Madras.

District Collectorate Records and *Athavanavyavaharatantramu* (A Mackenzie Manuscript) M.P.R. Reddy, ed.

Mackenzie Manuscripts & A.P. State Archives; *Grama Kaifiyattulu*, of Guntur, Nellore, Vijayanagaram etc published by A.P. State Archives.

Foreign Accounts

Barbosa, *An account of the countries bordering the Indian Ocean and their Inhabitants*.

Bernier, Francois, *Travels in the Mughal Empire 1656-68*, Delhi, 1968.

Bowry Thomas, *A Geographical Account of Countries round the Bay of Bengal*, Cambridge, 1995.

Jean Baptiste *Tavernier's Travels in India 1640-67*, 2 Vols. Trans. V. Ball, London, 1889, New Delhi, 1977 Indian Edition.

Jean De Thevenot, *The Indian Travels of the Venot and Careri*, ed. S.N. Sen, New Delhi, 1949.

Moreland, W.H. *Relations of Golkonda in the Early Seventeenth Century*, ed. 1608-22, London, 1931.

Nuniz Fernao, '*Chronicle of Pernao-Nuniz*', Trans. R. Sewell, *Forgotten Empire*, pp. 291-395.

Paes Domingo, '*Narrative of Domingo-Paes*', Trans. R. Sewell, *Forgotten Empire*, pp. 236-93.

Purchas, *His Pilgrims*, Glasgow, 1905-07.

Gazetteers and Manuals

Boswell, JAC, *Manual of the Nellore District in the Presidency of Madras*, Madras, 1875.

Brakenbury, C.F. *Madras District Gazetteers-Cuddapah*, Madras, 1915.

Carmichael, D.F. *Manual of the District of Vizagapatnam*, Madras, 1869.

Chetti, N.G.K. *Manual of Kurnool District*, Madras, 1886.

Francis, W. *Madras District, Gazetteers – Anantapur*, Madras, 1905.

Francis, G. *Vizagapatnam Gazetteer*, Madras, 1907.

Gazetteer of the Nellore District (brought upto 1938) Madras, 1938-42.

Gribble, J.D.B., *A Manual of the District of Cuddapah*, Madras, 1875.

Hemingway, F.R. *Madras District Gazetteer-Godavari*, Madras, 1907.

Imperial Gazetteer of Hyderabad State, Calcutta, 1909.

Imperial Gazetteer of India, Oxford, 1908.

Mackenzie Gordon, *A Manual of the Krishna District in the Presidency of Madras*, Madras, 1883.

Malidy, T.J. *Manual of the Ganjam District*, Madras, 1882.

Morris, Manual of the Godavari District, Madras, 1878.

Farmans and Sanads

Farmans of Bahamani and Qutbshahi periods in the Bande Nawaz Collection (Persian), copies preserved in A.P. Government State Archives.

Yusuf Hussain Khan (ed.) *Farmans and Sanads of the Deccan Sultans*, Published by State Archives, A.P. Hyderabad, 1963.

The Printed Primary Sources: Official

(Reports and other Government Publications)

- *Circuit Committee Report Vol.3009 and Orame's Report on the Havelis of Masulipatnam.*

- *Appendix to the Fifth Report from the Select Committee on the Affairs of the East India Company.*

1812 *The Fifth Report from the Select Committee on the Affairs of the East India Company,* Madras Presidency, London, 1812.

1812-13 *Minutes of Evidence taken before the Committee of the whole House on the Affairs of the East India Company* 1812-13.

1831 *Minutes of Evidence taken before the Select Committee on the affairs of the East India Company,* 1831.

1831-32 *East India Company – Selection of papers from the records at the East India House, Relating to the Revenue, Police, Civil and Criminal Justice under the Company's Government in India,* 4 Vols. London (1820-26).

Munro, Sir, Thomas, *Abstract of Correspondence between Sir Thomas Munro, the Board of Revenue and the Madras Government,* Madras, 1853.

Bour Bourdillon (Secretary to Madras Government), *Brief Statement of the Principal Measures of Sir Charles Trevelyan's Administration at Madras.*

Sullivan, J., *Report on the Ryotwari Settlement of the Madras Presidency,* Coimbatore Collectorate, 1823.

Proceedings of the Commission on Moturpha Taxes (1855).

Reports and other papers on the remission and resisting of revenue laws of the Madras Presidency.

Mirasi Right, Replied to the Seventeen questions proposed by the Government of *Fort St. George relating to the Miras Right,* Madras, 1814.

Bayley *Memorandum on Mirasi Tenures,* Madras, 1856.

Land Tenures, Selections from Records of Fort. St. George (Revenue) Series – No.XI *A Collection of papers relating to the value of land in the early years of the Nineteenth century.* The Government Press, Madras, 1906.

Maclean, *Manual of Madras Administration.*

Records of Fort. St. George, Selections from records of Madras Government, Bengal Government, Government of India, etc. 1600-1850

Salarjung, *Correspondence with British Government Files 1800-1860.*

Secondary Sources

Baden Powell, B.H., *The Land System of British India* 3 Vols, 1892..

" *The Short Account of the Land Revenue and its Administration in British India with a Sketch of the Land Tenures.*

Aiyangar, S.K. (ed.) *Sources of Vijayanagara History*, Madras, 1919.

Ali Asghar Bilgrami., *The Landmarks of Deccan.*

Arudra, *Samagrahandra Sahityamu: Tolirayala Yugam and Malirayala Yugam* (Telugu) Madras, 1965.

Atchi Reddy, M., *Lands and Tenants in South India – A Study of Nellore District 1850.*

Ayyangar, *Sources of Vijayanagara History.*

Baden Powerl, B.H., *The origin and growth of Village Community in India.*

Bava, B.K., ed. *Aspects of Deccan History*, Institute of Asian Studies, Hyderabad, 1975.

Beaglehole, T.H., *Munro and the Development of Administrative Policy in Madras 1792-1818.*

Bilgrami, A.A., *Landmarks of the Deccan*, Hyderabad, 1927.

Bilgrami & Willmott., *Historical and Descriptive Sketch of H.E.H. the Nizam's Dominions*, I & II, Bombay, 1884

Briggs, H.G., *The Nizam* 2 Vols.

Burton Stein., *Peasant State and Society in Medieval South India.*

Burton Stein., *The New Cambridge History of India – Vijayanagara*, 1919, New Delhi.

Cambell, G., *Extracts from Records in the Indian Office Relating to Famines in India*, 1793-1858, with remarks on the Famine of 1769-70 by W.W. Hunter.

Campbell, A.C. *Glimpses of the Nizam's Dominions*, Bombay, 1898.

Chatopadyaya, B.D., *Coins and Currency System in South India.*

Cunningham, A., *Coins of Medieval India.*

Daniel of Alice Thorne, *Land and Labour in India.*

Das, D., *Economic History of Decca.*

David Ludden., *Peasant History in South India.*

Desikachari, T., *South Indian Coins.*

Dharma Kumar., *Land and Caste in South India.*

Dharma Kumar., *The Cambridge Economic History of India 1757-1914.*

Dipakaranjan Das., *Economic History of Deccan.*

Dodwell, H., *The Private Diary of Ananda Ranga Pillai,* 12 Vols, Madras.

Dua, J.C., *Palegars of South India – Forms and Contents of their Resistance in Ceded Districts.*

Dua, J.C., *Palegars of South India,* 1996, New Delhi.

Due, J.C., *British Inam Policy and Palegar Resistance in Ceded Districts.*

Dutt, R.C., *The Economic History of India,* 2 Vols.

Edgar Thurston, *Monograph on the Cotton Industry in the Madras Presidency.*

Eenugula Veeraswamy, *Kasiyathra Charitra* (Telugu).

Eugenia Vanina., *Ideas and Society in India from the Sixteenth to the Eighteenth Century.*

Fawcett, Sir Charles., *English Factories in India 1670-77, 1678-84.*

Foster William., *John Company.*

Foster William., *English Factories in India 1655-60, 1661-64.*

Frykenburg, ed. *Land Control and Social Structure in Indian History.*

Gleig. G. R., *Life and Correspondence of Major General Sir Thomas Munro* 3 Vols.

Grant, Dugg, M.E., *General Survey of the Madras Presidency.*

Gribble, J.D.B. *A History of the Deccan,* 2 Vols. London, 1895-1924.

Griffiths, Pericival., *The British Impact on India.*

Gupta Sulek Chandra., *Agrarian Relations and the Early British Rule in India A Case Study of Ceded and Conquerred provinces.*

Gyan Prakash., *The World of Rural Labourer in Colonial India.*

Haig, W. *Historic Landmarks of the Deccan,* Allahabad, 1907.

Henry Heras., *The Aravidu Dynasty of Vijayanagara*, 1927, Madras.

Hiroshi Fukozawa., *The Medieval Deccan Peasants, Social Systems and States.*

Hiroyuki Kotani., *Western Indian Historical Transition*, 2002, New Delhi.

Indra Deva., *Folk Culture and Peasant Society in India.*

Irfan Habib., *The Agrarian System of Mughal India.*

Irfan Habib., *The Peasants in Indian History.*

Iswara Dutt, K., *Inscriptional Glossary of Andhra Pradesh*, Hyderabad, 1967.

Jaysree, K. *Agrarian Economy in Andhra under Vijayanagara.*

Kadiripati., *Sukasaptati* (Telugu).

Lovaday, A., *The History and Economics of Indian Famines.*

Madhava Rao., *18th Century Deccan.*

Mahalingam, T.V., *Economic Life in Vijayanagara*, Madras, 1951.

Mahalingam, T.V., *Administration and Social Life under Vijayanagara*, Madras, 2nd edn. 1969.

Mahalingam, T.V., *The Mackenzie Manuscripts* 2 Vols.

Maine., *Village Communities in East and West.*

Major, R.H., *The Vijayanagara Empire, Chronicles of Paes and Nuniz.*

Makenna, J., *Agriculture in India.*

Mathai John., *Village Government in British India.*

Metcalfe T.E., *Laissez faire and Tenant Right.*

Moreland, W.H., *The Agrarian System of Moslem India.*

Mukherjee, R.K., *Indian Land System.*

Narayanamatya Ayylaraju., *Hamsavimsati.* (Telugu)

Nilakanta Sastry & Nelaturi Venkataramanayya., *Further Sources of Vijayanagara.*

Nilamani Mukherjee., *Ryotwari System in Madras 1792-1827.*

Pattabi Rami Reddy, M., *East India Company in Andhra with Special Reference to Agrarian Relations 1760-1820.*

Rajayyan, K., *Administration and Society in the Carnatic*, 1966, Tirupati.

Ram Sharan Sarma., *Land Revenue in India.*

Ramaswami Naidu., B. *Memoir on the Internal Revenue System of the Madras Presidency.*

Randawa, M.S. *A History of Agriculture in India.*

Ratnam, R., *Agricultural Development in Madras State prior to 1900.*

Richards, J.F., *Mughal Administration in Golconda.*

Robert Sewell., *A Forgotten Empire, Vijayanagara.*

Romesh Dutt., *The Economic History of India, Land Problems in India.*

Romesh Dutt., *Economic History of India*, Vol.I & II.

Rothermund, D., *An Economic History of India.*

Sanjay Subramanyam, *Penumbral Visions, Making Politics in Early Modern South India.*

Satyanarayana, A., *Andhra Peasants Under British Rule, 1900-1940*, Manohar Publishers, New Delhi, India, 1991

Satyanarayana, K., *A Study of the History and Culture of the Andhras.*

Shah Rocco., *Golkonda and the Qutbshahis*, Lahore, 1920.

Sharada Raju., *Economic Conditions in Madras Presidency (1800-1850)*, Madras, 1941.

Sherwani, H.K., *The Bahamanis of the Deccan*, Hyderabad, 1953.

Sherwani, H.K., *History of the Qutbshahi Dynasty*, New Delhi, 1974.

Sherwani, H.K. ed. *History of Medieval Deccan*, Part I & II.

Sherwani & Joshi, P. ed. *History of Medieval Deccan (1294-1724)*, 2 Vols. Hyderabad, 1974.

Shrimali, K. M., *Agrarian Structure in Central India.*

Siddiqui Abdul Majeed., *History of Golkonda*, Hyderabad, 1956.

Sinha, J. C., *Economic Conditions of the Ceded Districts* (1800-1807).

Sinha, N. K., *Sir Thomas Munro and the Land Tax.*

Smith, R. B., *Irrigation in Madras Provinces.*

Soma Reddy, R., *Hindu Muslim Religious Institutions in Andhra Desa, 1300-1600*, 1984, Madras.

Soma Reddy, R. M.R.K. Sarma & Satyanarayana, A., (edited), *Agrarian Conditions in Andhra Desa 17th & 18th Centuries, A.D. Proceedings of the DRS Seminar*, 1997.

Srinivasan, T. M., *Irrigation and Water Supply – South India 200 B.C. to 1600 A.D.*

Sulekh Chandragupta., *Agrarian Relations and Early British Rule in India.*

Sundara Raja Iyengar., *Land Tenures in the Madras Presidency.*

Suravaram Pratapa Reddy, *Andhrula Sanghika Charitra* (Telugu).

Sutherland Lucy, S., *The East India Company in 18th Century Policies.*

Tapan Ray Choudhuri and Irfan Habib, *The Cambridge Economic History of India*, Vol.I, 1200-1700 & , Vol.II

Thurston, Edgar & Ranga Chari, K., *Castes and Tribes of Southern India*, 7 Vols. Madras, 1909.

Tiblyot Wyatt., *British India, 1600-1828.*

Tuktuk Kumar., *History of Rice in India.*

Varadharajan, L., *Indian in the 17th Century, Social, Economical and Political Memoirs of Francors Martin.*

Venkat Subba Sastri, K.N., *The Munro System of British Statemanship in India.*

Wilson, H.H., *A Glossary of Judicial and Revenue Terms and C. of British India*, Londo, 1875.

Wink, A., *Land and Sovereignity in India, Agrarian Society and Politics in the 18th Century.*

Zor., *Qutb Shahi Sultans and Andhra Sanskriti.*

INDEX

D

K

L

M

N

Q

R

S